A Legal Analysis of the Belt and Road Initiative

Giuseppe Martinico · Xueyan WU
Editors

A Legal Analysis of the Belt and Road Initiative

Towards a New Silk Road?

palgrave
macmillan

Editors
Giuseppe Martinico
DIRPOLIS Institute (Institute of Law, Politics and Development)
Sant'Anna School of Advanced Studies, Pisa
Pisa, Italy

Xueyan WU
School of Law
Chongqing University
Chongqing, China

ISBN 978-3-030-45999-4 ISBN 978-3-030-46000-6 (eBook)
https://doi.org/10.1007/978-3-030-46000-6

This Palgrave Macmillan imprint is published by the registered company Springer Nature Switzerland AG
The registered company address is: Gewerbestrasse 11, 6330 Cham, Switzerland

Contents

Notes on Contributors

Henrik Andersen is an Associate Professor at CBS Law, Copenhagen Business School, where he has worked since 2003. He has an interdisciplinary background with a B.Sc. and an M.Sc. in Commercial Law and Business Administration, and he holds a Ph.D. in WTO and EU antidumping law. Henrik Andersen is currently a Visiting Senior Fellow of International Economic and Financial Law at UCLan Cyprus, School of Law and he has been a visiting researcher at City University of Hong Kong; European University Institute; and University of Westminster. His main areas of research revolve around international economic law with particular focus on WTO law and its Dispute Settlement System; Trade between China and the EU; Rule of law developments in the WTO; The Chinese Belt and Road Initiative; and antidumping law. He has published with various publishers and journals, including *Journal of International Economic Law*, *Global Journal of Comparative Law*, Cambridge University Press, Routledge, and Kluwer, and he has been speaker at numerous international conferences and seminars in Europe and Asia. He is currently editor of *CBS Law Legal Research Paper Series* and *Journal of Malaysian and Comparative Law*. In addition, he has done reviews for various international journals and publishers, including Cambridge University Press, *Modern Law Review*, *Journal of Economics and International Finance*, and the *International Journal of Human Rights*, and he has done reviews for the Economic and Social Research Council in the UK.

Yongmei Chen is a professor of International Law and Director of the International Economic Law Department, School of International Law, Southwest University of Political Science and Law, China. Also a Ph.D. in Law, arbitrator of Chongqing Arbitration Commission and Hainan Arbitration Commission, China, executive member of the council of WTO Law Research Society of China Law Society, member of the Councils of Chinese Society of International Economic Law and China-ASEAN Legal Research Centre. Also a former visiting scholar at the School of Law, University of Leeds, UK (2015.10–2016.10), the School of Education, University of Oregon, United States (2014.09–2014.12) and at Law Faculty, Bond University, Australia (2007.09–2008.04).

Ming Du is Professor in Chinese Law and the Director of Centre for Chinese Law and Policy at Durham Law School. Prior to joining Durham in September 2019, he was Professor in Chinese and Comparative Law at the University of Surrey from April 2016 and Reader in International Business Law at Lancaster University from September 2013. He was raised in China and completed his Chinese law training at Tsinghua University School of Law in Beijing. He holds an LLM from Harvard Law School, where he was a Victor and William Fung Fellow and a DPhil from the University of Oxford (Brasenose College) where he was a Clarendon Scholar.

His current research focuses on the theoretical and structural issues of global economic governance (trade, investment and finance), China's approach to international law, and the development of the rule of law in contemporary China. He also retains a strong interest in corporate law and cross-border business transactions in which he practised as a qualified lawyer in both New York and Beijing for a number of years.

He sits on editorial boards of Chinese Journal of International Law (OUP), Chinese Journal of Comparative Law (OUP) and Manchester Journal of International Economic Law.

Imad Antoine Ibrahim is a Ph.D. Candidate in Law, Institute of Law, Politics and Development (DIRPOLIS), Sant'Anna School of Advanced Studies, Pisa, Italy. He is also a Research Associate at Global Law Initiative for Sustainable Development (gLAWcal), Essex, UK; Non-Resident Research Fellow at the Institute of Water Security and Science (IWSS), West Virginia University, United States; and Energy policy expert at the

Lebanese Oil & Gas Initiative—LOGI, Beirut, Lebanon. Master in European Interdisciplinary Studies, College of Europe, Bruges, Belgium. Bachelor in Law, Lebanese University 'Filiere Francophone de Droit', Beirut, Lebanon.

Shisong Jiang currently is a faculty member of the School of Law, Chongqing University (China). He obtained his Ph.D. in Politics, Human Rights and Sustainability from the Scuola Superiore Sant'Anna (Italy) and his Ph.D. in Law from the University of Antwerp (Belgium) in 2020. His research focuses on the sociology of international law, methodology of international legal scholarship, human rights law and social network analysis. His work has appeared in *The Journal of Human Rights*, *Asian Journal of International Law*, and *Journal of Chinese Political Science*, among other outlets.

Qingjiang Kong has been a full professor of law since November 2002. He is currently Dean of the School of International Law, China University of Political Science and Law. He is the Editor-in-chief of *The Chinese Journal of Global Governance* (Leiden and Boston: Brill). Specialising in international economic law, the WTO law and China issues, he has published more than 40 articles with international journals e.g. 3 articles with *Journal of International Economic Law* (JIEL), 3 with *Journal of World Trade* (JWT), 1 with *International and Comparative Law Quarterly* (ICLQ), 2 with *Heidelberg Journal of International Law* (ZaöV), 1 with *Journal of Intellectual Property Law & Practice* (JIPL&P), 1 with *Cambridge Journal of China Studies*. He is the author of 7 books (4 in English and 2 in Chinese), i.e. *China and the World Trade Organization: A Legal Perspective* (World Scientific Publishing, Singapore and London, 2002), *WTO, Internationalization of Intellectual Property Rights Regime in China* (Marshall Cavendish, Singapore, 2005), *China-EU Trade Disputes and Their Legal Management* (World Scientific Publishing, Singapore and London, 2012), *The Legal Environment for Chinese Trade in Textiles* (China Renmin University Press, 2005). A Study of *The Co-relation Between the Transplantability of International Economic Norms and National Economic Security* (Wuhan University Press, 2016) and *New Bank Insolvency Law in China and Europe, Vol. I: China* (Eleven International Publishing, 2017). His recent book is *Interpretation of the Foreign Investment Law of the People's Republic of China* (The Law Press, May 2019). He was heavily involved in the consultation process regarding the formulation of the Foreign investment Law of the People's Republic of

China. He has delivered a few lectures upon the invitations of such institutions as The Chinese Embassy in London and the People's Government of Gansu Province. He teaches International Economic law, International Trade Law, International Law on Intellectual Property Rights and related subjects, and etc. (email: qkong2000@cupl.edu.cn).

Huichun Liu is an associate professor of Guangzhou University, lawyer of Beijing DHH (Guangzhou) Law Firm, arbitrator of Guangzhou Arbitration Commission, and lawyer mediator of Guangzhou foreign-related Mediation Expert Tank. His research focus on the international economic law, international commercial arbitration law and international human rights conventions. He has published one book, co-translated two books, co-edited five books and published 30 articles in academic journals.

Giuseppe Martinico is an Associate Professor of DIRPOLIS Institute (Institute of Law, Politics and Development) at the Sant'Anna School of Advanced Studies, Pisa. Prior to joining the Sant'Anna School of Advanced Studies, he was García Pelayo Fellow at the Centro de Estudios Políticos y Constitucionales (CEPC), Madrid, and Max Weber Fellow at the European University Institute, Florence. He is also affiliated to several international research centres (among others, the Centre for Judicial Cooperation of the European University Institute, Florence, and the Centre for Studies on Federalism, Turin-Moncalieri). There he has been carrying out international projects related to comparative federalism and subnational constitutionalism, and to the constitutional dimensions of EU law and international human rights law (especially the European Convention on Human Rights). His research interests cover both comparative and European law, fields in which he published extensively, including two monographs in English (one with Elgar and one with Routledge) he has published extensively in international peer-reviewed journals in three languages (English, Italian and Spanish). His volumes have been reviewed in top-class reviews. As evidence of the impact of his research, his first monograph *L'Integrazione Silente* (Jovene, 2009) was quoted in the Opinion given by Advocate General Dámaso Ruiz-Jarabo Colomer in the Umweltanwalt von Kärnten and Alpe Adria Energia SpA case decided by the Court of Justice of the European Union (C 205/08). More recently he was also cited by Advocate General Cruz Villalón in his Opinion on the Gauweiler (OMT) case and by. Advocate General Tanchev in his Opinion (ft 45) on Case C-541/16 European Commission v Kingdom of Denmark.

Ernst-Ulrich Petersmann is Emeritus at the European University Institute, Florence. He was formerly Professor at the University of Geneva and its Graduate Institute of International Studies, and legal adviser in GATT and the WTO. His research focuses on International law, especially international economic law, environmental law and human rights law. He also works on European law, especially constitutional law and foreign relations law of the EU, especially German and Swiss public and constitutional law.

Xiaoling Tian has taught Intellectual Property law, Trademark law, Copyright law at Chongqing Jiaotong University and Southwest University of Political Science and Law since 2013. She got her Ph.D. in 2009 at Chongqing University and was a visiting scholar at Drake University (Iowa, USA) from 2012 to 2013. She is also an arbitrator of Chongqing Arbitration Commission.

Xueyan WU is an associate professor at the Law School of Chongqing University and an affiliate professor of the DIRPOLIS Institute of Scuola Superiore Sant'Anna. She is the executive director of the international law research centre on 'Belt and Road' of Chongqing University. Her research area includes international economic law, international environmental law and comparative law.

Wenge Zeng is a leading Professor in international law in the law school at Chongqing University, Director of the Belt and Road Initiative of international law research centre, law school, Chongqing University. He has been a visiting scholar in many countries and regions: Visiting Professor, School of Law, Washington University in Saint Luis, 2017–2018; Visiting Professor, Faculty of Law, University of Antwerp, October–November 2013; Visiting Scholar, School of Law, University of Florida, 2004–2005; Visiting Scholar, School of Law, University of Hong Kong, March–May 2004. Specialising in international economic law and international environment law, he has published over 200 articles in the international law area and the following books: *Special Safeguard Mechanism of Agricultural Products in WTO* (Wuhan: Wuhan University Press, 2012); *A Study on Legal System of the Special Economic Zone* (Beijing: University of International Business and Economics Press, 2012); *Addressing Climate Change from Legal Perspective* (Chongqing: Chongqing University Press, 2012); *Legal System of Agricultural Subsidy and Anti-subsidy* (Beijing: Law Press China, 2009); *Legal Study on Foreign Bank Risk Control* (Beijing: Beijing University Press, 2007); *Legal Regime of the Green Trade* *in China* (Beijing: Law Press China, 2007); New Perspectives of International Environmental Law (Chongqing: Chongqing University Press, 2005).

Lorenzo Zucca is Professor in Law & Philosophy. Lorenzo's special interests span from human rights law and philosophy to constitutional theory, with a focus on the relation between Church and State. He's now working on a project entitled 'The Uncertainty of Will,' which explores Shakespeare's vision on the connection between power and knowledge and examines its psychological and philosophical insights on human cognition and human institutions. He is the author of *Constitutional Dilemmas—Conflicts of Fundamental Legal Rights in Europe and the United States* (OUP, 2007) and numerous articles on human rights law and theory. His second monograph is entitled *A Secular Europe: Law and Religion in the European Constitutional Landscape* (OUP, 2012). This is a study of one of the most pressing problems in Europe and includes issues such as the protection of religious freedom, the limits of religious toleration, and a wider debate on European identity.

List of Tables

The Belt and Road Initiative: A Legal Analysis—An Introduction

Giuseppe Martinico and Xueyan WU

The Belt and Road Initiative (BRI) is a multi-functional strategy launched by the People's Republic of China, which is based on a variety of instruments and measures.

The priorities of the BRI are different and ambitious, namely policy coordination, infrastructure connectivity, unimpeded trade, financial integration, people-to-people bond[1] and development through six geographical corridors. As is evident, the realisation of this initiative will take ages and is part of a grand strategy, which may be read in different ways.

So far, the debate on the topic has mostly been dominated by scholars in international relations and geopolitics and economists (Xing 2019; Cheng et al. 2018; Mayer 2018). More recently, lawyers (Zhao 2018; Chaisse and Górski 2018; Shan et al. 2018) tried to enter into this

[1] Full text of the Vision for Maritime Cooperation under the Belt and Road Initiative, https://www.fmprc.gov.cn/mfa_eng/zxxx_662805/t1249618.shtml.

G. Martinico (✉)
DIRPOLIS Institute (Institute of Law, Politics and Development), Sant'Anna School of Advanced Studies, Pisa, Pisa, Italy
e-mail: giuseppe.martinico@santannapisa.it

X. WU
School of Law, Chongqing University, Chongqing, China
e-mail: wuxueyan@cqu.edu.in

G. Martinico and X. WU (eds.), *A Legal Analysis of the Belt and Road Initiative*, https://doi.org/10.1007/978-3-030-46000-6_1

interdisciplinary debate. However, with the above-mentioned exceptions, the very few legal analyses that exist on this ambit are still superficial. Western scholars frequently refer to the initiative as mere propaganda while the Eastern contributions on the topic are above all descriptive (however, germs of a proper and critical legal approach can be found in recent articles [Wang 2019]). This volume aims to overcome this divide, taking into consideration the different Eastern and Western perspectives.

What does the BRI mean for the existing multilateral organisations? What can it represent for the future of the European Union in the long run? What is the role of hard and soft law in the functioning of the Initiative? What does it represent from a legal theory perspective?

This book gathers scholars from different backgrounds and several countries to provide a cross-country discussion.

In their chapter, Qingjiang Kong and Ming Du explore the BRI as an attempt at filling the vacuum characterising the global governance and a manifestation of the Chinese ambition to serve as a global leader. Lorenzo Zucca investigates the BRI in the light of two competing visions of global order, the Western one, fostered mainly by the United States, and the Chinese one emerging from the BRI.

Ernst-Ulrich Petersmann explores the issue of the international settlement trade and investment disputes concerning the BRI from the viewpoint of the European Union. Rule of law is one of the most ambiguous concepts in constitutional and political theory and we have decided to gather two very different perspectives on it. Yongmei Chen explores the concept of the rule of law fostered by the BRI. As we will see, the rule of law ideal is one of the major sources of misunderstanding between Western and Eastern scholars and this chapter offers important clarifications.

Henrik Andersen's contribution looks at the BRI from the viewpoint of the rule of law to identify some problematic gaps in terms of legal certainty for international businesses and other stakeholders.

Giuseppe Martinico explores the significant role acquired by soft law instruments in the scope of the BRI, by reconstructing its concept in international and comparative law. In his chapter, Imad Antoine Ibrahim analyses the role of international water law in the implementation of the Belt and Road Initiative, arguing that this area of international law constitutes an appropriate regulatory framework on the basis of which China can base the implementation of the Initiative.

The BRI represents an interesting test to verify how the Chinese ambition will impact on international law. Against this background, in her chapter, Xiaoling Tian investigates some burning issues on intellectual property cooperation in the context of the BRI. In her chapter, Xueyan WU introduces the main features of Chinese investments in the countries involved in the BRI by examining the current insurance system and its gaps. Indeed, China has not yet established a comprehensive legal framework covering the political risks of overseas investment. In addition, the legal protection provided by Bilateral Investment Treaties against political risk is insufficient. It is time to reconstruct China's overseas investment insurance system and speed up the signing and revision of BITs with countries in the OBOR region and around the world.

In the final part of the book, specific aspects of the BRI are investigated.

Wenge Zeng offers a diachronic analysis of some efforts made by the Chinese government at the end of the nineties, in particular, the 'Go Out' Policy, to stress its continuity and discontinuity with the BRI.

Shisong Jiang approaches the BRI to reflect upon the broader issue of the Chinese conception of the international legal system, dealing with the role of cities in international law.

Huichun Liu offers a comparative analysis of the reconciliation legislation and the judiciary system of countries along the BRI.

The book aspires to contribute to the international debate by gathering scholars from different backgrounds (legal theorists, public international lawyers, comparative lawyers) in a way that they can offer their inputs and observations concerning the BRI.

Special acknowledgements go to Imad Antoine Ibrahim who assisted us in the latest phase of the editorial project. We hope that this book might prove interesting, as it is likely to facilitate an exchange of ideas and a comparison between different practices to mutual benefit and understanding.

This book originates from an international conference organised in Pisa on 24 May 2019 within the frame of the Sant'Anna Legal Studies initiative. STALS (Sant'Anna Legal Studies) is a project made possible thanks to the financial support offered by Scuola Superiore Sant'Anna, issued within the framework of the School's internationalisation policy. The conference was organised after the signature of the Memorandum of Understanding between China and Italy and was kindly funded by the Confucius Institute of Pisa. While finalising this collection, the coronavirus crisis exploded and our Chinese colleagues in particular have suffered from many inconveniences, so this book is dedicated to those who believe in transnational friendship even in hard times.

References

Chaisse, Julien and Górski, Jędrzej (eds.) (2018), *The Belt and Road Initiative Law, Economics, and Politics*, Brill, Leiden.

Cheng, Yu, Song, Lilei and Huang Lihe (eds.) (2018), *The Belt & Road Initiative in the Global Arena: Chinese and European Perspectives*, Palgrave, New York.

Mayer, Maximilian (ed.) (2018), *Rethinking the Silk Road China's Belt and Road Initiative and Emerging Eurasian Relations*, Palgrave, New York.

Shan, Wenhua, Nuotio, Kimmo and Zhang, Kangle (eds.) (2018), *Normative Readings of the Belt and Road Initiative: Road to New Paradigms*, Springer, Berlin.

Wang, Heng (2019), "China's Approach to the Belt and Road Initiative: Scope, Character and Sustainability", in *Journal of International Economic Law*, 22(1), 29–55.

Xing, Li (ed.) (2019), *Mapping China's 'One Belt One Road' Initiative*, Palgrave, New York.

Zhao, Yun (ed.) (2018), *International Governance and the Rule of Law in China under the Belt and Road Initiative*, Cambridge University Press, Cambridge.

Is the 'Belt and Road' Initiative the Chinese Vision of Global Governance?

Qingjiang Kong and Ming Du

The Leadership Vacuum in Global Governance Coincides with the Rise of China's Power and Ambition

It is not difficult to find that international order is now in an awkward position. On the one hand, today's world is undergoing unprecedented changes in a century. Sluggish recovery of the world economy, increasing polarisation between the poor and the rich, and rise of intermittent regional hot issues, emergence and spreading of non-traditional security issues such as terrorism, cybersecurity, sporadic outbreak of contagious diseases, climate change and trade war, all these are calling for joint efforts of the international community to maintain or create international order.

On the other, the international community is divided. A number of European countries have embraced nationalism, which was illustrated by the rise of the nationalist and even far-rightist political parties. The United Kingdom, a traditionally liberalist country, surprisingly turned to

Q. Kong (✉)
Centre for Global Governance and the Rule of Law, China
University of Political Science and Law, Beijing, China
e-mail: qkong2000@cupl.edu.cn

M. Du
Durham Law School, Centre for Chinese Law and Policy, Durham, UK

G. Martinico and X. WU (eds.), *A Legal Analysis of the Belt and Road Initiative*, https://doi.org/10.1007/978-3-030-46000-6_2

the Brexit. More notable than the Brexit is the US withdrawal from an array of international treaties and institutions.

As a result of the switch to nationalism and isolationism, anti-globalisation has become a trendy phenomenon in the Western world. Moreover, some have been obsessed with pursuing their own interests while giving up their leadership and even responsibility. They have even acted to sabotage the current international order which they had helped establish.

The outbreak and escalating of the unprecedented trade war between the United States and China highlighted the crisis of the global economic governance. It clearly showed that the World Trade Organization (WTO) and its rules cannot discipline its member, and stop the war.

Neither the WTO failed to provide the rules needed to address the so-called unfair trade practices, nor did it compel the two trade giant members in the world trading body to resort to its Dispute Settlement Mechanism (DSM) when the trade disputes arose around these issues. The flourishing of the regional trade agreements or free trade agreements between WTO members has in a way weakened the universality of trade rules. As more and more big players in the WTO such as the United States, the EU and Japan turned to this approach to trade rule-making, the WTO was cast in a darker shadow. The existing *deficit of global governance* is getting even worse.

Moreover, in addition to threatening to withdraw from the WTO on a few occasions, the United States took advantage of the consensus decision-making mechanism to block the appointment of Appellate Body (AB) members. Given the relevance of the AB to the functioning of the WTO, failure to appoint judges triggered a crisis of the DSM of the WTO, which has been acclaimed as the pillar of the multilateral trading system. It added to the uncertainty whether the WTO can survive. The United States is effectively relinquishing leadership in global governance.

Similarly, while feeling frustrated with the current trade norms that are viewed to be no longer capable of accommodating their interests, the United States has resorted frequently to national security exception in their tool kit. On the disguised excuse of national security, the United States levied additional 25 and 10% of tariffs against steel and aluminium, respectively, from the rest of the world in early 2018.

According to many international trade lawyers, frequently invoking broader national security claims is nothing but opening the Pandora's

Box, because broader security claims would subject a wide range of goods to 'legitimated' protectionist action. As a result, the free and open global trading system is at the risk of disintegration. While keeping a close eye on the new role of the emerging powers, major powers are becoming increasingly reluctant to provide public goods in the form of international order.

Amid the dire cry for joint efforts to save the WTO from the crisis, no WTO reform agenda has unfortunately been reached and possibly would not be reached in the near future, which means no reform would be initiated soon. The crisis is not only an indicator that the United States have given up is leadership as well as its responsibility as leading powers in the international trade community, and has gone so far as becoming a nuisance to the making of international trade norms.

There arises an urgent need of saving the multilateral trading system. What is needed is to prompt democratic decision-making process in international trade order and curbing the US unilateralism in particular. The U.S. retreat has created a leadership vacuum for the shaping of international order. A strong leadership is needed to replace the inward-looking United States in delivering public goods in this regard.

The leadership vacuum coincides with the rise of emerging powers like China, whose capacity and ambition are also rising in the twenty-first century. A fundamental change takes place with respect to the relationship between China and the rest of the world: China has risen to be the second-largest economy in the world; the largest exporter and the largest trader in goods; the third-largest source of outbound foreign direct investment; and the owner of the largest foreign exchange reserve. The economic power, its huge market potential and its gigantic financial capacity lend China support in its economic relationship with the emerging economies.

It can absorb the goods from the emerging economies in large scale, provide needed capital to them, making it an irreplaceable market for their goods and an important source for the influx of capital in these countries.

Moreover, the emerging economies are collectively a rising force in the global area. In terms of the total economic output, they are comparable to the established powers, and the multi-polarisation of the world economic pattern becomes evident. As a matter of fact, within the existing system, emerging economies have had difficulty expressing their wishes, their role in global governance is disproportionate to their powers.

The 'Belt and Road' Initiative

The 'Belt and Road' Initiative was first introduced by Xi Jinping in the fall of 2013 during visits to Kazakhstan and Indonesia, respectively. The initiative consists of two main components, the land-based 'Silk Road Economic Belt' and ocean-going 'Maritime Silk Road'.

To the surprise of many observers, the president's initiative was, to his Kazakhstani host, possibly a reminder only of their shared commercial ties along the Silk Road, stretching back millennia. During a September 2013 visit to Kazakhstan, which is later regarded as the place where this initiative sprouted, Xi Jinping spoke of the Silk Road, suggesting the long-time commercial links between China and its neighbour. Xi went on to propose the establishment of a Silk Road Economic Belt to bring new prosperity to Asia. The speech sounds a typical one on a diplomatic occasion and thus barely registered in the international media. It had even failed to attract adequate attention of the Chinese media, before Xi made a further reference of the Maritime Silk Road of the 21st Century in his Indonesia visit in October 2013. But less than two years later, when the National Development and Reform Commission, the Ministry of Foreign Affairs and the Ministry of Commerce jointly promulgated the Action Plan for the so-called Belt and Road Initiative on 28 March 2015 (National Development and Reform Commission, Ministry of Foreign Affairs and Ministry of Commerce 2015), the Initiative became a buzzword, and was formerly made the centrepiece of China's foreign policy and international economic strategy (Magnus 2015).

This modern-day Silk Road originally was intended to bind together 65 countries and 4.4 billion people from Xi'an in western China (the old imperial capital and the start of the original Silk Road), across Central Asia to the Middle East, Russia and Europe. The maritime road is designed to link the South China Sea to the Indian Ocean, east Africa, the Red Sea and the Mediterranean. Later it was open to all the countries interested and involved.

The sprout of the Belt and Road Initiative had its domestic economic background. China is in need of a new strategy to spur its sluggish economy. China had practised, in the past three decades, the opening-up strategy which focused on manufacturing and exporting cheap goods. With the rise of labour costs, labour-intensive goods are no longer competitive and labour-intensive industries move gradually to and aggregate in the neighbouring countries. The old-fashioned opening-up strategy faces huge challenges. China is struggling to manage a difficult transition to a 'new normal' of slower and more sustainable economic growth.[1] On the other hand, the overseas direct investment (ODI) surged in the past decade by 41.6% annually, making itself the third-largest source of ODI in the world in 2012, and a net exporter of capital in 2013. China needs a new, safe, balanced and efficient opening-up strategy to boost its economy, and particularly to nurture a new round of economic development.

The Belt and Road Initiative needs to be understood against the background of the current world economy. In face of the weak recovery of the global economy in the post-crisis era, the developed economies are still in the process of revival and adjustment. With the weak market demands and rising protectionism, they are not in a position to continue importing goods from emerging economies in large scale, unwilling to tolerate large trade deficits from the emerging economies. In the meantime, the developed economies and emerging economies worked together to upgrade the current trading system, which is expected to serve as catalyst for the world economic development; unfortunately, either side blamed the reluctance of the other side for failing to cooperate with itself.[2] Against this backdrop, the developed countries undertook, by their own, to shape high standard, exclusive rules for global trade and investment. As a result, the free and open global trading system is at the risk of disintegration and thus undermining the competitive advantages that the emerging countries and other developing countries have enjoyed under the existing global trading system and reducing the global market and the sources of investment influx to shrink.

Up to 2013, fundamental changes have taken place with respect to the relationship between China and the rest of the world: China has risen to be the second-largest economy in the world,[3] the largest exporter

[1] 'New normal', which is a popular term coined by President Xi during his May 2014 visit to Henan, a hinterland province, is referring to the current economic situation. According to Xi, the economy now features more sustainable, mid-to-high-speed growth with higher efficiency and lower cost, suggesting that the Chinese economy has entered a new phase that is different from the high-speed growth pattern exhibited in the past three decades.

[2] After the failure of the negotiations under the WTO's Doha Development Agenda in July 2008, several countries blamed each other for the breakdown. The United States and some European Union members blamed India for the failure of the talks. India claimed that its position was supported by over 100 countries.

[3] Since 2010, China has been the second largest economy after the United States.

and the second largest importer in goods (WTO Trade Database), the third-largest source of outbound foreign direct investment (*China Daily* 2014)[4] and the owner of the largest foreign exchange reserve. The economic power, its huge market potential and its gigantic financial capacity lend China support in its economic relationship with the emerging economies: it can absorb the goods from the emerging economies in large scale and provide needed capital to them, making it an irreplaceable market for their goods and an important source for the influx of capital in these countries. As one of the engines of the global economy, China has contributed substantially to the recovery of the world economy. According to the IMF, China contributed 27.8% to the world economic growth in 2014, topping the world in contribution to the global economic growth (IMF 2014). Some Chinese experts believe that China may raise 'China Proposal' or 'China Solution', making it part of the 'global solution' (Gao 2015: 7).

Nowadays, the emerging countries are collectively a rising force in the global area. In terms of the total economic output, they are comparable to the established powers, and the multi-polarisation of the world economic pattern becomes evident. Yet, the voice of the emerging economies is rarely heard in the discourse on global economic governance. The existing world economic structure and governance system were established under the US leadership and thus dominated by the US and European economies. The IMF committed to undertake reform so as to divert some voting rights to the emerging economies. Due to the US reluctance, no accomplishment has been achieved as planned.

It is not difficult to see that in the past decade, the WTO fades in the new discourse of free trade, while the bilateral or multilateral negotiation

[4] According to Xinhua News Agency, China's outbound direct investment (ODI) reached a record high of $108 billion in 2013, making it the world's third largest investor for the second year.

on FTAs flourishes.[5] Apparently, the accomplishment of freer trade calls for new platform and system.

As a matter of fact, within the existing system, emerging economies have difficulty expressing their wishes, their role in global governance is disproportionate to their powers. Now that there is no enough room for stock reform, one may naturally turn to incremental reform. The New Development Bank, which comprises Brazil, Russia, India, China and South Africa,[6] is a result of such an endeavour. Unfortunately, the NDB fails to have the geo-economical support.

The Belt and Road Initiative is not intended to make a fresh start, but to integrate the existing multilateral and bilateral mechanisms into a broader framework.

Focuses

One needs to turn to the Action Plan for a good understanding of the focuses of the SREB/MSR. The Action Plan outlines five tasks to be accomplished: (1) policy coordination, (2) facility connectivity, (3) unimpeded trade, (4) financial integration and (5) people-to-people Bond. Needless to say, none of these tasks is easy to be completed. Policy coordination calls for frequent diplomatic communications among the countries along the Silk Road with a view to promoting the mind meeting of the governments of these countries; facility connectivity requires, among

[5] The United States, Australia, Brunei Darussalam, Canada, Chile, Japan, Malaysia, Mexico, New Zealand, Peru, Singapore and Vietnam have just concluded the negotiation of the Trans-Pacific Partnership (TPP), which sets forth high standard trade rules for the Asia-Pacific region, and is supposed to deepen economic ties between these nations. In the meantime, it is also negotiating with European Union the Transatlantic Trade and Investment Partnership (TTIP), which is aimed at setting forth high standard trade and investment rules for the cross-Atlantic region. It is anticipated that given the importance of the two pacts' member economies in the world, when both the TPP and TTIP are completed, the US-led trading and investment rules will become really global rules. Some analysts have even suggested that the US may be trying to use the TPP as a means to undermine China's growing economic might in the region, and isolate China with the new global rules.

[6] On 14 July 2014, leaders of Brazil, China, India, Russia and India sealed on a deal in Fortaleza, Brazil for the founding of the New Development Bank. With each of the five signatories contributing $10 billion as its initial capital, the bank works on an equal-share voting basis. The NDB will have a president (an Indian for the first six years), a Board of Governors Chair (a Russian), a Board of Directors Chair (a Brazilian) and a headquarters (in Shanghai).

others, prioritising of the key projects along the Silk Road and first of all, gigantic inputs of resources by China, Asia Infrastructure Investment Bank (ASIIB) and other countries, as well as investors. Unimpeded trade and financial integration engender formidable work of institution-building among all the countries along the Silk Road, in the form of, for example, FTA or international financial infrastructure. People-to-people bond requires intercourse and interaction between the peoples of all the countries along the Silk Road despite the cultural disparity among them.

A close look at the Action Plan, however, will find that the road map is notable for its mixing of traditional Chinese diplomatic language (e.g. emphasising sovereignty and non-intervention) alongside a newer rhetorical focus on adherence to high standards and international norms. Full of Chinese-style language and rhetoric, the text of the Action Plan is not always comprehensible to outsiders. While using the poetic language to describe the Silk Road and calling for the revival and carrying-on of the spirit of the ancient trade routes, it fails to appease the worrisome link between the traditional tributary system and the modern-day Silk Road. As the Action Plan is not a representation of China's unilateral commitments, nothing therein can be suggested as joint commitments of the participating partners. Unfortunately, the Action Plan is full of such expressions as 'we shall' and 'we should', from the reiterated governing principles to suggested actions. Moreover, vague Chinese expressions and parallel constructions can be found, which adds difficulty to the interpretation of the Action Plan.

Despite the difficulty that all this leave for the interpretation of the Action Plan, it is clear that the SREB/MSR strategy is a development strategy and framework which focuses on connectivity and cooperation among countries primarily in Eurasia. 'Connectivity' and 'Cooperation' are the keywords of the SREB/MSR strategy, thus bringing forth the economic development of the Eurasia economies.

Initially billed as a network of regional infrastructure projects, the latest release of the Action Plan indicates that the scope of the SREB/MSR strategy has expanded to establish a free trade network, to promote free flow of capital, technology, personnel as well as goods, to promote the effective interaction between the East Asia economic circle and the European economic circle and now to include promotion of enhanced policy coordination across the Asian continent, financial integration, trade liberalisation and people-to-people connectivity.

Regarding connectivity, the SREB will on land, focus on jointly building a new Eurasian Land Bridge and developing China-Mongolia-Russia, China-Central Asia-West Asia and China-Indochina Peninsula economic corridors by taking advantage of international transport routes, relying on core cities along the Belt and Road and using key economic industrial parks as cooperation platforms. At sea, the Initiative will focus on jointly building smooth, secure and efficient transport routes connecting major seaports along the Belt and Road.[7]

With respect to cooperation which is a guarantee to the smooth unfolding and proper implementation of the SREB/MSR strategy, the Action Plan focuses on concerted work and move towards the objectives of mutual benefit and common security. To be specific, they need to improve the region's infrastructure, and put in place a secure and efficient network of land, sea and air passages, lifting their connectivity to a higher level; to further enhance trade and investment facilitation, establish a network of free trade areas that meet high standards, maintain closer economic ties and deepen political trust; to enhance cultural exchanges; to encourage different civilisations to learn from each other and flourish together; and to promote mutual understanding, peace and friendship among people of all countries.

Institutions

Empirically, it is almost certain that without facilitating institutions, there would not be smooth integration among various countries with various economic development, political structures and cultures; no ambitious plan like the SREB/MSR strategy can be properly implemented as planned. In the light of the ambitious goal of the SREB/MSR strategy, a high standard FTA and an efficient DSM, among others, are needed. Unfortunately, the existing institutions across the Asian continent are

[7] Interestingly, given its close ties with neighboring countries in South Asia, the ongoing China-Pakistan Economic Corridor and the Bangladesh-China-India-Myanmar Economic Corridor are pronounced to be closely related to the Belt and Road Initiative.

fragmented. There are already such institutions as Shanghai Cooperation Organization (SCO), ASEAN plus China (10 + 1), etc.[8] Unfortunately, none of these multilateral mechanisms is in a position to serve the SREB/MSR strategy well. Take as example the SCO[9] along the SREC and a FTA between China and the ASEAN[10] (CAFTA)[11] along the GMS. SCO was designed to be an organisation facilitating cooperation among its members regarding primarily security issues. The economic integration among the SCO member countries is slow and has borne no meaningful fruits,[12] due to the fact that the members lack the incentive to promote an FTA among themselves. Russia, an important member of SCO, has its own competing scheme. It has formulated a Eurasia Economic Union (EEU) with Kazakhstan and Belarus.[13] Needless to say, Russia has no capacity and leadership if it has the intention to expand and transform the EEU into a FTA for the countries across the Eurasia. Moreover, there

[8] Other institutions include Asia-Pacific Economic Cooperation (APEC), Asia-Europe Meeting (ASEM), Asia Cooperation Dialogue (ACD), Conference on Interaction and Confidence-Building Measures in Asia (CICA), China-Arab States Cooperation Forum (CASCF), China-Gulf Cooperation Council Strategic Dialogue, Greater Mekong Subregion (GMS) Economic Cooperation and Central Asia Regional Economic Cooperation (CAREC).

[9] SCO is a Eurasian political, economic and military organisation which was founded in 2001 in Shanghai by the leaders of China, Kazakhstan, Kyrgyzstan, Russia, Tajikistan and Uzbekistan. On 10 July 2015, the SCO decided to admit India and Pakistan as full members, and they are expected to join by 2016.

[10] ASEAN stands for the Association of Southeast Asian Nations, comprising Brunei, Cambodia, Indonesia, Laos, Malaysia, Myanmar, Philippines, Singapore, Thailand and Vietnam.

[11] The framework agreement was signed on 4 November 2002 in Phnom Penh, Cambodia, with the intention to establish a free trade area among the eleven nations by 2010. The free trade area came into effect on 1 January 2010. The ASEAN–China Free Trade Area is the largest free trade area in terms of population and third largest in terms of nominal GDP.

[12] Trade volume between China and other SCO member states jumped from US$12.1 billion in 2001 to US$130 billion in 2013. Their economic output totalled 14.9% of the world economy, compared with just 4.8% in 2001. However, SCO mechanisms for economic integration have so far ended up in such ones as the SCO Business Council and SCO Interbank Consortium.

[13] EEU is an economic union of states located primarily in northern Eurasia. A treaty aiming for the establishment of the EEU was signed on 29 May 2014 by the leaders of Belarus, Kazakhstan and Russia, and came into force on 1 January 2015. Treaties aiming for Armenia's and Kyrgyzstan's accession to the Eurasian Economic Union were signed on 9 October 2014 and 23 December, respectively.

is no point expanding the SCO to the rest of countries along the SREB; neither is there possibility of transforming the SCO into an FTA for the countries along the SREC.

So is the case with the CAFTA. It is a low standard FTA which has been far away from the forefront of FTAs. While the CAFTA used to be a focus for its 'Early Harvest Package' that China offered to the ASEAN members, it lacks visibility in the arena of FTAs—despite that both China and ASEAN are negotiating an upgraded version.[14] There is also no point expanding the CAFTA to the rest of the countries along the MSR.

In addition to the existing multilateral mechanisms, there are also established international forums and exhibitions at regional and subregional levels hosted by countries along the Belt and Road, as well as a few platforms such as Bo'ao Forum for Asia,[15] Belt and Road Forum for International Cooperation (Belt and Road Forum)[16] and China International Import Expo (CIIE).[17] These forums are conducive to the visibility of the Belt and Road Initiative, but it remains to be seen whether they are useful to carry on the strategy.

So is the case with various bilateral trade and investment agreements between the countries. China, for example, concluded trade and/or

[14] China and the ASEAN members have set a goal to conclude the negotiations on upgrading the China-ASEAN Free Trade Agreement by the end of 2015.

[15] Bo'ao Forum for Asia is a non-profit organisation that was initiated and supported by the Chinese government. It hosts high-level forums for leaders from government, business and academia in Asia and other continents to share their vision on the most pressing issues in this dynamic region and the world at large. BFA is modelled after the World Economic Forum held annually in Davos, Switzerland. Other platforms include China-ASEAN Expo, China-Eurasia Expo, Euro-Asia Economic Forum, China International Fair for Investment and Trade, China-South Asia Expo, China-Arab States Expo, Western China International Fair, China-Russia Expo, Qianhai Cooperation Forum, Silk Road (Dunhuang) International Culture Expo, Silk Road International Film Festival and Silk Road International Book Fair.

[16] The Beijing-based Belt and Road Forum was organised by China every other year. The first and second Belt and Road Forums, which were held on 14 May 2017 and 27 April 2019, respectively, focused on advancing connectivity, strengthening policy synergy and promoting green and sustainable development.

[17] In May 2017, Chinese President Xi Jinping announced at the Belt and Road Forum for International Cooperation that China will hold CIIE every other year, starting from 2018. The CIIE is a significant move for the Chinese government to open its market to the countries along the Belt and Road, a symbol of its commitment to trade liberalisation and economic globalisation. The first and second CIIEs were held in Shanghai in 2018 and 2020, respectively.

investment agreement with each country along the SREB/MSR. There is a network of such bilateral agreements of various natures, with various focuses and various degree of openness.

Should one existing agreement be selected and expanded into the framework agreement for all the countries along the Belt and Road, or should a regional FTA be contemplated, strong leadership would be needed. No other country than China has such leadership.

The core of the Belt and Road Initiative lies in the connectivity, of infrastructures in particular. The developing countries on the Eurasia lack in capital and technology. To meet the demands, the AIIB was founded. Up to 77 countries have committed to join the AIIB, making it a really international development bank, serving the economic development of Asia and beyond. It is anticipated that the AIIB will bring together the Chinese money, European expertise and the demands of Asia's developing economies, and lay down the financial foundation for the implementation of the Belt and Road Initiative.

In this regard, no one can afford ignoring the role of a working DSM in the implementation of the Belt and Road Initiative. Varied interests or varied perceived interests, varied legal systems, varied cultures among the countries are likely to give rise to disputes, which in turn hamper the smooth implementation of the strategy. Designing and having in place a DSM shall be given priority in all the agenda concerning the Initiative.

Implications

The release of this strategy attracted the eye of the world. Observers are mostly concerned with the objectives of Belt and Road Initiative and its influence; they focus more on the China's interests and the threats the strategy may cause rather than the economic output the plan will bring out as China always highlight. Some outside observers downplay the strategy as another symbolism showing Beijing is trying to claim a place as Asia's dominant economic and military power. It adds the annual Asia Pacific Economic Cooperation summit as a support example which 'is set to endorse for the first time a "blueprint on regional connectivity" over the next decade'. A reference to the APEC is strongly suggesting that the SREB/MSR strategy is an unwieldy attempt and merely a declaration of grandiose goal.

Indeed, the establishment of the Belt and the Road will not be an easy task. A great deal of deliberation and negotiation may be necessary among the countries along the Belt and the Road for generating necessary political interest in and support for these mega-connectivity projects and viewing mutual benefits in them and for harmonisation of customs and financial rules and regulations, removal/lowering of tariff and non-tariff barriers, trade and investment facilitation, etc., in order that desirable economic integration may be achieved. Negotiation at the bilateral and multilateral levels has to be carefully planned and commenced on all these matters and areas.

A major issue would be building or development of appropriate infrastructural facilities in all the counties along the Belt and Road for the unfolding and smooth operation of the Initiative. Many of the countries need financial and technical assistance in this regard. China might be required to provide a huge chunk of it. This will be a test of China's capacity and willingness to channel formidable resources to the regional infrastructure development. An early commencement of the functioning of the AIIB has been a major step forward in this arena. Even if enough resources can be made available to the infrastructures, there are also risks. For example, many of China's past bilateral investment deals in Africa and Asia based around access to commodity resources were not commercially viable, poorly implemented and, in some cases, unpopular locally.[18] Improperly implemented, the Initiative would well end up as little more than a series of expensive boondoggles.

Of course, it is premature to predict whether the Belt and Road Initiative is doomed to end in failure or will mark the start of a China era in global economic governance. But, it is instrumental to outline the problems and challenges facing the implementation of the strategy, and to explore the implications of the Initiative for China, if properly implemented, for the participating partners and for the global governance separately.

[18] China Harbor Engineering Co. Ltd., a wholly owned subsidiary of state-owned China Communications Construction Co., was contracted by the Sri Lanka government to invest US$1.5 billion to build Colombo Port City. It would build berths for vessels at the nearby port, hotels, shopping centres, office buildings and residential complexes, covering a total area of more than 5.3 million square meters. The deal was to give the Chinese investors 1.08 million square meters of land in the area, some of it outright and the rest on a 99-year lease. While the port project would have been the largest foreign direct investment Sri Lanka has received, the Chinese government held it dear as a pioneering project for the Maritime Silk Road initiative. However, the project spurred controversy in Sri Lanka, as some criticised it violated local laws and regulations and would damage the environment. Soon after the newly elected government came to office in March 2015, it announced its decision to hold off on the project while assessing its impact on the environment.

Implications for China

The Belt and Road Initiative is expected to feature prominently in China's next decade and guide national economic and social development strategy throughout that period. Its immediate implications are as follows:

The Initiative will secure the transport of oil and gas and other essential goods, and particularly access to the Central Asian energy resources needed to sustain China's economy.

The property and investment boom at home that they served has now ended, leaving China with significant overcapacity in industry and construction, deflation and rising debt management problems. The implementation of the Initiative can ease the entry of Chinese goods into regional markets, help make use of China's enormous industrial overcapacity, thus offsetting the effects of a falling investment rate and rising overcapacity at home.

China has been tired of accumulating endless volumes of US Treasury and other government bonds and now prefers more direct investment overseas to make a better use of its foreign exchange reserve (about $4 trillion) by making direct investment overseas rather than accumulating endless volumes of US Treasury and other government bonds. Equally important, the Initiative can improve internal economic integration between the country's advanced coastal and the more backward western provinces. These are the Initiative's intermediary implications.

With respect to the long-term implications, by linking the economies of Central Asia with western China, China is expected to bring further development and stability to restive and relatively underdeveloped Xinjiang and Tibet and cuts off any potential support that Uygur dissident groups may seek from fellow Muslims in Central Asia. With the unfolding of the Belt and Road Initiative, China will be in a position to promote the global use of RMB which is likely to lead to the internationalisation of RMB.

Implications for Partners

Needless to say, the Belt and Road Initiative will have its implications for the participating countries along the Belt and Road. Properly implemented, the Initiative will likely have an important effect on the region's economic architecture—infrastructure development, patterns of regional trade and investment. However, this rests on their own perception of interests therein and the extent of cooperation they offered. It is not surprising if they argue Initiative is too China-centric and that other participating states will reap only marginal benefits.

Implication for Global Governance

China has long expressed opposition to the dominance of the United States and the dollar in the global financial institutions, most notably the International Monetary Fund and World Bank.

The Belt and Road Initiative is the upgraded version of China's grand strategy of opening-up, as well as China's strategy for globalisation. Globalisation has been driven by the West. With the unfolding of the Initiative, non-Western countries are going to inject vitality. The Chinese version of globalisation needs to nurture shared interests, shared system and effective DSM.

Another concern is that some Western officials also fear a flood of Chinese development money will undermine governance standards at existing lending institutions like the World Bank, especially if China channels funds to its own companies, to politically motivated projects or to environmentally damaging ones.

An even deep concern beneath, which results from the distaste for the Chinese governance structure and state-led economic structure, is whether China will extend and deepen its global footprint without fundamental changes in political and economic philosophy.

Concluding Remarks

The Belt and Road Initiative is an ambitious economic vision of the opening-up of and cooperation among the countries along the Belt and Road. It is aimed to establish a free and open market system in the heartland of Eurasia and reshape the geo-economic order.

Inevitably, this will require China to project its growing power further. After all, this Initiative would simply be a commercial but truculent riposte to America's pivot to Asia. Important commercial consequences for the region and global companies will go hand in hand with unpredictable geopolitical implications in parts of the world where the United States—and even Japan, India and Russia—has material and competing interests. Against these backdrops, however, the operationality of the Initiative is in contrast with the grandiose discourse by the Chinese authorities.

References

China Daily (2014), "China: 2013 Outbound Investment Hits Record High", 10 September 2014, available at: https://www.chinadaily.com.cn/business/chinadata/2014-09/10/content_18572828.htm.

Gao, Hucheng (Minister of Commerce) (2015), "A Chinese Solution to the Promotion of Global Cooperation on Development", in *People's Daily*, 18 September 2015.

International Monetary Fund (2014), World Economic Outlook 2014.

Magnus, George (2015), "China's Great Economic Journey Takes It on to a New Silk Road", in *The Times*, 20 September 2015, available at: https://www.thetimes.co.uk/article/chinas-great-economic-journey-takes-it-on-to-a-new-silk-road-03ssdbtkxjc.

National Development and Reform Commission, Ministry of Foreign Affairs and Ministry of Commerce (2015), Vision and Proposed Actions Outlined on Jointly Building Silk Road Economic Belt and 21st-Century Maritime Silk Road, 28 March 2015.

World Trade Organization, WTO Trade Database (2013), available at: http://stat.wto.org/CountryProfile/WSDBCountryPFView.aspx?Language=E&Country=CN.

Two Conceptions of Global Order

Lorenzo Zucca

Introduction

The world is heading towards anarchy: international institutions are fragile and liberal constitutionalism is being tested everywhere. The number of failed or failing states is on the rise, and there is no foreseeable improvement in the horizon (Kaplan 1994).[1] *Pax Americana* has been characterised by a drive to export liberal constitutionalism coupled with a commitment to free trade. Whether this recipe has worked is debatable. Since the end of World War II, Europe has emerged from the ashes, but it is now struggling with several structural problems. The Middle East is more unstable than ever. South America is struggling with corruption and the rise of authoritarian rulers. Africa is still underdeveloped and poor. Finally, Asia is booming economically and is trying to find its own place in the global chessboard. The rise of China is proving very challenging for America at the economic and political level: Is Chinese economic success likely to upset the balance of world order? Is China going to shape the global order in its image?

[1] Robert Kaplan suggested it over twenty years ago.

L. Zucca (✉)
King's College London, London, UK
e-mail: lorenzo.zucca@kcl.ac.uk

G. Martinico and X. WU (eds.), *A Legal Analysis of the Belt and Road Initiative*, https://doi.org/10.1007/978-3-030-46000-6_3

I present, and contrast two opposite, and perhaps incompatible, conceptions of global order. The paper begins by presenting the dominant conception of the global order, the orthodox conception. The orthodox conception has two defining elements. Firstly, it has a normative commitment to liberal constitutionalism, which includes a principled commitment to democracy, human rights and the rule of law as the core ingredients of any well-ordered political society. Secondly, the global order relies on a web of international treaties that include the UN, NATO and WTO as well as the EU as core international institutions that protect and promote the liberal constitutionalist commitment. I attempt to show that the orthodox conception of global order is in being challenged for two reasons: the lack of support of core actors such as the United States and the lack of efficiency faced by international institutions when implementing their norms.

I contrast the orthodox conception with an emerging alternative conception of the global order implicitly put forward by China. My analysis of the Chinese conception begins with China's trade project known as the Silk Economic Road or as the Belt and Road Initiative (BRI). This project of global scope works along the following principles: 'The BRI is in line with the purposes and principles of the UN Charter. It upholds the Five Principles of Peaceful Coexistence: mutual respect for each other's sovereignty and territorial integrity, mutual non-aggression, mutual non-interference in each other's internal affairs, equality and mutual benefit, and peaceful coexistence'.[2] China is bent on capturing the global vacuum of power to put forward its new global trade initiative. China not only aspires to be the first economic power in the world, but it is slowly forming a coalition of states to support its renewed global ambitious at the political level. If it is true that China's government is becoming more authoritarian rather than less domestically, its official conception of global order is on paper more conciliatory and is inspired by the Confucian idea of *Tianxia* (all under heaven). *Tianxia* prioritises harmony over hostility, but it is unclear whether hostility can be completely ruled out or whether China reserves its power to flex its military muscles when harmonious relations cannot be built.

[2] Full text of the Vision for Maritime Cooperation under the Belt and Road Initiative, https://www.fmprc.gov.cn/mfa_eng/zxxx_662805/t1249618.shtml.

Some argue that there is only one conception of global order and dismiss competing conceptions as being anti-constitutionalist (Kumm et al. 2017). The challenge of the paper is to refrain from holding on to a moralising idea of global order and examine the alternative on its own merits. Only then we will be able to understand what went wrong with the present state of global order, and this will also inform the questions that we have in store for our uncertain future. The paper will proceed in five steps. Section 'The Orthodox Conception of Global Order' presents the Orthodox conception of global order. Section 'An Alternative: The Chinese Conception of Global Order' introduces the alternative conception supported by China. In section 'China's Engagement with Existing International Institutions', I examine China's engagement with existing international institutions. In section 'The Doubts and the Reality', I raise some doubts and questions about China's understanding of constitutionalism. In section 'The Future: Three Scenarios Plus One', I raise four possible scenarios on the future of global order. The conclusion suggests new avenues of research opened up by the confrontation of the two conceptions of global order.

The Orthodox Conception of Global Order

It is hard to be optimistic these days, especially when two pillars of global order such as the United States and the UK are questioning the terms of their participation in international institutions and their respect for international human rights and the rule of law at a supranational level. No countries have done more to help create the global order in which we live, although both the United States and the UK have behaved ambiguously in terms of their submission to that order (Kissinger 2015). For example, the UK played a crucial role in the drafting of the European Convention of Human Rights. Yet, today it contemplates pulling out of the system of control of human rights. The ambiguity is remarkable. The UK's relation to the EU is even worse as the present government is bent on severing its ties with Europe.

The two central commitments of global order are even more fiercely threatened by the Trump administration (Havercroft et al. 2018). The UN and NATO suffer from the president's churlish criticism that aims to diminish their status (Parker 2016). International trade partnerships signed by Obama are now dismissed, possibly leading to a challenge to the global architecture of trade (Peterson 2018). The imposition on tariffs on steel and aluminium imports means that the world trading system is on the verge of collapse (Rosyadi and Widodo 2018). Moreover, Trump does not seem to be concerned about the fate of the EU; he took a visit to Europe as an opportunity to lecture NATO and EU leaders, while he struck a weapons deal with Saudi Arabia (Posen 2018). This unilateral approach is only weakening the global order and favours a bargaining style of diplomacy. The lack of interest in Europe's future might signify that the tide has turned: America heavily invested in Post-War Europe through the Marshall Plan and was supportive at every step of European Integration, which has been a very successful peacemaker in modern history. The crisis of global order is evident. It can be measured by looking at the two main components of global law. Liberal Constitutionalism and International organisations have been weakened from the inside, and they are not appealing to emerging and developing countries. We need to look a little deeper into the Orthodox conception of global order to understand what its main traits are.

The orthodox conception of global order presented thus far has four characteristics. It is binary, top-down, moralising and Kantian. The orthodox conception is binary because it makes participation in the club conditional upon the respect of the core tenets of liberal constitutionalism. If a country does not respect those principles or does not want to abide by them, then the country is considered as an outcast (Brunkhorst 2018).

Secondly, it is top-down in the sense that an outcast can be admitted to the club after being judged by the elite members. Notice here that the judgement can be arbitrary as the conditions set by liberal constitutionalism are very loose (Epstein 2018).[3] A country can formally meet the conditions of being a democracy, respecting human rights and compliant with the rule of law, without being a just society. Think for example of post-apartheid South Africa: it entrenched a generous list of liberal principles in its constitution and has a newly established democracy; but it also with a de facto rule of one party and growing issues of distribution of wealth (Ignatieff 2017). Israel can also be mentioned here: a democracy with an activist judiciary and a strong sense of the rule of law is still deeply

[3] The very decision to admit China to the WTO was based on the false belief that such membership would have opened China as a market and it would have promoted democratisation at the political level. None of these two conditions materialised.

divided and at war with itself, and occupies the territories of another people, imposing on them military rule. At bottom, the decision to admit a country to the global club is political and not a neutral evaluation of the constitutional health.

Thirdly, it is moralising because elite countries treat outcasts as if they needed a lecture on their shortcomings and on their moral inadequacy for not being compliant members of the global community (Stuenkel 2017). Of course, the charge of immorality is based on cultural and political practices that are deemed to be defining the elite group, so the moral judgement is also a judgement of how much cultural and political diversity can be tolerated by the elite group (Stuenkel 2017). The irony of international law is that it inevitably defines itself as tolerant and pluralist. The problems with tolerance should be well known: it presupposes the moral inferiority of the person who is tolerated and yet grants a moral pass for the sake of necessary co-existence. Legal pluralism is not put under the appropriate scrutiny and presents many weaknesses. For example, legal pluralism is often confused with value pluralism (Zucca 2012a). The global order presents an immediate tension between the two: one thing is to acknowledge that different countries have different sources of legal normativity, another is to say that those sources must comply with liberal constitutionalist values. If the former is attempting to capture all the sources of law, the latter tends to exclude all those sources that are not compatible with the basic moral intuitions of the elite club. Tolerance and pluralism are in reality quite narrow when it comes to judge non-members, and they are also accompanied by moral lectures that highlight the limitations of tolerance rather than its open-mindedness (Zucca 2012b).

Fourthly, it is broadly speaking Kantian as it assumes that to have durable peace the world needs to be organised into republics:

> The republican constitution, besides the purity of its origin (having sprung from the pure source of the concept of law), also gives a favourable prospect for the desired consequence, i.e., perpetual peace. The reason is this: if the consent of the citizens is required in order to decide that war should be declared (and in this constitution it cannot but be the case), nothing is more natural than that they would be very cautious in commencing such a poor game, decreeing for themselves all the calamities of war. (Kant 1795)

The orthodox conception is sceptical as to whether durable peace and a global order can be achieved in a world in which some domestic constitutional systems are not republics. The orthodox conception of global order comes with a set of heavily loaded normative conditions that are no longer attractive to a growing number of states around the world. China, to begin with, does not seem to be willing to accept the previous conditions to make its own contribution to world order. It is time to ask whether China has an alternative conception of global order.

An Alternative: The Chinese Conception of Global Order

China's conception of global order comes in the wrappings of its global trade initiative called the new silk road or 'belt and road initiative' (Chinese Ministry of Foreign Affairs et al. 2015). Even if it does not come in an explicit political language, it can be reinterpreted in that way and contrasted to the orthodox model of global order.

The goal of China is to rebuild global trade routes between China, Europe and Africa and cover more than 60 countries and two-thirds of the global population. It is too early to evaluate the true potential of such an initiative, but it is high time to consider its implications for an alternative vision of global order through trade relations. China interprets the spirit of the Silk Road not only as an economic plan, but also as a political project:

> For thousands of years, the Silk Road Spirit – "peace and cooperation, openness and inclusiveness, mutual learning and mutual benefit" – has been passed from generation to generation, promoted the progress of human civilization, and contributed greatly to the prosperity and development of the countries along the Silk Road. Symbolizing communication and cooperation between the East and the West, the Silk Road Spirit is a historic and cultural heritage shared by all countries around the world. (Chinese Ministry of Foreign Affairs et al. 2015: 2)

It is unclear whether the historical project has ever gained the prominence that it claims to have had (Bowring 2017). But the narrative is very powerful in linking the past to newly found ambitions:

> The government's marketing of the BRI has thus played upon myths and half-remembered facts about China's past—"the glory of the silk routes," in Xi's words. At the same time, the narrative gives credence to the notion that, until the age of Western aggression, China always was the master of the region. From this perspective, its current claims to ownership of almost all the South China Sea is founded on a history of Chinese presence and of tribute to the emperor and the overland Silk Road as a mighty highway of Chinese commerce with the world. (Bowring 2017)

China plans to invest billions to build railways and maritime routes that easily amounts to the greatest project of economic collaboration ever initiated (Fan 2018). The Marshall plan would pale by comparison. This approach can be deemed a hands-on initiative to global development that hopes to foster political stability by promoting economic interdependence. It can be contrasted to the orthodox conception that insists that political stability will come from institution-building and from the privatisation of economic forces (Little 2018).

China is seizing an historic opportunity to lead the world on its own terms. The financial crisis of 2008 left United States and Europe deeply battered and inward-looking, and their role in developing the economic links with poorer countries has been one of withdrawal for fear of being caught in too big problems at a difficult moment. The way in which Greece has been treated by the EU is symptomatic of a top-down, moralising, make no prisoners approach to 'European solidarity' (Scholl and Freyberg-Inan 2018: 103). If that is the treatment reserved to a member of the elite group, one can easily imagine how a non-member country would be treated.

By contrast, China is throwing its huge economic weight behind a hands-on-initiative that has no moral strings attached. If we compare it to the orthodox conception, China's initiative is non-binary, bottom-up, non-moralising and is closer in spirit to Montesquieu than to Kant. Firstly, it is non-binary, or in the very words of its vision documents: 'The Initiative is open for cooperation. It covers, but is not limited to, the area of the ancient Silk Road. It is open to all countries, and international and regional organizations for engagement, so that the results of the concerted efforts will benefit wider areas'.[4]

[4] Full text of the Vision for Maritime Cooperation under the Belt and Road Initiative, https://www.fmprc.gov.cn/mfa_eng/zxxx_662805/t1249618.shtml.

Secondly, it is a bottom-up initiative. It does not aim to form an elite group but aims instead to gather together and create bridges, road and ports between all the countries that expect a mutual benefit from this project. The New Silk Road aims to build new infrastructures and enhance old ones so as to increase the economic flow along the route. All the parties interested in such a plan can join the group.[5]

Thirdly, it is a non-moralising initiative. No lectures are offered on the way. China and Asia know well how humiliating it was to receive moral lectures from the United States and Europe (Stuenkel 2017). This is not to say that the lectures were not legitimate, but it means instead that the way in which China proposes to engage with other countries is first and foremost based on mutual economic advantage and does not come with any moral strings attached. China does not want to replicate a model of global order that is too culturally and politically limited in its own eyes. For this reason, it decided to sever the economic project from any other immediate political or moral goal. However, this does not mean that political and cultural collaboration is not encompassed. The plan is to improve on the economic links in a way that brings different countries closer; the cultural and political rapprochement is meant to be an outcome of the economic collaboration.

Fourthly, it is reminiscent of Montesquieu. The idea of '*doux commerce*' and of its positive impact on different countries comes from the French writer; China is officially interested in an idea of global order that could be more pluralist and tolerant than the one we have taken to be the western blueprint of the orthodox global order. Peace, from this perspective, would not come from the necessary embrace of republican government, but it would come instead from the natural opening that is brought about by the intensification of trade relations.

It may be asked at this point what is the political vision of China's economic project. It certainly does not have a liberal constitutionalist core as it is non-judgemental in terms of political performance and human rights record. It does not have minimum political requirements, but it does have a commitment to the rule of law as assisting the efficient functioning of markets. The rule of law by itself does not amount to a political vision. To understand what China might mean by global order, we need to look at

[5] 'We welcome companies from all countries to invest in China, and encourage Chinese enterprises to participate in infrastructure construction in other countries along the Belt and Road, and make industrial investments there'.

the philosophical roots of its project: China is trying to resuscitate Confucian thought, and in particular his conception of *tianxia* (All under Heaven) as a core idea of global order.

Zhao Tingyang is a popular philosopher in China. His last book is entitled 'The Tianxia system: An introduction to a Philosophy of a World Institution' (Tingyang 2011). Tingyang aims to show that Confucius has an answer to the present state of global anarchy. Economic globalisation, he argues, cannot be met with national protectionism and global conflict, as Trump seems to be inclined to do. Such a political response is outdated and unlikely to succeed. Instead, the modern world could benefit from embracing *Tianxia* (All under Heaven), which is an ancient Chinese concept that can be translated as 'harmonious co-existence'. *Tianxia* has three different dimensions as it refers to the physical world (the earth under the sky), the general will of the people and the idea of global order. We could say that it has a physical, a psychological and a political component. The three components must work together to transform global hostility into global hospitality. The idea of hospitality can be grasped in opposition to hostile ideas such as Carl Schmitt's enemy or Huntington's clash of civilisation. China's *tianxia* attempts to bring everyone together in order to defuse conflicts and promote global harmony. History, Tingyang claims, shows a successful precedent with the Zhou's dynasty, circa 3000 years ago. Now, it is time to bring China back as a global leader capable of managing conflicts and maintaining peace and harmony despite diversity.

Tingyang explains the psychological mechanism of *tianxia*. In a world where every party seeks the maximisation of self-interest to the detriment of other parties, *tianxia* calls for the minimisation of hostility. The psychological mechanisms that promote self-interest are to be avoided as they favour conflict and trade wars. Instead, the only strategy that is worth spreading is one that calls for de-escalating conflicts and negotiating solutions to the problem in a spirit of global collaboration. *Tianxia* promotes mutual recognition and what Tingyang calls relational rationality: self-improvement and self-assertion cannot happen to the detriment of someone else; it can only happen if it is compatible with improvement and assertion of someone else. Either we rise together, or we fall together: this sends a not so veiled criticism of Trump's worldview, that seems to be bent on fuelling trade wars and political conflicts. The connection between *tianxia* and the silk road is easy to establish. Both of them are essential elements of Xi Jinping's political philosophy, which has been entrenched in the Chinese Constitution in its last amendment on 11 March 2018.[6]

China's Engagement with Existing International Institutions

On 11 December 2001, China joined the WTO. The intent was to integrate China in the global economy and to nudge China towards democratisation of its constitutional and institutional framework. The Western theorem is simple: trade will exert pressure on government to open up its markets and democratise its institutions. Free trade goes hand in hand with liberal democracies. China proved the theorem wrong: free trade boomed, but government became more authoritarian and personalised, and China's markets proved to be hard to enter. Andrew Nathan noted very aptly: 'Ten years ago the journalist James Mann published a book called *The China Fantasy*, in which he criticized American policymakers for using something he called "the Soothing Scenario" to justify the policy of diplomatic and economic engagement with China. According to this view, China's exposure to the benefits of globalization would lead the country to embrace democratic institutions and support the American-led world order. Instead, Mann predicted, China would remain an authoritarian country, and its success would encourage other authoritarian regimes to resist pressures to change' (Nathan 2017).

By signing the WTO accession Treaty, China also agreed to a term of 15 years as non-market economy member, after which it could apply for a full status of market economy. On 15 November 2017, the US administration filed a 40 pages memorandum in support of EU's claim that China should not be given the status of market economy at the WTO. The United States is trying with every means to limit the influence of China within global institutions, but this strategy is unlikely to bear any positive outcome. Indeed, Trump's move to impose tariffs on steel and aluminium belies a considerable change of mind in the Sino-American relation: if the WTO cannot contain China's rise, then the WTO must be

[6] I say more about China's constitutional amendment below, section 'The Doubts and the Reality'.

abandoned, and old-fashioned protectionism is to be reintroduced giving rise to the prospect of legal challenges and trade wars (Guo et al. 2018).

China's New Silk Road is compatible with and perhaps even enhances the role of international institutions. On paper, it declares to be 'in line with the purposes and principles of the UN Charter. It upholds the Five Principles of Peaceful Coexistence: mutual respect for each other's sovereignty and territorial integrity, mutual non-aggression, mutual non-interference in each other's internal affairs, equality and mutual benefit, and peaceful coexistence'. To this extent, China's New Silk Road contributes to the upkeep of the global order through the respect of law and the promotion of economic collaboration. Global order acquires a more instrumental role in this vision, and a non-moralising attitude.

When it comes to global institutions of trade such as the WTO, China looks more likely to sustain them than the United States does at the moment (Davis 2018). During the last World Economic Forum, China defended the WTO and global trade in general, while the American administration denounced them (Elliot and Wearden 2017). America's decision to impose tariffs on steel and coal imports is an open declaration of trade wars (Verma 2018); its principle flies in the face of open trade as protected by the WTO, and it is hard to believe that steel and coal will be the only objects of protection (Verma 2018). The EU and China could take the legal route at first, but in the present circumstances an international legal dispute may not yield any concrete result. An alternative response to the United States would be to impose tariffs on American products, but that would escalate a trade war that the American administration seems keen on having. The end game of this affair could be the delegitimisation of international institutions such as the WTO (Verma 2018).

China has benefited immensely from global trade and from membership to the WTO. Its present position of dominance is due to the opening of the markets to China. China is paradoxically the only hope to save the global order of trade presided by the WTO. Perhaps the American threat of dismantling international institutions is aimed precisely at bringing China to the negotiating table, so as to agree on a new regulatory framework for trade. China could take the lead on this too by opening a new round of negotiations in Beijing, since the West has failed to come to a conclusion to the previous set of negotiations launched in Doha in 2001.

Perhaps China supports the existing global institutions only insofar that they guarantee its present economic dominance. But for the moment, it is clear that China has a greater interest in protecting the WTO than the Trump administration. It is only mildly ironic that the best hope for international trade, the WTO and other international institutions is China. America's Trump seems to believe that its own economic problems come from trade regulations, in particular the restriction on tariffs and on state aids. UK's brexiteers think very much along the same line: the economic problems for the UK derive from EU restrictive regulation to free trade as well as the prohibition of state aids to companies. Tories focus on the possibility of a more lucrative set of free trade agreements, whereas the labour party is supporting brexit to the extent that the EU is regarded as an obstacle to re-nationalisation as well as state intervention in the national economic sector.

The WTO provides a trade framework which has guaranteed and secured China's performance in the last 15 years. There is nothing to gain from plunging into a situation of uncertainty by scrapping the WTO: if it works, don't fix it. Of course, the problem is that it works for China, but not so well for the United States. Trump's administration does not have the clout and the respectability to push for a reform; instead, it challenges the system to see how far it can be pushed before it breaks.

In the meanwhile, China has not been waiting still. While participating in what it perceives as Western global institutions of free trade, China has set up a number of parallel global economic institutions that gather the BRICs countries and other participants from the southern hemisphere (Stuenkel 2017). Oliver Stuenkel identifies twenty-two global institutions that range from the Asian Infrastructure Investment Bank to the Free Trade Area of the Asian Pacific (Stuenkel 2017). These institutions are not alternatives to the existing institutions, but are parallel: they work with similar rules and comparable framework. They offer similar benefits to other international institutions, and China can control them more easily. Participation in those institutions does not preclude participation to the traditional ones. However, it is clear that if the WTO were to be abandoned, then China would have some fall-back institutions to work within its area of influence.

The two conceptions of global order developed so far can be identified by their geographical scope: a Western and an Eastern. The Orthodox conception is the preserve of the West. The other conception is driven by China and has a regional as well as a global dimension. China wants to establish its range of influence and its scope of governance in the Asian Pacific, which is at the moment a region full of potential as well as risk (Auslin 2017). China is strengthening economic and political ties with all the countries in the region so as to be recognised as the leader. The BRI takes regional dominance to a higher level and attempts to connect Asia with Africa and Europe, thereby widening the reach of influence. Finally, parallel institutions of economic governance are completing the picture of an increasingly more regulated area of global economic order designed by China, to foster Chinese interests while creating stronger bonds with the rest of the world, while the West and International institutions designed by the West are being strained under the pressure of increased competition and inability to cope.

Some suggest that China is exclusively interested in the economic aspect of global institutions, but there is ample evidence that China's global efforts are designed to give China an important political role, not only an economic one (The National Bureau of Asian Research). In this, China is abetted by Western institutions that are resisting China's influence, and this can only have the consequence of pushing China to invest more on the parallel set of institutions so as to mitigate the negative effects of a possible failure of global institutions.

The Doubts and the Reality

China is no democracy and has a negative human rights record. Some Chinese Constitutional Scholars conclude that its constitution is 'lettre morte' (Zhang 2010) while others notice its quiet transformation towards a system of checks and balances (Lin 2015). An immediate caveat must be added: most of these debates are of limited value as their starting point is a narrow definition of constitutionalism that boils down to an idealised caricature of the American experience (Dowdle 2010). Starting from such premise, it is hard to achieve a balanced assessment of the Chinese constitutional experience. What emerges is that the roots of China's constitutional experience are far removed from liberal constitutionalism as it has developed in the West.

It is also clear that China is not interested in separation of powers and limited government. Xi Jinping, the ruling president, consolidated his authoritarian rule through constitutional amendment on 10 March 2018 (Hancock 2018). The Chinese Constitution of 1982 set a limit of two terms to presidential rule, but Xi Jinping led the National People's

Congress to remove that limit and open the door to a lifelong rule of chairman Xi. This puts China in a similar situation as Russia, Turkey and other countries that have decided to lift constitutional limits to lifelong presidencies. Whether this can be equated to the emergence of authoritarian rules should be established separately. If it is true that presidential regimes tend to limit the number of terms that a president can run for, it is not the hallmark of a despotic rule.

However, China went further by amending the Preamble of the Constitution to include a reference to 'Xi Jinping Thought' as a source of constitutional ideology (Buckley 2018). The ideology focuses on three pillars to strengthen China's power: the Nation, the Party and the Man. The Nation is presented as a unitary concept despite the ever-growing complexity of Chinese society. The country's economic performance globally has boosted the morale of the nation, and Xi Jinping wants to bring China to the next level: political dominance is on his agenda. The means to achieve this are twofold: the modernisation of the army and the BRI.

China's conception of global order can be clarified in the light of Xi Jinping Thought. Xi Jinping is keen to give China a new central position in the world. It could do this trough trade but does not exclude flexing its military muscles (Marcus 2018). The investment in the BRI is matched by military investment at home (China Power 2019). China's ruling motto is 'all under heaven (*tianxia*)', and the BRI stresses the importance of partnership, but China does not hide the fact that global order comes with an hierarchy in which China is the presiding power. China aims to secure the status of a global superpower by economic domination; the BRI is designed to create strong bonds of economic dependence with a large number of willing economic partners. Economic bonds, in Xi Jinping's vision of foreign affairs, will be the bedrock upon which solid political relations can be established and secured. Failing that, of course, China reserves the right to use its increasing military power in order to keep dissenters at bay and to incentivise political resolution of international disputes.

Xi Jinping's second pillar is the party, which is not a novelty in Chinese politics, although Xi Jinping reinforces its grip on power by stressing that the alternative to one-party rule is chaos and corruption as it happens in the rest of the Western world. Xi Jinping has also adapted party marketing to the modern technological world, by strengthening his control over the internet and new social media. The one-party rule is presented as the solution to political problems besetting modern liberal democracies and not as the problem.

The third pillar of Xi Jinping Thought is the Man: personal rule is considered as a fundamental tenet for a successful country. Xi Jinping happens to be such a strong and decisive ruler, whose stature reaches comparable heights as Mao, and whose virtue possibly goes further. Mao was known to be a man of his time with an allergy for traditional Chinese thinking; Xi Jinping blends instead a modern vision with Confucian values. China and Xi Jinping draw their legitimacy on their claim of historical continuity with a glorious past and a tradition of thought. The central political notion in Confucius is *tianxia*, which is presented as a possible solution to world order problems; Xi Jinping officially embraces tianxia, but this will not screen him from having to make difficult choices as to the future shape and design of world order.

The Future: Three Scenarios Plus One

The real test for international institutions comes at a historical moment of economic downturn. The EU, the WTO, the UN and NATO are only as strong as they are capable to meet these challenges. The Orthodox global order depends in great part in the ability of those institutions to provide solutions to concrete problems as well as in their capacity to maintain the social capital of trust. If we take the EU, for example, the situation is at present ambivalent. The way in which the EU is dealing with Brexit negotiation seems to point to a great ability to win while sitting on the negotiating table: Britain has been forced to agree on most of the strict requirements of the EU on EU citizens, the Irish border and the divorce bill. However, the EU is not yet capable of stirring positive political emotions for an entity that has monstrous administrative traits. It is unclear whether it is capable to build a social capital of trust by simply delivering solutions to problems of negotiation. There are other problems, chiefly among which, the issue of solidarity among those states that do support the EU. Italy and Greece have been made to kneel to the pressure of the supranational administration, but the price to pay for that is the resurrection of national populism and protectionism even where the EU was highly respected and praised.

The present world, however, shows that the orthodox conception of global order is not faring very well: there are legitimate doubts as to whether its main actors are still committed to it. Not only that, the liberal constitutionalist package is not sufficient to guarantee the stability of any country or its successful participation in the global order. Liberal constitutionalism seems high in moral judgement but short in delivering the policies that would help poorer countries to improve on their economic record. China's New Silk Road initiative functions the other way around: it is very undemanding in terms of moral evaluation, but very high in policies that assist with the creation of infrastructures that boost the economic performance.

Den Xiaoping's words illustrate where China still stands today:

> National Sovereignty is far more important than human rights, but the Group of Seven (or eight) often infringe upon the sovereignty of poor, weak countries of the Third World. Their talk about human rights, freedom and democracy is designed only to safeguard the interests of the strong, rich countries, which take advantage of their strength to bully weak countries, and which pursue hegemony and practice power politics. (Majie 2002: 81)

China's assessment of Western politics of domination is harsh. It might have sounded as an excuse for its poor record up until a few years ago. With hindsight, it has to be interpreted in a more nuanced way. China is serious about creating actual conditions of economic development for third world countries. Of course, it hopes to benefit from this both at the economic and political level. Mutual economic benefits are immediate, while political benefits depend on the success of the economic relations. It also highlights a certain hypocrisy of the ruling group of countries, whose recent record on economic development is increasingly more limited. This is not to say that China provides a magic wand with which it will cure global ills. It simply means that China has an ambitious position on how to promote global order through the strengthening of economic ties; implicitly, China also has a clear idea of what global order should look like: International institutions can be supported to the extent that they facilitate global trade and provide legal predictability (Zhang 2015).

Uncertainty characterises our present predicament. There is no way to know where we are headed but we can distinguish three broad scenarios: status quo, anarchy or reform. Status quo means to maintain things as they are. But make no mistake: to do so, it would not be effortless and cheap. Huge efforts would be required to strengthen the legitimacy of existing institutions and the efficiency with which they are capable of enforcing their norms. To maintain the status quo, a concerted effort of all major global actors would be required. At the moment, those conditions are not met.

A failure of the global order would push us towards a system of greater anarchy, with no paramount co-ordination. Political and Economic relations between countries would be regulated by bilateral treaties, and they would suffer from great imbalance of power. Some countries may believe they can gain from such an uncertain situation. The UK, for example, believes that it would be better off if it went *solo*, negotiating its way through the maze of an unregulated world. Whether it has the skills to do and whether it can punch above its weight are questions open to empirical verification. It is not hard, however, to predict a very challenging route ahead. It is also not so hard to predict that the economy of any country thrives in an ordered environment and suffers from a lack of predictability and uncertainty. This is true for any country, but in particular for the small ones that cannot retaliate against bigger entities. China would also suffer from global anarchy, but it could rely at least on the parallel institutions that it has created so far.

The United States seems equally bent on abandoning its international commitments rather than playing by the rules of the institutions that it itself heavily contributed to create (Prakash and Dolsak 2017). Ambivalence towards international institutions is not a new thing. The United States and the UK enjoy creating institutions for other countries but have a mixed record when it comes to participation and engagement in them. The United States and the UK like to export constitutionalism, but they find it difficult to be bound by global constitutional rules. China—and possibly any superpower who is in control of the rules of the game—is not unlike that in so far that it likes to have a framework in which other actors respect the rules, but it does not enjoy playing by the rules itself. Without a globally concerted action, anarchy is the most likely scenario. Existing international institutions will not disappear, but they will become increasingly more redundant and less efficient. Other institutions will appear and will make claims as to their authority to rule over some disputes (Stuenkel 2017).

The third scenario is reform of existing institutions. This is by far the most difficult scenario as it is extremely hard to create consensus on a framework of rules for the whole world. Also, major concessions would have to be made: China and other rising economies would have to be given a greater role and a greater responsibility within reformed institutions. More importantly, America and China would have to agree that the world has changed and so the conception of global order would have to reflect a new configuration of economic and political power. It would require for both China and the United States to put world order before their national interest, and this—despite their rhetoric—is highly unlikely. Instead, a confrontation between the two could lead towards the least desirable outcome: war.

The tension between two conceptions of global order can be lethal. America and China are facing off: America is the established power, while China is the rising power. This has been called Thucydides's Trap, from the original account of the war between Sparta, the established power, and Athens, the rising power (Allison 2017). The same situation arose at the end of the nineteenth century between England, the established power, and Germany, the rising power. We know how the confrontation ended and the way it shaped the twentieth century.

China and America do not have to fall in such a trap, but it is not something to be ignored. At present, the United States finds itself in a difficult position: if it supports existing institutions, China is likely to become the first economic power in the world, and politically it is going down an authoritarian route. The alternative is not more palatable: international institutions are abandoned and the global order collapses into global anarchy. Ideally, there would be a third alternative that unlocks the deadlock, but it is very hard to conceive the possibility of agreeing on a new global framework. Thus, for the moment, the only option is to work with the framework we have and involve all the participants to collaborate to maintain and possibly reform existing institutions. On a very optimistic day, one could even venture that Trump's threat to abandon global institutions is only just that: a threat. Its purpose could be to incentivise collaboration, without which everyone would have to lose something when left in a state of uncertainty about global rules. But one has to be very optimistic, to envisage that. A more pessimistic version of the story is that the confrontation is inevitable, and that is the gist of Thucydides's Trap.

Conclusion

This paper presented two distinct, perhaps incompatible, conceptions of global order. Whether the two conceptions of global order can coexist or whether one prevails over the other is a central dilemma of global governance. As we saw, the orthodox conception has a twofold commitment to international institutions and to liberal constitutionalism. The Chinese conception only stresses the importance of a stable order in which international institutions can guarantee the respect of the rule of international law. This predicament opens up a very important line of enquiry: what is the relationship between the two conceptions of global order? There are five possible combinations to explore in future:

1. The orthodox conception and the Chinese conception are in direct competition, and the orthodox conception is superior.
2. The orthodox conception and the Chinese conception are in direct competition, and the Chinese conception is superior.
3. The orthodox conception and the Chinese conception are not in direct competition, but stand in a relationship of priority or sequencing, with the orthodox conception prior to (i.e. identifies the preconditions for) the Chinese conception in practice.
4. The orthodox conception and the Chinese conception are not in direct competition, but stand in a relationship of priority or sequencing, with the Chinese conception prior to (i.e. identifies the preconditions for) the orthodox conception in practice.
5. The orthodox conception and the Chinese conception are neither in direct competition nor do they stand in a relationship of priority or sequencing; rather, each is appropriate in different contexts.

It is impossible to predict what we have in store for the future. Any of the five options above are conceptually possible. What we do know, however, is that the orthodox conception is in crisis and does not seem to be capable to sustain those international institutions that are central to the project of global order, nor is there an impression that liberal constitutionalism is spreading through the globe as successfully as in the past. America is not responding well to China's economic rise. China's full participation in international organisations is contested, and tariffs to protect against China's exports have been implemented. China needs to show goodwill when it comes to opening its markets to the external world, but it should also be put in a position of responsibility towards making international institutions more efficient for the interest of global order. China is playing this role with the parallel global institutions that it helped set up with its BRICS coalition.

Is it therefore time to abandon an idealistic idea of global order of free republics? It is too early to answer that question. For the moment, we can note that the link between free trade and progressive democratisation seems to be an illusion. If anything, the rise of trade friendly authoritarianism is undeniable, and the success of China makes that model more appealing rather than not. Can trade-friendly authoritarian regimes promote order at the global level? This can only be the case if their interests are not hampered by other countries, but tensions and conflicts, at the economic and at the political level, are inevitable. In that event, would international institutions be capable to offer commonly agreeable decisions?

To present two conceptions of global order should not be confused with defending any of the two. More work will need to be done on every front, including the normative front. But that was not the goal of this paper. This paper aimed to sketch two conceptions that are likely to be with us for the foreseeable future, even if we cannot predict their mode of interaction. This reflects the uncertain age in which we are living, where pillars of global order such as the United States and the UK are taking an ever-growing nationalist and protectionist stance while authoritarian regimes such as China are the last hope for the respect of international institutions. These are fascinating and terrifying times for a student of global order. Thus ends, or perhaps begins, the tale of two conceptions of global order:

> It was the best of times, it was the worst of times, it was the age of wisdom, it was the age of foolishness, it was the epoch of belief, it was the epoch of incredulity, it was the season of Light, it was the season of Darkness, it was the spring of hope, it was the winter of despair, we had everything before us, we had nothing before us, we were all going direct to Heaven, we were all going direct the other way — in short, the period was so far like the present period, that some of its noisiest authorities insisted on its being received, for good or for evil, in the superlative degree of comparison only. (Dickens 1874)

Acknowledgements I greatly benefited from comments of the participants at the conference on Global Constitutionalism at IDC, Herzliya. I am particularly grateful to Adam Shinar, Michael Giudice, Federico Ortino for very helpful comments on the written text.

References

Allison, Graham (2017), *Destined for War: Can America and China Escape Thucydides's Trap?* Houghton Mifflin Harcourt, Boston and New York.

Auslin, Michael (2017), *The End of the Asian Century: War, Stagnation, and the Risks to the World's Most Dynamic Region*, Yale University Press, New Haven and London.

Bowring, Philip (2017), "China's Silk Road Illusions", in *The New York Review of Books*, 25 October 2017, available at: https://www.nybooks.com/daily/2017/10/25/chinas-silk-road-illusions/.

Brunkhorst, Hauke (2018), "Some Conceptual and Structural Problems of Global Cosmopolitanism", in Giri, Ananta Kumar (ed.), *Beyond Cosmopolitanism: Towards Planetary Transformations*, Palgrave Macmillan, Singapore, 299–326.

Buckley, Chris (2018), "Xi Jinping Thought Explained: A New Ideology for a New Era", in *The New York Times*, 26 February 2018, available at: https://www.nytimes.com/2018/02/26/world/asia/xi-jinping-thought-explained-a-new-ideology-for-a-new-era.html.

China Power (2019), "What Does China Really Spend on Its Military?", available at: https://chinapower.csis.org/military-spending/.

Davis, Christina (2018), "It Is Up to China to Save the Global Trading System", in *Financial Times*, 9 March 2018, available at: https://www.ft.com/content/6d85636e-22ca-11e8–8138-569c3d7ab0a7.

Dickens, Charles (1874), *A Tale of Two Cities*, Piccadilly, London.

Dowdle, Michael (2010), "Of Comparative Constitutional Monocropping: A Reply to Qianfan Zhang", in *International Journal of Constitutional Law*, 8(4), 977–984.

Elliott, Larry and Wearden, Graeme (2017), "Xi Jinping Signals China Will Champion Free Trade if Trump Builds Barriers", in *The Guardian*, 18 January 2017, available at: https://www.theguardian.com/business/2017/jan/17/china-xi-jinping-china-free-trade-trump-globalisation-wef-davos.

Epstein, Richard (2018), "The Wrong Rights, or: The Inescapable Weaknesses of Modern Liberal Constitutionalism", in *The University of Chicago Law Review*, 85(2), 403–423.

Fan, Jiayang (2018), "A New Silk Road: China Is Investing Billions in Building Pathways to Europe, Central Asia, and the Middle East", in *The New Yorker*, 8 January 2018, available at: https://www.newyorker.com/magazine/2018/01/08/a-new-silk-road.

Guo, Meixin et al. (2018), "The Day After Tomorrow: Evaluating the Burden of Trump's Trade War", in *Asian Economic Papers*, 17(1), 101–120.

Hancock, Tom (2018), "China Votes to Allow Xi Jinping to Rule for Life", in *Financial Times*, 10 March 2018, available at: https://www.ft.com/content/bc8ab2bc-24fe-11e8-b27e-cc62a39d57a0.

Havercroft, Jonathan et al. (2018), "Editorial: Donald Trump as Global Constitutional Breaching Experiment", in *Global Constitutionalism*, 7(1), 1–13.

Ignatieff, Michael (2017), *The Ordinary Virtues: Moral Order in a Divided World*, Harvard University Press, Cambridge and London.

Kant, Immanuel (1795), "Perpetual Peace: A Philosophical Sketch", available at https://www.mtholyoke.edu/acad/intrel/kant/kant1.htm.

Kaplan, Robert (1994), "The Coming Anarchy: How Scarcity, Crime, Overpopulation, Tribalism, and Disease Are Rapidly Destroying the Social Fabric of Our Planet", in *The Atlantic*, February 1994, available at: https://www.theatlantic.com/magazine/archive/1994/02/the-coming-anarchy/304670/.

Kissinger, Henry (2015), *World Order*, Penguin Books, New York.

Kumm, Mattias et al. (2017), "Editorial: The End of the 'West' and the Future of Global Constitutionalism", in *Global Constitutionalism*, 6 (1), 1–11.

Lin, Yan (2015), "Constitutional Evolution Through Legislation: The Quiet Transformation of China's Constitution", in *International Journal of Constitutional Law*, 13(1), 61–89.

Little, Daniel (2018), *The Paradox of Wealth and Poverty: Mapping the Ethical Dilemmas of Global Development*, Routledge, New York and Oxon.

Majie, Zhu (2002) "Deng Xiaoping's Human Rights Theory", in Xintian, Yu (ed.), *Cultural Impact on International Relations*, The Council for Research in Values and Philosophy, Washington, DC, 79–90.

Marcus, Jonathan (2018), "The 'Globalisation' of China's Military Power", in *BBC News*, 13 February 2018, available at: https://www.bbc.com/news/world-asia-china-43036302.

National Development and Reform Commission, Ministry of Foreign Affairs, and Ministry of Commerce of the People's Republic of China (2015), "Vision and Actions on Jointly Building Silk Road Economic Belt and 21st Century Maritime Silk Road", 28 March 2015, available at: https://reconasia-production.s3.amazonaws.com/media/filer_public/e0/22/e0228017-7463-46fc-9094-0465a6f1ca23/vision_and_actions_on_jointly_building_silk_road_economic_belt_and_21st-century_maritime_silk_road.pdf.

Nathan, Andrew (2017), "The Chinese World Order", in *New York Review of Books*, 12 October 2017, available at: http://www.nybooks.com/articles/2017/10/12/chinese-world-order/.

Parker, Ashley (2016), "Donald Trump Says NATO Is 'Obsolete,' UN is 'Political Game", in *The New York Times*, 2 April 2016, available at: https://www.nytimes.com/politics/first-draft/2016/04/02/donald-trump-tells-crowd-hed-be-fine-if-nato-broke-up/.

Peterson, John (2018), "Present at the Destruction? The Liberal Order in the Trump Era", in *The International Spectator*, 53(1), 28–44.

Posen, Barry (2018), "The Rise of Illiberal Hegemony: Trump's Surprising Grand Strategy", in *Foreign Affairs*, 97(2), 20–27.

Prakash, Aseem and Dolsak, Nives (2017), "International Organizations and the Crisis of Legitimacy", in *Open Global Rights*, 9 June 2017, available at: https://www.openglobalrights.org/international-organizations-and-crisis-of-legitimacy/.

Rosyadi, Saiful Alim and Widodo, Tri (2018), "Impact of Donald Trump's Tariff Increase Against Chinese Imports on Global Economy: Global Trade Analysis Project (GTAP) Model", in *Journal of Chinese Economic and Business Studies*, 16(2), 125–145.

Scholl, Christian and Freyberg-Inan, Annette (2018), "Imagining Another Europe: Building a Pan-European Counter-Hegemonic Bloc Around an Anti-Austerity Master Frame", in *Comparative European Politics*, 16(1), 103–125.

Stuenkel, Oliver (2017), *Post-Western World: How Emerging Powers Are Remaking Global Order*, Polity, Cambridge.

The National Bureau of Asian Research (2020, May 8), China's Belt and Road Initiative: Political and Strategic Implications of a Chinese-led Regional Infrastructure, available at: https://www.nbr.org/program/chinas-belt-and-road-initiative-political-and-strategic-implications-of-a-chinese-led-regional-infrastructure/.

Tingyang, Zhao (2011), *The Tianxia System: An Introduction to the Philosophy of World Institution*, China Renmin University Press, Beijing.

Verma, S.K. (2018), "WTO and the Regulation of International Trade Law", in Nirmal, B. C. and Singh, Rajnish (eds.), *Contemporary Issues in International Law*, Springer, Singapore, 263–272.

Zhang, Qianfan (2010), "A Constitution Without Constitutionalism? The Paths of Constitutional Development in China", in *International Journal of Constitutional Law*, 8 (4), 950–976.

Zhang, Feng (2015), *Chinese Hegemony: Grand Strategy and International Institutions in East Asian History*, Stanford University Press, California.

Zucca, Lorenzo (2012a), "Monism and Fundamental Rights", in Dickson, Julie and Elefteriadis, Pavlos (eds.), *Philosophical Foundations of European Law*, Oxford University Press, Oxford, 331–353.

Zucca, Lorenzo (2012b), *A Secular Europe: Law and Religion in the European Constitutional Landscape*, Oxford University Press, Oxford.

International Settlement of Trade and Investment Disputes Over Chinese 'Silk Road Projects' Inside the European Union

Ernst-Ulrich Petersmann

Introduction: Multilevel Governance of Transnational Public Goods Connecting East and West

All human societies use law as an instrument for social ordering. Yet, even though *homo sapiens* seems to have evolved in Africa, legal civilisations emerged in the villages, cities, kingdoms and empires in Asia, Europe and around the Mediterranean Sea thousands of years ago. Up to the nineteenth century, the economies of China and India were as important as those of European empires. The scientific revolutions since the sixteenth century, and the industrial and legal revolutions since the eighteenth century, enabled the industrialised countries in Western Europe and North America to dominate international economic relations and their legal regulation during the nineteenth and twentieth centuries. Following World War II, almost all Asian trading nations joined the World Trade Organization (WTO) and the Bretton Woods institutions; they used these multilateral legal and dispute settlement systems for reforming their national and regional economic, trading and legal systems in Asia, thereby lifting more

E.-U. Petersmann (✉)
European University Institute, Florence, Italy
e-mail: ulrich.petersmann@eui.eu

G. Martinico and X. WU (eds.), *A Legal Analysis of the Belt and Road Initiative*, https://doi.org/10.1007/978-3-030-46000-6_4

than a billion of poor people in China, India and other Asian countries out of poverty. While Western countries continue to dominate the legal design of worldwide economic organisations like the 1994 WTO and the 1944 Bretton Woods institutions, Asian countries became locomotives driving economic growth not only for their own populations but providing goods and services also for people all over the world. Many Western industrialised countries continue struggling with the economic, social and political adjustment problems resulting from Asia regaining its major share in the world economy, as the shares and political influence of North America and Europe relatively shrink in the twenty-first century. The hegemonic assault by the United States (US) Trump administration on multilateral trade and environmental agreements since 2017 (cf. Petersmann 2018a), the emergence of China as the biggest trading nation with—soon—the world's largest economy, and the Belt and Road Initiative (BRI) launched by President Xi Jinping in 2013 for strengthening trade, investment and infrastructure cooperation with 65 Asian, African and European countries along the ancient territorial and maritime Silk Roads, are historical turning points in designing economic, legal and political cooperation between East and West. While the US Trump administration's *bilateral 'trade wars'* (e.g. against China) reflect US attempts at maintaining economic, technological and military US hegemony, Europe emphasises its different strategic self-interest in maintaining and adjusting *multilateral trade and investment systems* as legal basis for mutually beneficial cooperation with Asia.

During most of its history of more than 5000 years, China perceived itself as the 'Middle Kingdom' maintaining 'suzerain-vassal' relationships with several of its neighbouring countries. Law played only a secondary role in Chinese society due to the primary importance given to feudal hierarchies, social stratification, and traditional family and kinship systems. The two intellectual Chinese traditions of *Confucianism* and *legalism* contributed to the imperial administration's increasing use of 'rule by administrative decrees'; yet, even though 'humane governance' and promotion of social welfare were accepted as moral responsibilities of Chinese rulers and as parts of their 'mandate from heaven', little attention was given to individual rights; litigation was discouraged, and 'rule of law' in the substantive sense of independent judicial protection of individual rights against abuses of state powers was hardly known (cf. Carty and Nijman 2018). The late Qing government's isolation policy in the eighteenth century contributed to

China's fall under the rule of imperial powers. The communist revolution during *Mao Zedong's* era (1949–1978) led to impoverishing economic policies and 'social dis-embedding' (e.g. due to food crises and the 'cultural revolution'). The reforms and 'open door policies' under *Deng Xiaoping's* rule (1979–1989) introduced a 'socialist market economy with Chinese characteristics' and economics-driven legal reforms ushering in China's accession to the WTO in 2001. China's government used WTO law also for introducing judicial reforms and for embedding its 'one state, two systems' policies into international law, for instance by accepting four WTO memberships of China, Hong Kong, Macau and Taiwan (cf. Wu 2012). The BRI continues to be primarily motivated by domestic policy goals (e.g. to improve access to resources and export markets); it can be viewed as the 'third opening' of China's liberalisation policies beginning in 1978 and embedded into multilateral WTO market access commitments since 2001. Yet, whereas democratic and republican city states (e.g. in ancient Greece, Italy, Germany and other northern European states belonging to the 'Hanseatic League') and their 'constitutional checks and balances' protected decentralised, competitive legal structures promoting free and prosperous societies in many parts of Europe (cf. Scheidel 2019),[1] there are no signs of China's totalitarian 'communist party state' accepting constitutionalism and legal decentralisation as reasonable self-restraints protecting citizens against abuses of political power. Nor is China transforming its 'one state, two systems' agreements into a constitutional confederation protecting human and constitutional rights of citizens in all four Chinese customs territories.

According to K. Mahbubani, Singapore's long-time ambassador to the United Nations (UN), the 'biggest gift the West gave the Rest was the power of reasoning', which 'seeped into Asian minds gradually, through the adoption of Western science and technology and the application of the scientific method to solving social problems' (Mahbubani 2018: 11 ff):

[1] Scheidel (2019) explains the widening economic gap between Europe after the fall of the Roman empire and other parts of the Old World in terms of (1) Europe's legal decentralisation (unleashing 'competitive fragmentation of power', economic rivalries, growth and 'renaissance modernity' in many parts of Europe) and (2) the later industrial revolutions as the two 'great divergences' differentiating Europe from the 'agrarian paternalism' in China.

"East Asian societies, especially Japan and the 'Four Tigers' (South Korea, Taiwan, Hong, Kong and Singapore) were the first to absorb these ideas and practices, such as free market economics and empirical scientific research".... "This spread of Western reasoning ... triggered three silent revolutions that explain the extraordinary success of many non-Western societies in recent decades".... "The first revolution is political. For *millenia*, Asian societies were deeply feudal. The people were accountable to their rulers, not rulers to their people. 'Oriental despotism' was a fair description of the political environments in all corners of Asia"... "The rebellion against all kinds of feudal mind-sets which gained momentum in the second half of the twentieth century was hugely liberating for all Asian societies"... "in a big shift from previous 'despotic' assumptions, most Asian leaders now recognized that they are accountable to their people".... "The second revolution is psychological: the Rest are going from believing that they were helpless voyagers in a life determined by 'fate' to believing that they can take control of their lives and rationally produce better outcomes"... "In the last thirty years, we have carried more people over the threshold of university education than we have in the previous 3'000 years"... "The third revolution is in the field of governance"... "Fifty years ago, few Asian governments believed that good rational governance could transform their societies. Now most do".... "In China, India and Indonesia, more than 90 per cent of young people named technology as the factor that made them most hopeful for the future".

Decolonisation, universal recognition of human rights and multilevel governance of Public Goods (PGs) through national and international organisations are among the biggest political achievements during the second half of the twentieth century. The shift of power to Asia has, however, failed to effectively protect human rights and multilevel, *democratic* governance of PGs in many Asian countries. Globalisation continues to transform most *national* into *transnational PGs* like rule of law, rules-based trading systems, protection of the environment, mitigation of climate change, and protection of many of the 17 'Sustainable Development Goals' (SDGs) adopted by all UN member states. Yet, the collective action problems require limitations of intergovernmental power politics through 'constitutionalization' of discretionary foreign policies aimed at transforming *national* into *multilevel governance of transnational PGs* for the benefit of citizens. Such multilevel constitutionalism continues being resisted by many governments (cf. Petersmann 2020a), often due to feudal, religious and other power-oriented—rather than humanist and democratic—world views neglecting the close interrelationships between transnational economic and non-economic 'overlapping PGs' (e.g. between a rules-based world trading system, climate change mitigation and the 17 SDGs). The US Trump administration's assault on the WTO legal and dispute settlement system risks undermining protection also of many *non-economic PGs*. Will China's BRI and bilateral agreements with more than 60 countries participating in trade, investment and infrastructure cooperation along the territorial and maritime Silk Roads offer Asian leadership for rules-based protection of transnational PGs and peaceful settlement of related trade and investment disputes? This contribution discusses some of the related legal questions by using the example of disputes over 'silk road projects' financed and operated by Chinese State-Owned Enterprises (SOEs) in European states, where Chinese SOEs bought and administer parts of the Piraeus harbour in Athens (Greece), construct a railway linking Belgrade (Serbia) to Budapest in Hungary, and improve China's 'Silk Road connections' with Europe through numerous other investments. This BRI cooperation with 17 Central, Eastern and Southern European countries is coordinated through annual '17+1' Ministerial meetings and a secretariat in Beijing (with 'national coordinators' in each of the 17 partner countries). Yet, also this BRI cooperation is not treaty-based due to China's preference for legal flexibility and administrative discretion.

Can China's Bilateralism Be Reconciled with the EU's Multilateral Approaches to International Law?

National legal traditions in Asian countries differ from democratic constitutionalism (e.g. in ancient Athens) and republican constitutionalism (e.g.in ancient Rome), which continue to shape the national and European legal systems in the 27 constitutional democracies of the European Union (EU). The ancient constitutional theories of justice (as expressed in the publications of Greek and Roman philosophers like Plato, Aristotle and Cicero) justifying law, republican governance, rules-based self-regulation in 'private law societies', constitutional 'checks and balances' and judicial remedies by procedural, constitutional, distributive, corrective, commutative justice principles and equity have no equivalent in Chinese legal traditions. Nor does the transformation of agreed principles of justice in national and European constitutional law systems—such as the European Charter of Fundamental Rights (EUCFR) recognising civil, political, economic and social, human and constitutional rights of EU citizens as multilevel, constitutional restraints on the legislative, executive and judicial powers of EU institutions—have a parallel in the legal system of the People's Republic of China (PRC). Citizens are not allowed to invoke China's national Constitution in Chinese courts as a basis for individual rights. The basic principles of democratic constitutionalism—like free democratic elections of representative national and European parliaments, and independent, multilevel judicial protection of human and constitutional rights of citizens against abuses of executive and legislative powers—remain alien to the totalitarian claim of China's Communist Party (CCP) to unlimited political powers over state institutions and private citizens (cf. Li and Jian 2018; Petersmann 2018b). The recognition of 'inalienable' and 'indivisible' civil, political, economic, social and cultural human rights in UN law and EU constitutional law, and their effective domestic protection inside the national legal systems of EU member states, reflect regulatory approaches to the complex interactions between civil societies and their interdependent legal, political, economic, social and cultural systems, which are fundamentally different from the PRC's regulatory approaches (e.g. vis-à-vis minoritarian Tibetan and Uighur cultures, political dissidents, human rights advocates, economic competition, political, social and labour rights). The different legal cultures risk provoking conflicts if, for example, Chinese SOEs implementing 'Silk Road projects' inside the EU (like construction of transport links) fail to respect human, labour, environmental or judicial rights protecting workers and citizens inside EU member states; or when foreign direct investors from the EU are denied 'access to justice' in Chinese jurisdictions and are forced to accept the formation of 'CCP committees' also inside foreign firms operating in China.

Such risks of conflicts among diverse national legal systems are amplified by the fact that important UN conventions (e.g. on civil, political and labour rights) and international dispute settlement jurisdictions (e.g. by the International Tribunal for the Law of the Sea) ratified by EU member states have not been accepted by China. The EU proposals for creating multilateral investment court systems have, so far, also not been supported by China; yet, at an informal meeting of WTO trade ministers on 24 January 2020 at the World Economic Forum in Davos, China was among 43 WTO members committing themselves to using Article 25 of the Dispute Settlement Understanding (DSU) for an *interim* appellate arbitration review pending the resolution of the WTO Appellate Body (AB) crisis triggered by the US blocking of AB nominations. The implementation of the BRI reflects preferences of Chinese authorities and SOEs for informal bilateralism (e.g. based on 'memoranda of understandings'), avoidance of multilateral treaties, and settlement of disputes by political negotiations or mediation and arbitration proceedings inside China rather than by international adjudication.[2] The protection standards and dispute settlement provisions in China's bilateral investment treaties do not follow a uniform pattern; they have, so far, rarely been invoked by Chinese or foreign companies (cf. Shan 2015, 2020; Chaisse 2019). China's 'socialist market economy with Chinese characteristics' differs fundamentally from the multilevel constitutional design of the EU's 'competitive social market economy' (Article 3 Lisbon Treaty). For example:

- The risks of domestic market distortions resulting from the totalitarian control by the CCP of state bodies, other public bodies (like thousands of SOEs) and private bodies (including also thousands of private companies) are not effectively limited by multilevel competition laws, policies and judicial remedies similar to those inside the EU.[3]
- The risks of public and private distortions of WTO market access commitments aimed at non-discriminatory conditions of trade, undistorted price competition, reciprocity and transnational rule of law are not effectively limited by 'common market law' (e.g. similar to EU common market rights, judicial remedies, and constitutional 'checks and balances') and reciprocal opening of market access (e.g. to government procurement).

[2] On the dispute resolution culture in East Asia, its preferred use of arbitration and mediation, and the advantages of using commercial arbitration for the settlement of disputes over BRI investments rather than the Chinese ordinary, judicial system, see: Yuhong Chai (2018). Many of the 51 WTO members participating in the BRI are less developed countries with comparatively less developed judicial systems and hardly any effective, regional court systems outside Europe.

[3] Cf. 'China grants immunity to executives to bolster private sector' (*Financial Times* of 15 December 2019, reporting that 'Chinese prosecutors are dropping criminal charges against business owners in a desperate effort to rescue the country's ailing private sector' so as to 'help companies grappling with one of the country's worst debt crises', thereby 'putting the economy above the strict implementation of the law').

- The gigantic size of China's domestic market (18% of the world population), its totalitarian control and direction (e.g. through direct and indirect subsidisation of SOEs) and inadequate protection of intellectual property have entailed structural over-production (e.g. of steel, cement, aluminium, solar panels) and counterfeiting, with the exportation of surplus products and of counterfeited goods causing major disruptions in third countries (e.g. more than 80% of all counterfeit and pirated products seized in 2013 in seven EU countries originated in China). Chinese restrictions of internet governance, distortions of the digital economy and political uses of digital control technologies prompt technological rivalries and conflicts between Chinese and foreign interests (e.g. over technology transfers imposed on foreign companies, 5G network technologies).
- China's export-oriented trade mercantilism has entailed 'one-way traffic' on the railways connecting China with Europe, with many trains returning empty to China.
- China's claims to unilateral appropriation of more than 80% of the South China Sea—in violation of its multilateral legal obligations under the UN Convention on the Law of the Sea (UNCLOS), as formally established through legally binding arbitration awards[4]—reveal hegemonic ambitions in China's maritime 'Silk Roads' policies.
- China's strategy of low wages and of denial of labour and trade union rights has prompted China to ratify only 26 of the 177 International Labour Organization (ILO) Conventions (e.g. refusing to ratify the ILO Conventions on forced labour, freedom of association, and the right to collective bargaining and disregarding recommendations made by ILO monitoring committees).

Mutually beneficial trade and investment cooperation for creating transnational infrastructures of (rail)road, maritime and internet connectivity among countries along the Silk Roads meets the criteria of

[4] See China's rejection of the arbitration award of 12 July 2016 under UNCLOS Annex VII concerning the Chinese claims to control more than 80% of the South China Sea without regard to UNCLOS obligations: Permanent Court of Arbitration Case No 2013-19 in the matter of the South China Sea Arbitration (*The Republic of the Philippines* v. *The Peoples Republic of China*). The award is published on the PCA website at www.pcacases.com/web/view/7.

'aggregate PGs'.[5] Whereas informal bilateralism may entail abuses of power asymmetries imposing superior interests of the stronger partner, rules-based and transparent multilateralism protects weaker countries against abuses of power. US governments have taken an antagonistic view of the BRI in view of their strategic rivalries with China. The EU's multilateralism pursues no hegemonic foreign policies. At a 2017 BRI Forum in China, EU delegates surprised their Chinese hosts by turning down an offer to sign a declaration supporting the BRI by financing infrastructure investments inside the EU. Even though the EU describes China as a 'systemic rival promoting alternative models of governance', it has not opposed the participation of EU member states in various BRI projects financed by Chinese SOE, notably in Southern, Central and Eastern European states. Europeans criticise BRI governance, inter alia, for lack of transparency, reciprocity and of respect for competition, environmental, labour and human rights standards by Chinese SOEs. At another BRI Forum in April 2019, President Xi Jinping pledged a more open approach and—in response to problems of over-indebtedness of some borrowing countries—respect for financial sustainability. The more the US Trump administration rejects multilateral agreements in favour of unilateral power politics and 'bilateral deals' undermining the WTO and the 2015 Paris Agreement on climate change prevention, the more obvious become the increasing conflicts between three different, geopolitical policy paradigms:

- US leadership for *multilateral, neoliberal trade liberalization*, deregulation and privatisation of economic activities since World War II continues to be driven by domestic interest group politics, resulting in increasing social inequalities inside the United States and in US

[5] On the defining characteristics and different kinds of 'pure PGs' (whose use is 'non-rival' and 'non-excludable' like human rights) and 'impure PGs' (like 'club goods' excluding free-riders, common pool resources with rival uses), the related 'collective action problems', and their limitation through 'multilevel constitutionalism' and multilevel governance institutions see Petersmann (2017, Chapter 2), Jingxia (2018). As 'market failures' (like free-riding) impede the decentralised provision of PGs, and the 'aggregation' and transformation of national PGs into transnational PGs (like transnational rule of law, climate change mitigation) is made difficult by collective action problems among self-interested state actors with different preferences and interests, there is no universal solution or strategy for 'republican governance', i.e. the 'building blocks' and production processes for transnational PGs may differ depending on the particular regulatory challenges.

non-participation in important worldwide agreements (like UNCLOS, many multilateral human rights treaties, criminal law treaties and environmental treaties). The underlying economics is based more on utilitarian 'Chicago school' reasoning (e.g. market-driven maximisation of 'Pareto-' and 'Kaldor-Hicks-efficiencies') than on 'constitutional economics' (e.g. increasing economic and social welfare through democratic regulation of 'market failures' and related 'governance failures' in order to better satisfy general preferences of consumers and citizens). Neoliberal US leadership has ended with President Trump's mercantilist power politics shunning legal constraints in both domestic and foreign policies. The Trump administration's external mercantilism and domestic neoliberalism disdain 'judicialization' of dispute settlements in worldwide agreements (like the WTO), notably in view of their judicial limitations of US abuses of trade remedy laws.

- China's totalitarian *state capitalism* denies effective legal constraints on the CCP's political monopoly and economic dirigisme; notwithstanding China's continuing support for multilateral WTO negotiations and WTO dispute settlement procedures, China prefers administrative discretion and legal flexibility in bilateral BRI cooperation, thereby enabling China to use power asymmetries to its advantage (e.g. in the South China Sea).
- *European ordo-liberalism* rejects neoliberal 'market fundamentalism' advocating for a minimal state; it emphasises the need for 'strong states' legally limiting 'market failures', 'governance failures' and 'constitutional failures' (cf. Petersmann 1983; Slobodian 2018). The EU's ordo-liberal '*economic constitutionalism*' uses multilateral treaty disciplines for limiting market failures and governance failures also in multilevel governance of transnational PGs and international dispute settlement through rules-based trade and investment liberalisation, adjudication, protection of the environment and of human and constitutional rights as foundations of the EU's 'competitive social market economy'. Reconciling European multilateralism with Chinese bilateralism will require multilateral, rules-based approaches to protecting transnational rule of law and respect for human rights, as prescribed in the EU's foreign policy constitution (cf. Petersmann 2020a).

Trade and Investment Disputes Between China and the EU

BRI projects financed and carried out by Chinese companies continue to be based on flexible legal instruments (like memoranda of understandings) that tend to avoid multilateral BRI treaties and institutions.[6] China's BRI projects are often based on informal, bilateral and state-centred practices compared with the US post-war leadership for the multilateral Bretton Woods Agreements, GATT, the WTO and multilateral trade adjudication. China has been a party to the World Bank Agreement establishing the International Center for the Settlement of Investment Disputes (ICSID) for more than 25 years; it has also complied with most adverse WTO dispute settlement rulings (cf. Zhou 2019). These ICSID and WTO dispute settlement procedures are also available for the settlement of trade and investment disputes linked to BRI projects. Yet, China's BRI dispute settlement strategy has prioritised commercial arbitration in China's International Commercial Court (CICC) of the Supreme People's Court (cf. Jiang 2020), other Chinese arbitration institutions like the China International Economic and Trade Arbitration Commission (CIETAC) and its Silk Road Arbitration Center in Xi'an, and cooperation with other arbitration centres in Asia (e.g. in Hong Kong, Singapore), Africa and Europe (cf. Gu 2020). The lack of a multilateral dispute settlement strategy distinguishes the BRI from the past US leadership for multilateral dispute settlement systems in GATT, ICSID, the WTO and regional Free Trade Agreements (FTAs). Instead, China follows diverse, complementary dispute settlement methods and emphasises the advantages of political dispute settlement methods over third party adjudication.

At least seven different kinds of BRI disputes should be distinguished; their often 'overlapping jurisdictions' may lead to 'strategic forum shopping':

- International *trade disputes* tend to be settled by China through multilateral WTO dispute settlement procedures or through bilateral and regional negotiations. The 2010 ASEAN-China FTA (as

[6] The 2015 Agreement establishing the Asian Infrastructure and Investment Bank (AIIB) and the 2001 Shanghai Cooperation Organization—even though initiated by China and having their headquarters at Beijing—have mandates far beyond BRI cooperation.

amended in 2018) provides for settlement of disputes through consultations, mediation, conciliation or arbitration.

- *Investment disputes* tend to be settled through bilateral negotiations in the context of China's more than 130 Bilateral Investment Treaties (BITs) rather than through the very small number, so far, of ICSID or the United Nations Commission on International Trade Law (UNICITRAL) arbitration proceedings involving the PRC or companies from the PRC.
- *Financial disputes* seem to be settled through bilateral negotiations, arbitration and other jurisdictions in China rather than through multilateral treaty institutions like the Asian Infrastructure and Investment Bank (AIIB), which provides for settlement of disputes concerning loans from this bank through UNCITRAL arbitration.
- *Intellectual property disputes* may be settled through Chinese jurisdictions (like China's Patent office and Chinese courts) or through WTO, the World Intellectual Property Organization (WIPO) and other multilateral dispute settlement procedures.
- *Commercial disputes* are settled through Chinese courts and commercial arbitration procedures, subject to various limitations of the legal admissibility of ad hoc arbitration inside China (e.g. private ad hoc arbitration may be allowed inside China only inside Free Trade Zones and certain arbitration centres).
- As regards *maritime disputes*, China refused participating in the UNCLOS dispute settlement procedures initiated by the Philippines and rejected the UNCLOS arbitration award of 2016 concerning the South China Sea.
- As regards *energy trade and investment disputes*, China is not among the more than 75 members of the 1998 Energy Charter Treaty, which provides for international state-state and Investor-State Arbitration (ISA) of energy disputes and related investments.

This potential diversity of BRI disputes seems to confirm that creating a single dispute settlement mechanism for settling all potential BRI disputes would be neither feasible nor desirable. Yet, the pragmatic 'trial and error' approach of China vis-à-vis dispute settlement of BRI projects may be insufficient, for instance regarding countries that are not WTO members, with which China has not concluded a BIT or an FTA, or whose domestic judicial systems for the settlement of economic disputes are not reliable (e.g. due to lack of rule of law, of judicial independence, lack of trade law and financial law traditions or concerns about the enforcement of arbitral awards).[7] The diversity of dispute settlement fora for BRI-related disputes invites 'forum shopping', for instance in case of disputes over intellectual property rights protected by WIPO conventions, the WTO Agreement on Trade-Related Intellectual Property Rights (TRIPS) and international investment law. So far, China seems to have initiated hardly any WTO disputes and investment arbitration disputes related to Silk Road projects. If borrowing and host countries asked for adjustments to Silk Road Projects (like Malaysia due to its financial difficulties to pay its debts vis-à-vis China), political dispute settlements and contract re-negotiations were the preferred methods of agreed dispute settlement. Like China, also many other Asian countries often prefer political rather than judicial dispute settlement methods (as illustrated by the rejection of ICSID by India, Thailand and Vietnam). The disregard for the WTO legal obligation (under Article IX:1 WTO Agreement) to appoint vacant WTO AB positions by majority votes, if necessary, illustrates that some WTO members may not be unhappy about the US initiative to destroy the WTO AB review system, which—as of 11 December 2019—is no longer capable of accepting new appeals or completing all the 13 pending appellate review procedures. The draft Regional Comprehensive Economic Partnership (RCEP) Agreement between China and 14 other Asian countries, which is scheduled to be finalised in 2020, does not provide for a regional judicial and appellate review system that could compensate for the likely breakdown of the international rule of law at the worldwide level of WTO governance.

The prioritisation of bilaterally agreed, political dispute settlements has also become characteristic for the EU's external trade, investment and economic cooperation agreements. In EU treaty practices, disputes tend to be settled in bilateral treaty committees; treaty provisions for international arbitration have, so far, been rarely invoked by the EU (e.g. recently for the settlement of disputes over Korea's compliance with rules on worker rights in the EU-Korea FTA). This preference of both China and the EU for settling international financial and investment disputes

[7] On the risks of non-enforcement of arbitral awards in Asian BRI countries (e.g. due to invocation of the 'public policy exception' in Article V:2,b of the New York Convention on the Recognition and Enforcement of Foreign Arbitral Awards), and on the advantages of harmonising the 'public policy concept' in the cross-border enforcement of arbitral awards among Asian countries, see: Weixia Gu (2018).

politically stands in sharp contrast to the legalisation and judicialisation of trade, investment and financial disputes inside the EU. The Achmea judgement of the EU Court of Justice (CJEU) of March 2018[8] on the inconsistency of BITs among EU member states with EU constitutional law and its judicial remedies entails that—according to the EU Commission—'all investor-State arbitration clauses in intra-EU BITs are inapplicable and that any arbitration tribunal established on the basis of such clauses lacks jurisdiction due to the absence of a valid arbitration agreement'.[9] In a Declaration of 15 January 2019 on the legal consequences of the Achmea judgement and on investment protection, 22 EU member states committed to terminate their—altogether more about 80—intra-EU BITs by December 2019, if possible; they will no longer interpret the Energy Charter Treaty as including ISA clauses applicable in relations among EU member states.[10] Some of the EU's constitutional guarantees of fundamental rights and economic freedoms also protect Chinese investors and workers inside the EU. For instance, according to Article 15:3 EUCFR, '(n)ationals of third countries who are authorized to work in the territories of the Member States are entitled to working conditions equivalent to those of citizens of the Union'. Article 17:1 EUCFR provides:

> Everyone has the right to own, use, dispose of and bequeath his or her lawfully acquired possessions. No one may be deprived of his or her possessions, except in the public interest and in the cases and under the conditions provided for by law, subject to fair compensation being paid in good time for their loss. The use of property may be regulated by law in so far as is necessary for the general interest.

Hence, EU fundamental rights may be relied upon to ensure adequate protection also of Chinese investors and of their workers carrying out Silk Road projects inside EU member states. Past infringement actions by the EU Commission underscore its willingness to act on its own to

[8] Case C-284/16, *The Slovak Republic* v. *Achmea BV*, ECLI:EU:C:2018:158, 6 March 2018.

[9] Cf. *Protection of Intra-EU Investment, Communication from the Commission to the European Parliament and the Council*, COM (2018) 547 (19/7/2018), at p. 26.

[10] See: https://ec.europa.eu/info/publications/190117-bilateral-investment-treaties_en.

protect foreign investors inside EU member states from measures taken by their host states, rather than leave it only to those investors to seek judicial remedies.[11] The jurisprudence of the CJEU continues clarifying investor protection under EU law by member state courts in the wake of the *Achmea* judgement. This may incentivise also foreign investors, or their workers, to seek damages in host country courts for failures to comply with investment protection obligations and fundamental rights under EU law. In such disputes related to Silk Road investment projects inside EU member states, national and European courts—and, if the aim of concluding an EU-China BIT by the end of 2020 should be realised, also ISA composed of professional judges—may be legally bound to apply European fundamental rights and constitutional law as parts of the applicable law. As the demands of justice, and of legal and judicial justification, may differ according to the particular contexts, the principles of justice applicable to market and business transactions, labour contracts, 'justice at the workplace', and 'just compensation' for direct or indirect expropriation of property rights in EU-China relations may differ from those developed by national and European courts for foreign investments by EU citizens among EU member states. Yet, human rights (including human rights at work and to own private property)—as a type of fundamental rights focusing on respect for everyone's dignity and humanity—are recognised as 'general principles of the Union's law' (cf. Article 6 Lisbon Treaty on European Union [TEU]) that protect Chinese workers and investors inside the EU no less than workers and investors with EU passports. EU human rights law, constitutional law and social legislation tend to limit 'market failures' and 'governance failures' (e.g. public and private abuses of power like gender, racial and other discrimination, forced labour, child labour, other abuses of power in the workplace) much more strictly than in authoritarian Asian countries, which protect much lower minimum standards of welfare and well-being (e.g. in terms of legal prohibition of gender and racial discrimination and other abuses

[11] Cf. the judgment in *Commission* v. *Hungary*, Case C 235/17 (May 21, 2019). See also Communication from the Commission to the European Parliament and the Council Protection of intra-EU investment, COM/2018/547 final (Brussels: European Commission, 2018) (providing 'guidance to help EU investors to invoke their rights before national administrations and courts and to help Member States to protect the public interest in compliance with EU law'.)

of power). As Chinese SOEs may not be used to respecting civil, political, economic, social and cultural rights and the ordo-liberal competition and social laws in social market economies, their implementation of Silk Road projects inside EU member states may give rise to legal conflicts (e.g. about 'justice at work' in the power relationships between Chinese employers and their employees inside EU member states if liberal values like equal individual freedoms, privacy and co-determination of workers are disregarded); the settlement of such conflicts inside the EU may entail judicial dispute settlement procedures different from ISA, mediation and conciliation. It remains to be seen whether the ongoing negotiations on reforms of ICSID and UNCITRAL arbitration procedures, and the EU proposals for a multilateral investment court system, will strengthen the public law dimensions of investor-state disputes in ways that will also be accepted by China; or whether the jurisprudence of the CJEU and of the European Court of Human Rights (ECtHR) on protecting human rights as worker rights (e.g. based on EU anti-discrimination law, Articles 8, 11 and 14 European Convention on Human Rights) will strengthen the legal disciplines for foreign investors inside the EU and the protection of their workers (e.g. against being treated like commodities or robots), for instance by limiting the terms of labour contracts through mandatory principles of constitutional law and human rights law aimed at guaranteeing 'justice at work for all' (cf. Collins 2019).

Conclusion: Multilevel Protection of Rule of Law in Silk Road Investment Projects?

International trade, competition, investment, social and environmental laws need new rules in order to better take into account the risks of market failures and governance failures (including climate change) in relations between neoliberal economies (e.g. in Africa, the Americas and Asia), state-capitalist economies (e.g. in China and many of its Asian BRI partner countries) and ordo-liberal economies (e.g. in Europe). The more globalisation transforms *national* into *transnational PGs* (like transnational connectivity among BRI countries, climate stability) which no state can unilaterally protect without international law and cooperation, the more multilevel governance of transnational PGs requires multilevel protection of transnational rule of law; also the legitimacy of economic, financial and investment cooperation in the implementation of BRI projects depends on rules-based legal frameworks, impartial dispute settlement procedures, predictability and compliance of governance with the 'rule of law' as 'a principle of governance in which all persons, institutions and entities, ... including the State itself, are accountable to laws that are publicly promulgated, equally enforced and independently adjudicated, and which are consistent with international human rights norms and standards' that have become part of universally recognised human rights principles.[12]

The trade wars between China and the United States since 2018 were caused by (1) geopolitical rivalries and mercantilist zero-sum conceptions of international trade advocated by the US Trump administration; (2) American neoliberal interest group politics (e.g. increasing recourse to illegal 'trade remedies' and US disruption of the WTO dispute settlement system); and (3) systemic conflicts between China's totalitarian state-capitalism and liberal interpretations of WTO law (Petersmann 2020b). The 'phase-one economic and trade agreement between China and the USA', signed on 15 January 2020, reflects these systemic conflicts: while the Preamble acknowledges that it is 'in the interest of both countries that trade grow', the agreement leaves—arguably WTO-inconsistent, illegal—discriminatory US tariffs on imports from China worth up to $360 bn in place; it includes discriminatory commitments of China to increase its purchases of US goods and services up to a total amount of $200 bn during 2020/2021, thereby strengthening China's state-capitalist quantitative trade management; other agreed provisions (e.g. on 'forced' technology transfer, currency manipulation) aim at rules-based market-opening and at legal disciplines limiting market distortions in China, without mentioning discriminatory US restrictions on Chinese technology firms like Huawei; the bilateral dispute settlement procedure provides for the possibility of unilateral, discriminatory trade sanctions inconsistent with WTO rules and WTO dispute settlement procedures. The incoherent character of this partial 'trade truce' is also illustrated by the absence of rules on many of the systemic US complaints of Chinese trade distortions (e.g. by industrial subsidies, SOEs, China's technology policies and cyber theft); the hegemonic, geopolitical rivalries underlying this 'phase-one truce' suggest that the US trade war risks continuing indefinitely. Similarly, the agreement announced by the United States, the EU and Japan in January 2020 on tougher subsidy disciplines aimed at Chinese SOEs remains unenforceable

[12] UN General Assembly Resolution A/RES/67/97 (2012) on 'The Rule of Law at National and International Levels'.

due to the simultaneous US disruption of the WTO legal and dispute settlement system.[13] Continuing trade conflicts appear unavoidable not only between China's totalitarian state capitalism (e.g. denying constitutional 'checks and balances' limiting the CCP's powers and state-interventions) and the interest group-driven, American neoliberalism, where economic and environmental lawmaking are dominated by rent-seeking interest groups and by their financial support for congressmen and trade politicians; as illustrated by the US sanctions against Chinese technology companies, the US trade war against China and the increasing use by the United States of trade sanctions as a foreign policy instrument also affect third countries and the future of the WTO.

Following the 2016 'Brexit referendum' and the US election of President Trump, the executive trade policies of both the British and US governments increasingly avoided multilateral legal disciplines, parliamentary and judicial control also in relations with European trading partners (cf. Petersmann 2020b); this increasing recourse to intergovernmentalism and power-related conflicts (e.g. between EU law and Anglo-Saxon deregulation of product, production, tax, competition and environmental standards) is likely to further undermine multilateral trade rules and adjudication. Other WTO member countries increasingly emulate the US tactics of preventing judicial clarifications of WTO rules. For example, a draft WTO panel report of spring 2019 on China's complaint against EU anti-dumping measures found that Section 15 of China's WTO Accession Protocol does not prevent other WTO members from applying non-discriminatory 'distortion of competition principles' in their application of anti-dumping laws to imports from China; China's suspension of this WTO complaint after the interim review of the panel findings ushered in the non-publication and non-adoption of this panel report and

[13] Due to the illegal 'blockage' by the US of the appointment of AB members since 2017, there was only one single AB member left as of 11 December 2019; this rendered the AB uncapable of admitting new appeals and prompted both the US and other WTO members to prevent adoption of adverse panel reports by 'appealing into the void'; cf. E. U.Petersmann (2020c). At an informal WTO ministerial meeting during the Davos World Economic Forum in January 2020, the EU and 16 other WTO members (including China) agreed to using voluntary arbitration pursuant to Article 25 DSU as a temporary substitute for appellate review until the WTO AB would become operational again. In the meeting of the WTO Dispute Settlement Body on 27 January 2020, the United States blocked, once again, Mexico's request—on behalf of 120 WTO members—to initiate the procedure for appointing the six vacant AB positions.

of its important clarification of WTO legal disciplines. As China refused to accept the Organization for Economic Co-Operation and Development (OECD) principles on artificial intelligence, and its 'Made in China 2025' program aims at import substitution and technological independence (e.g. replacing foreign by domestic computers in all government offices), EU countries have introduced stricter surveillance of foreign direct investments from China (notably in information and communication technology sectors). Many WTO members continue to criticise China for not adequately meeting its transparency requirements under WTO law (e.g. regarding subsidies, sub-central government measures, China's obligation to translate its regulations into English). The more the US assault on the WTO legal and dispute settlement system limits political and judicial clarifications of the often contested meaning of WTO rights and obligations, the more China may find it preferable to prioritise its bilateral BRI and RCEP projects for constructing a China-centred 'Eurasian trading system', which could replace the United States as China's main export market and enable state-capitalist economies to become 'rule-makers' defending their authoritarian control of economies and polities also in transnational cooperation.

Since China's first BIT concluded in 1982, China accepted full ICSID jurisdiction since 1998 and pre-establishment national treatment commitments since 2013 (subject to exceptions). China concluded more than 50 BITs with BRI partner countries; but the number of FTAs concluded by China remains much smaller (cf. Jingxia 2018). China's new foreign investment legislation approved in 2019 reflects the changing investment policies; yet, it is widely criticised as 'a missed opportunity' to stop the downward trend, since 2015, of foreign direct investment in China.[14] The number of ICSID arbitration procedures for settling disputes involving China as a respondent (three cases only by July 2017), or introduced by Chinese investors abroad as complainants (five ISAs by July 2017), remains exceptionally low (cf. Hong and Yoen Lee 2018). China has played a leading role in the adoption of the 2017 'Guiding Principles for Global Investment Policymaking' by the G20. Yet, EU officials criticise China for the 'snail pace progress' in the many years of negotiations on a China-EU investment agreement and for making access of European companies to the Chinese market often conditional on joint ventures

[14] See: 'China's new foreign investment law is a missed opportunity', *Financial Times*, 24 December 2019.

and technology transfers. The recent EU Regulation for reviewing Foreign Direct Investment (e.g. screening Chinese takeovers of strategic European industries and of critical information technologies and infrastructures) reflects the EU's cautious attitude vis-à-vis Chinese SOEs and Chinese geopolitical influence. The advisory opinion by the CJEU of 30 April 2019 on the consistency with EU law of the investment court system of the Comprehensive Economic and Trade Agreement (CETA) of the EU with Canada sets out clear constitutional limits for future ISA in a China-EU investment agreement.[15] In view of China's non-participation in the UNCLOS arbitral proceeding initiated by the Philippines against China in 2013 and China's non-recognition of the arbitral award of 2016 rejecting China's claims to more than 80% of the South China Sea, it remains doubtful whether China will support the EU proposals for a multilateral investment court. It remains to be seen how China—in case the US assault on the WTO dispute settlement system should adversely affect also other WTO governance functions (like the WTO negotiations on electronic commerce, where China's insistence on protection of 'cyber sovereignty' and national data storing requirements conflicts with US positions)—will respond to the dismantling of the WTO provisions for horizontal and vertical separation of legislative, administrative and judicial WTO governance powers and mutual 'checks and balances'. The US trade war against China risks undermining the important role which international law has so far played in furthering economic and legal reforms inside China.

The systemic conflicts between Chinese state-capitalism, Anglo-Saxon neoliberalism and European ordo-liberalism embedded into rights-based, multilevel constitutionalism suggest increasing bilateral and regional challenges to the WTO legal and dispute settlement system. BRI projects are driven by Chinese economic, political and legal interests, for instance in Chinese top-down governance (e.g. prioritising bilateral contractual arrangements exploiting power asymmetries), China's preference for

[15] Opinion 1/2017 CJEU of 30 April 2019, ECLI:EU:C:2019:341. In Opinion 1/2017, the ISA procedures in the CETA were found to be consistent with EU law in view of the legal limitations of the potential reach of ISA by CETA guarantees of, inter alia, the legal autonomy of EU law, the EU judicial system, the democratic 'regulatory freedom' to protect non-economic PGs, and of fundamental rights (e.g. of access to judicial remedies, equal treatment) as protected in the EUCFR.

maintaining legal flexibility and China's self-interest in becoming a 'rule-maker' in new policy fields like the cyberspace and patent registration. The EU is currently designing a multilateral counter-strategy, for instance insisting on China's compliance with EU law in carrying out BRI projects inside the EU (e.g. respect for EU regulations for public procurement procedures in case of large infrastructure projects like the new high-speed train connections between Belgrade and Budapest). From the EU perspective, BRI-related trade and investment disputes may be better settled through WTO and investment arbitration than through Chinese court and arbitration proceedings applying Chinese law, whose consistency with EU constitutional law guarantees (like individual rights to effective remedies and to a fair trial, cf. Article 47 EUCFR) appears doubtful. Currently, 17 EU member states are members of the China-led AIIB, and 11 participate in BRI projects, which are discussed in a 17+1 institutional framework. Agreement on common EU positions on China's BRI initiative would be facilitated by conclusion of the proposed EU-China investment agreement and by China's accession to the WTO Government Procurement Agreement so as to protect reciprocal market access rights, investor rights and other fundamental rights and judicial remedies. The breakdown of the WTO dispute settlement system risks adversely affecting the impact of WTO law on China's continuing 'rule by law construction'. The constitutional requirement of the EU under Article 3 of its Lisbon Treaty to contribute—also in its external relations—to 'the sustainable development of the Earth', 'free and fair trade', 'the protection of human rights' and 'to the strict observance ... of international law' will be closely watched by European civil societies and democratic institutions in future EU cooperation with China. Notably in the implementation of the EU's 'new green deal' for climate change mitigation through reduction of greenhouse gas emission, the EU's introduction of taxes on carbon-emissions and related 'border carbon adjustments' is likely to give rise to increasing conflicts with other WTO members (like China, India and the United States as the countries with the largest carbon emissions). China's use of WTO law for promoting 'rule by law' in China's multilevel governance of transnational trade reflects a 'thin', formal conception of rule of law that does not meet all the formal criteria (like publicity, prospective application, generality, clarity, consistency, performability, stability over time, congruity between the positively enacted and actually practised law) and institutional criteria (like an independent judicial system) of what L. Fuller called the 'internal morality of law' (cf. Fuller 1977: 46 ff). China's legal system and ‘rule by law’ are even less consistent with substantive conceptions of rule of law, notably with the human and constitutional rights protected by EU law, by UN human rights and labour rights conventions or by the definition of ‘rule of law’ in UN reports.[16] This systemic rivalry between China’s totalitarian state-capitalism (e.g. using extremely low labour costs and state subsidies for its export-led growth model) and Europe’s rights-based ‘social market economy’ (based on multilevel human rights and democratic constitutionalism) is likely to remain a source for regular economic conflicts in the cooperation among China and Europe, which would be resolved best through multilateral, rules-based legal and dispute settlement systems. It remains paradoxical that—even though the WTO remains the only worldwide organisation capable of negotiating multilateral competition and legal disciplines for SOEs, state subsidies and other market distortions—the US Trump administration has given up Western leadership for using WTO law and dispute settlement procedures as constraints on systemic, competitive distortions and abuses of power inside China.

References

Carty, Anthony and Nijman, Janne (2018), *Morality and Responsibility of Rulers. European and Chinese Origins of a Rule of Law as Justice for World Order*, Oxford University Press, Oxford.

Chai, Yuhong (2018), “Regional Dispute Resolution: An International Civil Dispute Resolution Model for East Asia”, in Yun, Zhao (ed.), *International Governance and the Rule of Law in China Under the Belt and Road Initiative,* Cambridge University Press, Cambridge, 261–294.

Chaisse, Julien (2019), *China’s International Investment Strategy. Bilateral, Regional and Global Law and Policy*, Oxford University Press, Oxford.

[16]Cf. Report by the Secretary-General on the Rule of Law and Transitional Justice in Conflict and Post-Conflict Societies (UN Security Council, 23 August 2004), which defines the rule of law as a ‘principle of governance in which all persons, institutions and entities, public and private, including the State itself, are accountable to laws that are publicly promulgated, equally enforced and independently adjudicated, and which are consistent with international human rights norms and standards. It requires as well measures to ensure adherence to the principles of supremacy of law, equality before law, accountability to the law, fairness in the application of the law, separation of powers, participation in decision-making, legal certainty, avoidance of arbitrariness and procedural and legal transparency’.

Collins, Hugh (2019), Justice at Work, *LSE Law, Society and Economy Working Papers* 18/2019.
Fuller, L.F. (1977), *The Morality of Law*, Yale University Press, New Haven, CT.
Gu, Weixia (2018), "Enforcement of Arbitral Awards in Asia Under the Belt and Road Initiative", in Zhao, Yun (ed.), *International Governance and the Rule of Law in China Under the Belt and Road Initiative,* Cambridge University Press, Cambridge, 277–294.
Gu, Weixia (2020), "Belt and Road Dispute Resolution: New Development Trends", in *Chinese (Taiwan) Yearbook of International Law and Affairs*, 36, 151–169.
Jiang, Huiqin (2020), "Demystifying China's International Commercial Court Regime: International or Intra-National?", in *Chinese (Taiwan) Yearbook of International Law and Affairs*, 36, 171–198.
Jingxia, Shi (2018), "The Belt and Road Initiative and International Law: An International Public Goods Perspective", in Zhao, Yun (ed.), *International Governance and the Rule of Law in China Under the Belt and Road Initiative,* Cambridge University Press, Cambridge, 9–31.
Li, Tao and Jian, Zuoli (2018), "Human Rights, Justice and Courts in IEL: A Critical Examination of Petersmann's Constitutionalization Theory", in *Journal of International Economic Law*, 21(1), 193–212.
Mahbubani, Kishore (2018), *Has the West Lost? A Provocation*, Penguin Books, United Kingdom.
Petersmann, Ernst-Ulrich (1983), "International Economic Theory and International Economic Law—On the Need of a Legal Theory of International Economic Order", in MacDonald, Ronald St John and Johnston, Douglas Millar (eds.), *The Structure and Process of International Law*, Nijhoff Publishers, The Hague, 227–261.
Petersmann, Ernst-Ulrich (2017), *Multilevel Constitutionalism for Multilevel Governance of Public Goods—Methodology Problems in International Law*, Hart, Oxford.
Petersmann, Ernst-Ulrich (2018a), "The 2018 Trade Wars as a Threat to the World Trading System and to Constitutional Democracies", in *Trade, Law and Development*, 10(2), 179–225.
Petersmann, Ernst-Ulrich (2018b), "International Economic Law Without Human and Constitutional Rights? Legal Methodology Questions for My Chinese Critics", in *Journal of International Economic Law*, 21(1), 213–231.
Petersmann, Ernst-Ulrich (2020a), "Lessons from European Constitutionalism for Reforming Multilevel Governance of Transnational Public Goods in Asia?", in Chaisse, Julien (ed.), *EU Leadership and Global Power Shifts: What Lessons for Asia?* Hart, Oxford, 217–237.
Petersmann, Ernst-Ulrich (2020b), "Economic Disintegration? Political, Economic and Legal Drivers and the Need for 'Greening Embedded Liberalism'", in *JIEL*, 23 (2020, forthcoming).

Petersmann, Ernst-Ulrich (2020c), "Between 'Member-Driven Governance' and 'Judialization': Constitutional and Judicial Dilemmas in the World Trading System", in lo, Chang-fa, Nakagawa, Junji and Chen, Tsai-fang (eds.), *The Appellate Body of the WTO and Its Reform*, Springer, Singapore, 15–42.

Scheidel, Walter (2019), *Escape from Rome: The Failure of Empire and the Road to Prosperity*, Princeton University Press, Princeton, NJ.

Shan, Wenhua (2015), *China and International Investment Law: Twenty Years of ICSID Membership*, Brill Nijhoff, Leiden.

Shan, Wenhua (2020), *China and International Dispute Resolution in the Context of the Belt and Road Initiative*, Oxford University Press, Oxford.

Slobodian, Quinn (2018), *Globalists. The End of Empire and the Birth of Neoliberalism*, Harvard University Press, Cambridge, MA.

Un Hong, Dae and Yoen Lee, Ju (2018), "Why Are There so Few Investor-State Arbitrations in China?" in *China and WTO Review*, 4, 35–65.

Wu, Chien-Huei (2012), *WTO and the Greater China: Economic Integration and Dispute Resolution*, Martinus Nijhoff Publishers, The Hague.

Zhou, Weihuan (2019), *China's Implementation of the Rulings of the World Trade Organization*, Hart, Oxford.

The Construction of the Rule of Law of OBOR Through Implementation of TFA

Yongmei Chen

Introduction

According to the official documents of the Chinese government, the OBOR initiative advocates international cooperation, and the main content of OBOR international cooperation is the cooperation of trade and investment. On 28 March 2015, the "*Vision and Actions on Jointly Building Silk Road Economic Belt and 21st-Century Maritime Silk Road*" (《推动共建丝绸之路经济带和 21 世纪海上丝绸之路的愿景与行动》, hereinafter referred to as "Vision and Actions on OBOR") jointly issued by the National Development and Reform Commission, the Ministry of Foreign Affairs and the Ministry of Commerce clearly stated that the cooperation of investment and trade is a key content. In May 2017, *Joint Communique of the Leaders Roundtable of the "Belt and Road" Forum for International Cooperation* (《"一带一路"国际合作高峰论坛圆桌峰会联合公报》) jointly issued by President Xi and the heads of states of 28 countries also stated in the 'Cooperation Objectives', 'We reiterate the importance of expanding economic growth, trade and investment based

Y. Chen (✉)
School of International Law, Southwest University of Political Science and Law, Chongqing, China
e-mail: chenym226@126.com

G. Martinico and X. WU (eds.), *A Legal Analysis of the Belt and Road Initiative*, https://doi.org/10.1007/978-3-030-46000-6_5

on a level-playing field, market rules and universally recognized international norms'. Judging from the actual progress of OBOR international cooperation, trade and investment are also top priorities (Liu and Wang 2018: 18). In the field of trade, China's total imports and exports to the BRI countries in 2018 totalled 8365.7 billion yuan, an increase of 13.3% over the previous year. Among the total number, exports took up 4674.8 billion yuan, an increase of 7.9%; imports summed up in 3797.9 billion yuan, an increase of 20.9%.[1] In the field of investment, from January to November 2019, Chinese companies invested 12.78 billion US dollars in non-financial direct investment in 56 BRI countries, accounting for 12.9% of the total amount during the same period. The investment mainly went to Singapore, Laos, Vietnam, Indonesia, Thailand, Pakistan, United Arab Emirates (UAE), Malaysia, Cambodia and Kazakhstan. In terms of foreign contracting projects, Chinese companies have newly signed 6055 foreign contracted engineering projects in 61 BRI countries, with a new contract value of 127.67 billion US dollars, accounting for 61.2% of the total new contracted value of China's foreign contracted projects during the same period, an increase of 41.2%; the completed turnover was 74.61 billion US dollars, accounting for 55.3% of the total during the same period, an increase of 1.3%.[2]

However, in addition to geographical differences, the BRI countries differ in the level of economic development. Generally speaking, the level of economic development and the degree of trade facilitation tend to show a positive correlation: the more developed a country's economy is, the higher the per capita GDP is, and the stronger its ability to trade and invest abroad is, the more it would actively promote trade and investment facilitation cooperation. In less developed countries, the degree of marketisation is not high; the corresponding market economy system is incomplete; the laws are not sound and the transparency is low; and the degree of trade and investment facilitation is not high. All the above, status quo directly affects the volume of trade and investment in their countries. The difference in the economic development level of these countries not only determines their differences in the basis and level of trade and

[1] National Bureau of Statistics of the People's Republic of China, http://www.stats.gov.cn/tjsj/zxfb/201902/t20190228_1651265.html (accessed on 3 February 2020).

[2] The Ministry of Commerce of the People's Republic of China, http://www.mofcom.gov.cn/article/tongjiziliao/dgzz/201912/20191202924464.shtml (accessed on 3 February 2020).

investment facilitation, but also causes the differences in their goals and demands in trade and investment cooperation, which leads to the lack of consistency in countries' measures to promote trade and investment facilitation (Zhang and Fan 2016: 27).

Most of the BRI countries have major deficiencies in terms of market access, border management, infrastructure and operating environment and so on. In terms of market access, there are serious trade and investment protection problems, such as self-protective exclusion in Central Asia and the Commonwealth of Independent States (CIS) countries; border management procedures are cumbersome without standardised procedures; and port management is inefficient. In terms of infrastructure, the port facilities, information and communication facilities as well as logistics facilities are relatively backward, which affects paperless customs clearance applications and e-commerce development, and the construction of port management platform. In terms of the operating environment, the situation in many regions is volatile; it is difficult to keep policy coherence and stability. Many BRI countries have weak legal systems and lack effective legal foundations and institutional guarantees for trade and investment (Zhang and Fan 2016: 27).

If the problems such as infrastructure can be solved through investment and construction, then the biggest obstacle appearing on the implementation of OBOR initiative should be that most BRI countries have a low level but high risks of rule of law. The risks include both abstract legal and policy risks and concrete measures risks. To strengthen the rule of law communication and cooperation is an important measure to address these risks because the implementation of OBOR initiative requires the protection of the rule of law. In fact, the construction and cooperation of the rule of law are also the due meanings of the policy coordination in the "Five-Pronged Approach"[3] of OBOR initiative. On this basis, the construction of the OBOR rule of law and the implementation of the OBOR initiative can be promoted smoothly.

Recognising the importance of the rule of law cooperation and international rule of law on the implementation of OBOR initiative, the Chinese Ministry of Foreign Affairs and the Chinese Law Society jointly held the first Forum on the Belt and Road Legal Cooperation in Beijing from 2 July to 3 July 2018. "*Statement of the Co-Chairs of the Forum on*

[3] 'Five-Pronged Approach' refers to policy coordination, connectivity of infrastructure, unimpeded trade, financial integration and closer people-to-people ties.

the Belt and Road Legal Cooperation" (《"一带一路"法治合作国际论坛共同主席声明》) was issued as an important achievement of the meeting. According to the statement, on the one hand, it is necessary to carry out cooperation on the rule of law based on the principles of mutual consultation, co-construction and sharing, in order to consolidate the foundation of the rule of law for the construction of OBOR; on the other hand, the countries should observe and improve the relevant systems of international rules with the existing international cooperation mechanisms and by exploring the establishment of new mechanisms to build a stable, fair, transparent and non-discriminatory rule and institutional framework for OBOR. In order to trade with the BRI countries smoothly, it is necessary for China to pay special attention to and put extra emphasis on the reform and improvement of the legal system for the facilitation of China's customs trade, and to timely transform and implement the international treaties and the rules regarding trade facilitation. Several studies have also shown that trade facilitation will strongly promote global economic and trade growth and it will especially benefit developing countries and SMEs[4] (Zhou 2017: 10). To this end, China chooses to finance the implementation of OBOR rule of law cooperation training project to promote and deepen OBOR rule of law exchanges and cooperation. Therefore, the implementation of OBOR initiative will make outstanding contributions in strengthening the dialogue and coordination of laws and policies in countries along the route, and strengthening the development of the international rule of law (Han 2018: 24).

We believe that building an OBOR rule of law system should be an important mission for the construction of the rule of law in China and the reform of the global governance system (Liu 2017: 126). The OBOR is a new platform for practising the international rule of law and a new impetus for promoting the international rule of law. With the continuous development of OBOR construction and the gradual deepening of

[4] Hoekman Shepherd researched with the data from World Bank and corporate survey to show that shortening export time through trade facilitation measures will significantly promote exports of small and micro-manufacturing enterprises; Saporto et al. found that if countries strictly implement trade facilitation measures, the trade cost will be reduced by 16.5% in low-income countries, 17.4% in low- and middle-income countries and 14.6% in high- and middle-income countries. According to the latest estimates by the OECD and the Peterson Institute for International Economics, the effective implementation of trade facilitation measures can at most increase the exports of developed and developing members by 4.5 and 9.9%, respectively, each year, which would increase global GDP by 960 billion US dollars.

cooperation in the rule of law, the international rule of law will be further enriched from the conceptual and practical level, and the development of the international rule of law will be further promoted.[5] In this context, this article aims to demonstrate the OBOR rule of law construction from the perspective of TFA implementation, that is, how China implements TFA and promotes its implementation in the BRI countries, while addressing the challenges China face and pointing out the way forward. This article consists of an introduction, conclusion and main body which is divided into three parts. Given that the international cooperation of the OBOR initiative mainly happens in the field of trade and investment, after the introduction, the second part takes trade as its starting point to demonstrate the bi-directional relationship between the OBOR rule of law construction and the implementation of TFA. Built upon the second part, the third part analyses China's implementation of TFA, especially the implementation of TFA provisions related to Article X (Publication and Administration of Trade Regulations), Article VIII (Fees and Formalities connected to Importation and Exportation) and Article V (Freedom of Transit) of GATT1994, as well as the practices that promote the BRI countries to implement the relevant TFA provisions. Next, in the fourth part, the article points out the challenges China still faces and the outlook of possible actions China will take.

The Bi-Directional Relationship Between the Construction of Rule of Law of OBOR and the Implementation of the Trade Facilitation Agreement

The OBOR rule of law construction is carried out at both the international level and the domestic level. At the international level, as a part of the international economy, OBOR is a transnational economic region that achieves trade liberalisation. Therefore, in the process, it is necessary to promote economic growth in member countries, establish unified markets, coordinate and reach consensus on economic policies, and resolve legal issues in cooperation by signing treaties or with existing ones. In

[5] Statement of the Co-Chairs of the Forum on the Belt and Road Legal Cooperation, http://www.xinhuanet.com/politics/2018-07/03/c_1123073746.htm (accessed on 3 February 2020).

addition, "Vision and Actions on OBOR" clearly advocates strengthening the role of multilateral cooperation mechanisms. Therefore, OBOR rule of law construction relies on the operation of the existing multilateral cooperation mechanisms that include the WTO, the Shanghai Cooperation Organization, the ASEAN Plus China, the Asia-Pacific Economic Cooperation, the Asia-Europe Meeting, the Asian Cooperation Dialogue, the AsiaInfo Conference, the China-Arab Cooperation Forum and China-Gulf Cooperation Council Strategic Dialogue, Greater Mekong Subregional Economic Cooperation and Central Asian Regional Economic Cooperation (Wang 2017: 32). At the domestic level, what and how China, who initiated OBOR, should do in the construction of domestic rule of law is of paramount importance to the OBOR rule of law construction. At the same time, only when the BRI countries are promoted to implement international legislation can the rule of law mechanisms that solve problems about regional economic cooperation be provided. Because OBOR international cooperation is mainly trade and investment cooperation, there is a bi-directional relationship between OBOR rule of law construction and the implementation of the Trade Facilitation Agreement.

Promotion of Implementation of TFA Through OBOR Rule of Law Construction

The content of the OBOR law should include not only the existing bilateral, regional and multilateral trade and investment treaties and agreements signed by China and relevant countries and regions, but also the latest developments in international economic and trade rules. OBOR law should construct international trade laws with trade facilitation as the core, focus on innovating international investment laws by emphasising on the improvement of infrastructure in the BRI countries and construct international financial laws for the development of financial institutions such as the Asian Infrastructure Investment Bank and the Silk Road Fund. An important objective of OBOR achieving the rule of law is to build an international treaty system that represents the fruits of the twenty-first-century international economic law development (Liu 2017: 129).[6]

[6] The content of the OBOR law suggested by Chinese academics refers to Naigen Zhang (2016), "The Reconstitution of Rules on International Trade in 'One Belt and One Road' Initiative", in *Law Science*, 61(5), 93–99.

In the field of international trade law, specifically, TFA is the first multilateral agreement reached in the WTO since its establishment in 1995 and the most historic multilateral achievement with the greatest commercial value. China and the BRI countries should work jointly to sort out the existing bilateral and multilateral trade agreements and promote the implementation of TFA in the BRI countries and regions with trade facilitation as the core. Trade facilitation is particularly crucial for the construction of OBOR. An important goal of OBOR is to achieve the exchange of goods and services in its region. The core is to facilitate such an exchange (Zhu and Li 2016: 58). OBOR should pay special attention to legal issues such as customs clearance of goods, commodity inspection and quarantine, quality standards and e-commerce rules. Through the simplification of procedures, the coordination of applying laws and regulations, and the standardisation and improvement of infrastructure, a coordinated, transparent and predictable business environment is created.

Promoting the parallel operation between OBOR construction and TFA implementation is not only in the interest of China but also a common pursuit of relevant countries and regions. It is also destined by the OBOR rule of law construction. OBOR Initiative and TFA share the same international and regional background, a common vision and mission, and both reflect the common aspirations of countries around the world of pursuing cooperation and development (Zhang 2017: 8).

As we know that the TFA includes the release and clearance of goods, cooperation with border agencies, freedom of transit, and customs cooperation etc., and has established and improved a series of rules for customs trade facilitation. Take the certified operator system as an example, TFA provides specific standards and trade facilitation measures for certified operators in a generalised or enumerated manner respectively. Specific standards focus on compliance and safety, while procedural simplification, cost and time reduction are key considerations of trade facilitation measures. These rules are conducive to the trades among the BRI countries, but meanwhile, they bring forth new requirements of trade facilitation in the BRI countries. Therefore, the construction of OBOR's trade facilitation rules should comply with the relevant requirements and regulations of the TFA (Zeng 2018: 18). In other words, we believe that the implementation and practice of the TFA should be the priority of the OBOR rule of law construction in trade facilitation. Undoubtedly, promoting the implementation of TFA in the BRI countries is China's focus of work to accomplish the goals of OBOR and its focus on achieving the rule of law.

Promotion of OBOR Rule of Law Construction Through Implementation of TFA

As mentioned earlier, the BRI countries have an imbalanced economy but great potential for economic and social development. These countries currently lack integral capabilities or balanced abilities to implement TFA. Therefore, combining the implementation of OBOR initiative with that of TFA has important practical significance for China and other countries, especially those involved in the joint construction of the OBOR rule of law. Take the Pakistani Expressway funded by the Asian Infrastructure Investment Bank (AIIB) as an example. This expressway section is one of the BRI 'China-Pakistan Economic Corridor' projects which bridge the distance between mainland China and the Arabian Sea, shorten the transportation cycle and reduce the logistics cost. Therefore, the TFA and the BRI are closely linked by the infrastructure.

Trade facilitation creates a coordinated, transparent and predictable environment for international transactions through the simplification of procedures, the coordination of applying laws and regulations, and the standardisation and improvement of infrastructure. It is based on internationally recognised standards and practices. In short, trade facilitation, basing on the reduced transportation costs by interconnectedness, simplifies and coordinates international trade system and its procedures in order to cut down transaction costs (Feng and Li 2015: 4).

Across the entire TFA agreement, effective trade facilitation assistance is the key to the effectiveness of the TFA and to ensure that the trade volume of developing countries, especially the least developed countries, increases, and that the trade processes are simplified and convenient. Although the TFA provides that members can apply for an extension of the transition period when their implementation capacity is lacking,[7] the transition period is only meant to postpone the date of member countries starting to implement TFA, instead of solving their difficulties regarding implementation in the long run. The TFA can only be effectively implemented when the international community provides members in difficulties of implementation with capacity-building assistance and support.

[7] See TFA art. 17.2, 17.3.

To put it in detail, the provisions in the first part of the TFA on customs clearance and in the second part on capacity-building assistance are consistent with China's BRI purpose of accelerating the construction of big customs clearance; that is, both of them are intended to achieve trade facilitation by improving the infrastructure standards of countries. According to the special and differential treatment provisions in the TFA, 'capacity-building assistance and support should be provided to developing and least developed countries'. Although such provision sets obligations for developed countries in the form of a principle, the requirement is in line with providing funds and technical support for infrastructure construction in the BRI countries in OBOR implementation. Therefore, the connectivity of infrastructure is the commonality of BRI and TFA, and infrastructure is a nexus between BRI and TFA. The construction of BRI infrastructure will drive the implementation of TFA which will promote the OBOR rule of law construction.

If the TFA can be well implemented in the BRI countries, it will not only promote the OBOR rule of law construction, but also serve as a significant inspiration and reference for the WTO system and multilateral trade negotiations. The TFA defended the central role of the WTO in the international trade governance, solved the difficulty of the Doha Round being stuck in traditional issues for many years, successfully incorporated the first new international trade rules into the multilateral trading system, and added new contents to the governance on the trade of goods. The TFA has achieved reductions in trade costs at a deeper level by providing for joint actions between regulatory agencies in various countries (such as inter-customs information exchange mechanisms and cooperation between border regulators), and has achieved a trade promotion effect that cannot be achieved with unilateral actions, thereby setting a precedent for the expansion of future cooperation mechanisms and models of multilateral trade institutions. At the same time, the TFA's open negotiation approach that includes all members is distinct from the previously small-scale, group-based, closed and "greenhouse" style negotiation model of the WTO. This bottom-up negotiation process where all participants jointly lead the negotiated issues ensures the maximum political and economic interests of all parties. In addition, the TFA legally binds all WTO members equally, but the degree and duration of its implementation vary according to different members' levels of development. The

TFA also assesses different developing and least developed members' ability to implement each of the trade facilitation measures and provides corresponding capacity-building and technical support assistance based on the assessment, instead of adopting a 'one-size-fits-all' special and differential treatment. Its successful implementation in the BRI countries will also serve as an extremely useful reference for the formulation of other new agreements in future WTO negotiations (Sheng 2016: 10).

China's Implementation of the TFA and Its Promotion on the BRI Countries Implementing the TFA

The TFA is the first multilateral trade agreement China has entered into after joining WTO. As the world's largest trading country in goods, China has attached great importance and provided great support to TFA. China actively participated in and promoted the TFA negotiations, and submitted and co-signed successively eight proposals which covered not only the publication and implementation of trade regulations, risk management, follow-up inspections and other specific trade facilitation measures, but also comprehensive issues such as the determination of members' needs and priority concerns, technical assistance and capacity-building support.[8] During the adoption of the TFA protocol, China has repeatedly stressed that the implementation of TFA is in the interests of all members, calling on all members to pay attention to the demands of developing members, to earnestly help realise the development goals of the Doha Round and to comprehensively promote the implementation of the decisions of the Bali Ministerial Conference in a balanced way. On 4 September 2015, China submitted a letter of acceptance to the WTO Director General, announcing that China had formally completed the domestic procedure of approval for the TFA protocol and became the 16th member to accept TFA. With the TFA formally entering into force, its formal implementation will promote the reform of China's port system. In addition, the

[8] The Ministry of Commerce of the People's Republic of China, the head of the WTO Department of the Ministry of Commerce interprets the Trade Facilitation Agreement, http://www.mofcom.gov.cn/article/ae/ai/201501/20150100864841.shtml (accessed on 3 February 2020).

promotion of trade facilitation cannot be separated from the development of electronic and information technology. Therefore, the implementation of the TFA is also an important opportunity for China's customs modernisation.

Commitments Made by China

As mentioned above, the TFA has given special and differential treatment to developing and least developed members, allowing them to adjust the implementation of the terms in the agreement and the time limit for implementation according to their own capabilities. Based on that, on 30 June 2014, China sent a letter to the Chairman of the Preparatory Committee for Trade Facilitation, submitting one month in advance China's notification of Category A measures[9] under TFA. The notice designates most of the clauses in Section I[10] of TFA as Category A measures, except the following clauses: (a) Article 7.6 of TFA: Establishment and Publication of Average Release Times; (b) Article 10.4 of TFA: Single Window; (c) Article 10.9 of TFA: Temporary Admission of Goods and Inward and Outward Processing; (d) Article 12 of TFA: Customs Cooperation.[11] Therefore, according to the provisions of Section II[12] of TFA, except for the measures covered by the above clauses, China promises to implement the trade facilitation measures covered by all the other clauses immediately after the agreement enters into force (i.e. 22 February 2017).

[9] According to the provisions of Article 14 of TFA, developing countries may decide on their own the measures to be implemented in Section I immediately after the entry into force of the agreement (i.e. Category A measures), or the measures to be implemented after a transitional period (i.e. Category B measures), or the measures to be implemented after a transitional period and through capacity building and acquisition of implementation capacity (i.e. Category C measures), and notify the WTO.

[10] TFA mainly consists of Preamble, Section I, Section II, Section III and Annex 1. The Section I consists of Articles 1–12, which stipulates the substantive obligations of each member in terms of trade facilitation, involving information publication, advance rulings, release and clearance of goods, customs cooperation, etc., with a total of about 40 trade facilitation measures.

[11] Notification of Category A Commitments under the Agreement on Trade Facilitation, Communication from China, 30 June 2014.

[12] The Section II of TFA consists of Articles 13–22. It mainly stipulates the special and differential treatment that developing and the least developed countries can enjoy when implementing the Section I of TFA, which is embodied in implementation period and capacity building.

Measures Taken by China

In fact, many WTO agreements are related to TFA. For example, as far as GATT1994 is concerned, TFA is the clarification and improvement of Article X (Publication and Administration of Trade Regulations), Article VIII (Fees and Formalities connected to Importation and Exportation) and Article V (Freedom of Transit) of GATT1994. The following paragraphs will conduct a preliminary review on China's implementation of TFA mainly at three aspects: (a) freedom of transit, (b) fees and formalities connected to importation and exportation and (c) publication and administration of trade regulations.[13]

Freedom of Transit

The relevant clause of TFA is Article 11. In accordance with *the Customs Law* (《海关法》), *General Administration of Customs Decree No. 38 "Measures of the People's Republic of China on Customs Supervision of Transit Goods"* (1992) (《海关总署令第 38 号《中华人民共和国海关对过境货物监管办法》(1992)》) and *General Administration of Quality Supervision, Inspection and Quarantine Decree No. 159,*[14] *62,*[15] *136*[16] and *118,*[17] China has established customs and quality inspection procedures related

[13] The full implementation of TFA by China refers to *Trade Facilitation Annual Report of China*, published annually by Beijing Ro-code Trade Security and Facilitation Research Center, http://www.re-code.org/ (accessed on 3 February 2020).

[14] *Decree No. 159 of the General Administration of Quality Supervision, Inspection and Quarantine of the People's Republic of China "Administrative Measures for Inspection and Quarantine of Entry and Exit Non - edible Animal Products"*. (国家质量监督检验检疫总局令第159号《进出境非食用动物产品检验检疫监督管理办法》).

[15] *Decree No. 62 of the State General Administration of Quality Supervision, Inspection and Quarantine "Administrative Measures for Inspection and Quarantine of Import and Export Genetically Modified Products"*. (国家质量监督检验检疫总局令第 62 号《进出境转基因产品检验检疫管理办法》).

[16] *Decree No. 136 of the State General Administration of Quality Supervision, Inspection and Quarantine "Measures for the Supervision and Administration of Inspection and Quarantine of Imported and Exported Meat Products"*. (国家质量监督检验检疫总局令第 136 号《进出口肉类产品检验检疫监督管理办法》).

[17] *Decree No. 118 of the State General Administration of Quality Supervision, Inspection and Quarantine "Measures for Supervision and Administration of Inspection and Quarantine of Import and Export Feed and Feed Additives"*. (国家质量监督检验检疫总局令第 118 号《进出口饲料和饲料添加剂检验检疫监督管理办法》).

to transit transport and has not imposed disguised restrictions on transit transport. The provisions of Article 11 of TFA have been implemented in China, and China's current customs system basically meets the requirements of TFA.

For example, Article 11.5 of TFA encourages members to provide physically separate infrastructure (such as passageways, berths and similar facilities) for transit transport where feasible. In order to promote the construction of OBOR initiative, especially the construction of the "Silk Road Economic Belt", China initiated the establishment of the AIIB and the "Silk Road Fund" to strengthen infrastructure construction along the OBOR. One of the first projects of AIIB is "Tajikistan Dushanbe - Uzbekistan Border Highway Improvement Project". As these new domestic and foreign investment and financing institutions gradually increase their investment in the infrastructure of OBOR, there is great hope for the construction of Euro-Asian special transit railway. Therefore, the implementation of the OBOR Initiative will greatly promote the implementation of TFA, especially the realisation of transit trade facilitation (Zhang 2017: 7). Article 11.16 of TFA stipulates that all members shall strive to cooperate and coordinate with each other to enhance freedom of transit. Such cooperation and coordination may include, but is not limited to, understandings on (a) costs; (b) formalities and legal requirements; and (c) the actual operation of the transit system. China has successively signed bilateral customs cooperation and mutual assistance agreements with Russia (1994), Kyrgyzstan (1996), Kazakhstan (1997), Armenia (2015) and Belarus (2015), and these agreements stipulate mutual customs assistance on the facilitation of goods transit. In addition, China is pushing for the early signing of a customs cooperation agreement with Tajikistan and accelerating negotiations to reach a free trade agreement with EAEU (Eurasian Economic Union) so as to provide necessary conditions for future customs cooperation (Zhang 2017: 8).

Fees and Formalities Connected to Importation and Exportation

The relevant articles of TFA are Articles 6, 7.1, 7.7, 10.1, 10.4, 10.5, 10.6 and 10.9. As far as Article 6 of TFA "Disciplines on Fees and Charges Imposed on or in Connection with Importation and Exportation and Penalties" is concerned, in recent years, China's customs and quality inspection agencies have made great efforts and yielded remarkable results in publishing charging information and reducing charging items. Among them, the business charges involving customs and quality inspection agencies as well as the service charges implemented through the third-party agencies attached to the above agencies have been further cleaned up and standardised. Starting from 1 April 2017, the inspection and quarantine department completely lifts the entry-exit inspection and quarantine fees. In terms of publishing charging information, China's customs and quality inspection agencies have published relevant charging information such as charging types, charging standards, charging basis and reasons on the portal website.[18] The relevant requirements of Article 6 of TFA have been fully implemented in China Customs.

As far as Article 7.1 of TFA "Pre-arrival Processing" is concerned, China already has relevant laws and regulations, but the implementation of declaring in advance system is not sufficient. Article 9[19] of the Administrative Measures of the Customs of the People's Republic of China on Manifests of Inbound and Outbound Means of Transport and Article 1[20] of the Announcement No. 74 of the General Administration of Customs on Clarifying the Requirements for the Administration of Imported and Exported Goods in Declare in Advance stipulate that imported goods can be declared to the Customs three days in advance after the inbound

[18] For the current administrative charges of the customs, see: http://www.customs.gov.cn/customs/302249/302303/302305/index.html (accessed on 3 February 2020).

[19] Article 9 of the *Administrative Measures of the Customs of the People's Republic of China on Manifests of Inbound and Outbound Means of Transport* (《中华人民共和国海关进出境运输工具舱单管理办法》) stipulates that: 'The manifest transmitter shall transmit other data of the original manifest to the Customs before the inbound goods and articles arrive at the destination port. After the customs accepts the transmission of the main data of the original manifest, the consignee and the entrusted customs declaration enterprise may go through the customs declaration formalities for goods and articles'.

[20] Article 1 of the *Announcement of the General Administration of Customs No. 74 of 2014 "Announcement on Clarifying the Requirements for the Administration of Import and Export Goods in declare in advance"* (海关总署公告 2014 年第 74 号《关于明确进出口货物提前申报管理要求的公告》) stipulates that: 'The consignee or consignor of import and export goods and the entrusted customs declaration enterprise declare in advance shall first obtain the data of the manifest or bill of lading. Among them, the imported goods from declare in advance shall be declared to the customs after they are transported by the inbound means of transport and before they arrive at the customs supervision place. Goods exported from declare in advance shall be declared to the customs within 3 days before the goods arrive at the place under customs supervision'.

means of transport are shipped and before they arrive at the place under customs supervision, which provides legal basis and guarantee for the early declaration system. It meets the requirements of Article 7.1.1 of TFA. In practice, on the basis of Announcement No. 74 of the General Administration of Customs, although some local customs have also started to clarify and publish the specific operational details of early declaration in their own customs areas, such as Shanghai Customs and Changsha Customs,[21] there are still some problems and obstacles in the concrete implementation of the system. The main obstacles are the operational habits of manifest declaration enterprises and the fear of possible customs penalties if the manifest data in declaring in advance are wrong. The premise of declaring in advance is that manifest data should be transmitted in advance. In addition to cargo owners' need to strengthen information communication and transmission with customs declaration enterprises, shipping agents or shipping companies (sea transportation), airlines or ground agents (air transportation), the customs should strengthen publicity and fault tolerance mechanisms for manifest declaration enterprises and encourage enterprises to send manifest data in advance, so as to ensure the practical implementation of declare in advance. In addition, for imported goods, according to Article 6 of Announcement No. 74, imported goods declared in advance shall be subject to the tax rate and exchange rate implemented on the date when the means of transport carrying the goods declare their entry. This regulation pushes enterprises to face changes in tax rates and exchange rates when the means of transport declare their entry into the country, so enterprises need complicated operations such as tax refund and compensation according to the actual situation.

As far as Article 7.7 of the TFA "Trade Facilitation Measures for Authorized Operators" is concerned, China has fully implemented the

[21] *Shanghai Customs Announcement No. 1 of 2017 Announcement on Clarifying Matters Related to the Customs Clearance Operation Mode of Export "Declare in Advance, Arrival, Inspection and Release", Changsha Customs Announcement No. 2 of 2017 Announcement on Matters Related to the Implementation of the Customs Clearance Mode of Export "Declare in Advance, Arrival, Inspection and Release".* (上海海关公告2017年第1号《关于明确出口"提前申报、运抵验放"通关作业模式有关事项的公告》, 长沙海关公告2017年第2号《关于实施出口"提前申报、运抵验放"通关模式相关事宜的公告》).

AEO[22] Trade Facilitation Measures Clause. Article 4 of the *Interim Measures of the People's Republic of China on Credit Management of Customs Enterprises* in 2014 (2014年《中华人民共和国海关企业信用管理暂行办法》) clearly states that authorised enterprises are Authorized Economic Operators of the China Customs. China Customs shall carry out mutual recognition of AEOs with customs of other countries or regions in accordance with the law, and shall provide mutual recognition of AEO enterprises with corresponding customs clearance facilities. According to the provisions of the *Customs Certification Enterprise Standard, Decree No.82 of the General Administration of Customs* (海关总署令第 82 号《海关认证企业标准》), the authorisation standard is divided into four parts: internal control, financial status, compliance standards and trade safety.[23] These standards meet the requirements of Article 7.7.2 of TFA. The five aspects of facilitation measures stipulated in Article 7.7.3(b)(c)(d)(e)(g) of TFA have also been implemented, while the rest remains to be implemented. At present, the customs of China and other countries or regions actively carry out mutual recognition of AEO. For example, China, Singapore, South Korea, Hong Kong, EU, New Zealand and Switzerland have mutually recognised AEO. China Customs is stepping up AEO mutual recognition cooperation with the customs of major trading countries such as the United States, Japan and Australia, and other BRI countries such as Russia, Kazakhstan, Malaysia, Israel and South Africa. Its goal is to achieve more than 80% of the total exports value of AEO mutual recognition countries or regions by 2020.[24] In short, China's AEO system has been fully brought into line with international standards. In terms of advanced authorised enterprises, China has fully met TFA requirements in terms of cargo clearance and inspection ratio, delaying payment of customs duties, shortening clearance time and using guarantees before taxes.

[22] AEO means 'Authorized Economic Operator'. AEO system is a management system introduced by the World Customs Organization (WCO) in order to realise WCO SAFE (Framework of Standards for Global Trade Safety and Facilitation), build a partnership between customs and the business sector, and realise the objectives of trade safety and facilitation.

[23] Articles 1 and 3 of *Customs Certification Enterprise Standard* (《海关认证企业标准》).

[24] General Administration of Customs of the People's Republic of China, AEO mutual recognition between China and Switzerland will take effect on September 1 (《中国-瑞士海关AEO互认9月1日起实施》), http://www.customs.gov.cn/customs/302249/302425/721329/index.html (accessed on 3 February 2020).

As of the end of June 2018, of the 33 BRI countries within AEO systems, China has achieved mutual recognition with 14 countries and is stepping up mutual recognition negotiations or communicating mutual recognition cooperation intentions with the remaining 19 countries, striving to achieve mutual AEO recognition with customs of all BRI countries within AEO systems who have the willingness to cooperate by 2020 (Gu 2018: 3). Local customs have achieved good results in promoting the implementation of the AEO in OBOR construction. For example, Guangzhou Customs relying on the mutual support of international customs AEO expands the inter-customs cooperation of the BRI countries and regions, selects 3789 enterprises with import and export trade with important BRI countries such as India, Israel, Kazakhstan and Brazil to be included in the annual list of certified enterprise cultivation plans and actively carries out the cultivation of certified enterprises.[25] In countries and regions that recognise each other, goods of AEO-certified enterprises can be given facilitated treatment which reduces repeated declaration and inspection, and effectively saves time and cost. Such treatment has extremely important significance for enterprises to expand the international market, to improve international influence and competitiveness and to promote the process of international trade facilitation.

As far as Article 10.1 of TFA "Formalities and Documentation Requirements" is concerned, China's customs system is relatively complete and clear in terms of import, export and transit-related procedures. Chapter II "Declaration Requirements" and Chapter IV "Declaration Documents" in Decree No. 103 of the *General Administration of Customs "Administrative Provisions of the Customs of the People's Republic of China on Declaration of Import and Export Goods"* (2004), (海关总署令第 103 号《中华人民共和国海关进出口货物申报管理规定》) clearly stipulate the declaration procedures and document requirements for import and export goods. Article 8 of *Decree No. 38 of the General Administration of Customs "Measures of the Customs of the People's Republic of China on Supervision of Transit Goods"* (《中华人民共和国海关对过境货物监管办法》) stipulates that transit goods shall be declared when entering the

[25] The General Administration of Customs of the People's Republic of China, Guangzhou Customs 10 Key Measures to Promote the Implementation of "the Belt and Road" Initiative Construction (《广州海关10项重点举措推动落实"一带一路"建设》), http://www.customs.gov.cn/customs/302249/302425/636714/index.html (accessed on 3 February 2020).

country, and the relevant documents to be submitted shall be listed. In general, China Customs has fully implemented Article 10.1. For example, in order to ensure the efficient operation of the Central Asian Railway Express (Nantong-Hailaton, Afghanistan), Nantong Customs affiliated to Nanjing Customs implements a convenient combination of customs clearance such as export to declare in advance, arrival for inspection and release, paperless customs clearance, paperless customs transfer and "palm logistics" to shorten customs clearance time and improve customs clearance efficiency. At the same time, Nantong Customs strengthens the cooperation of port law enforcement, optimises the cooperation between customs and inspection, promotes 'one-stop' operations and realises the exchange of logistics information with railway departments.[26]

As far as TFA Article 10.4 "Single Window" is concerned, it is included in Category B measures of all China's TFA commitments; that is, China would implement it after the transition period. The indicative implementation date for the "Single Window" is 22 February 2020 (the final implementation date is to be determined), which is the same as that for other Category B measures.[27] Therefore, accelerating the construction and comprehensively promoting the application of the "Single Window" fully demonstrate China's fulfilment of WTO commitments and its implementation of high-level trade and investment liberalisation and facilitation policies. In practice, China first piloted a UN-developed Single Window project of international trade in the Shanghai Free Trade Zone in June 2014. After the initial success of the "Single Window" pilot in Shanghai, its promotion quickly spread to Fujian, Tianjin, Guangdong and other coastal provinces and cities. After five years of reform and innovation, fully implemented on 19 July 2019, China's Single Window project of international trade has been carried out in the entire country and achieved great results. So China has met the requirements of the TFA Article 10.4 in advance.[28]

[26] The General Administration of Customs of the People's Republic of China, China-Arab Customs Exchange Talks on "Market Procurement" Integrating into "the Belt and Road" Initiative (《中阿海关交流畅谈"市场采购"融入"一带一路"》), http://www.customs.gov.cn/customs/302249/302425/636664/index.html (accessed on 3 February 2020).

[27] China's Notification of Category Commitments under the TFA, G/TFA/N/CHN/1, 6 June 2017.

[28] https://tfadatabase.org/notifications/implementation (accessed on 3 February 2020).

China's Single Window project of international trade is built on governmental public platforms at both national and local levels. At the national level, the basic functions of the "Single Window" are coordinated and promoted. They mainly include relevant national departments' supervision on and service for international trade, cross-department information sharing and networking applications, and the establishment of relevant national standards for the "Single Window" (China International Trade Data Element Country Standards, etc.), the establishment of a Single Window legal framework for China's international trade and information exchange agreements with relevant countries. At the local level, the expansion of the "Single-Window" service functions actually required by the business of import and export enterprises is carried out. It mainly includes local government services, local port logistics services, local big data services and financial services, international freight services and other functions. Provinces and cities may entrust enterprises to manage and operate a Single Window public platform for local international trade. For example, in addition to the 12 functions including the state unified development license, customs declaration and export tax rebate, the Single Window of local international trade in Shanghai and Fujian also has 10 functions developed at the local level (Meng 2019: 50).

As far as Articles 10.5 "Preshipment Inspection" (PSI) and Article 10.6 "Use of Customs Brokers" of TFA are concerned, China Customs doesn't require 'pre-shipment inspection related to tariff classification and customs valuation', which meets the requirements of Article 10.5 of TFA. China Customs does not mandate the use of customs brokers. The consignor and consignee of import and export goods can decide to make customs declaration by themselves (registration of foreign trade operators and registration of customs declaration enterprises are required) or ask brokers to make customs declaration on their behalf, which meets the requirements of Article 10.6.

As far as Article 10.9 of TFA "Temporary Admission of Goods and Inward and Outward Processing" is concerned, China has fully implemented the requirement of temporary import of goods. The "Administrative Measures of the Customs of the People's Republic of China for Temporary Entry and Exit of Goods" clearly stipulates temporary import for exhibitions, sports, news, science and education, medical treatment, sample goods, charity and other activities.[29] In November 2016, the Customs issued a Notice on Cancelling the Administrative Examination and Approval Items of "Temporary Entry and Exit Goods" and cancelled the administrative examination and approval items of "Temporary Entry and Exit Goods". Applicants can directly go through the import and export declaration procedures of temporary entry and exit goods and submit relevant materials without going through the examination and approval procedures in advance.[30]

With regard to inbound and outbound processing, inbound processing has been carried out in China for more than 30 years, and a relatively complete "bonded" management system for inbound processing trade has been established.[31] In terms of outbound processing, starting from 2012, China Customs began to launch outbound processing pilot projects in some enterprises. In 2015, with the construction of the free trade zone, the General Administration of Customs allowed Fujian, Guangdong, Tianjin and other free trade zones to carry out overseas

[29] See *Decree No. 212 of the General Administration of Customs, "Administrative Measures of the Customs of the People's Republic of China for Temporary Entry and Exit Goods"* (《中华人民共和国海关暂时进出境货物管理办法》) and *"Acceptance Form for Administrative Examination and Approval of the Customs of the People's Republic of China (Administrative Examination and Approval Items for Temporary Entry and Exit Goods)"* (《中华人民共和国海关行政审批受理单(暂时进出境货物的核准行政审批事项)》).

[30] See the General Administration of Customs of the People's Republic of China, *Notice on Cancelling the Administrative Examination for Approval Items of "Temporary Entry and Exit Goods"* (《关于取消"暂时进出境货物的核准"行政审批项目的提示》).

[31] The inbound processing trade management system includes: *Decree No. 219 of the General Administration of Customs "Measures of the People's Republic of China on Supervision of Customs Processing Trade Goods"* (《中华人民共和国海关加工贸易货物监管办法》; *Decree No. 155 of the General Administration of Customs "Administrative Measures of the People's Republic of China on Unit Consumption of Customs Processing Trade"* (《中华人民共和国海关加工贸易单耗管理办法》); *Announcement of the General Administration of Customs No. 21 of 2014 "Announcement on Relevant Issues Concerning the Implementation of the Measures of the People's Republic of China on Supervision of Customs Processing Trade Goods"* (《关于执行<中华人民共和国海关加工贸易货物监管办法>有关问题的公告》; *Decree No. 150 of the General Administration of Customs "Measures of the People's Republic of China on the Supervision of Customs Processing Trade Enterprises on the Internet"* (《中华人民共和国海关加工贸易企业联网监管办法》; *General Office of the State Council of the People's Republic of China [1999] No. 35 "Notice on Further Improving the Opinions on the Margin Account System of Processing Trade Banks"* (《关于进一步完善加工贸易银行保证金台帐制度意见的通知》), etc.

processing pilot projects.[32] In December 2016, the General Administration of Customs promulgated the Announcement on Issues Related to Outbound Processing Business,[33] further regulating outbound processing business. It can be said that outbound processing is currently in its infancy and needs further development.

According to Xiamen Customs, in the process of outbound processing, the Customs only levies taxes on the value-added part. The policy helps enterprises save about 30% of import and export duties and value-added taxes on general trade, thus greatly reducing the operating costs and gaining wide recognition from enterprises. In order to enable more enterprises to enjoy the bonus of the "outbound processing" policy and actively participate in the cooperation of OBOR national production capacity, Xiamen Customs has set up a special window for outbound processing business. For eligible enterprises, the onsite customs will directly handle outbound processing account books. Xiamen Customs will also explore the promotion of enterprise independent verification and automatic verification modes to further simplify the verification procedures for outbound processing account books. Xiamen Customs also takes the initiative to coach enterprises to carry out "general certification" to ensure the smooth development of related businesses.[34]

[32] In 2015, the General Administration of Customs mentioned in *"Several Measures to Support and Promote the Construction and Development of China (Fujian) Pilot Free Trade Zone"* (《关于支持和促进中国（福建）自由贸易试验区建设发展的若干措施》), *"Several Measures to Support and Promote the Construction and Development of China (Tianjin) Pilot Free Trade Zone"* (《关于支持和促进中国（天津）自由贸易试验区建设发展的若干措施》) and *"Several Measures to Support and Promote the Construction and Development of China (Guangdong) Pilot Free Trade Zone"* (《关于支持和促进中国（广东）自由贸易试验区建设发展的若干措施》) the need to support the implementation of outbound processing business in the above-mentioned free trade zone. Xiamen, Dalian and other customs have also started outbound processing overseas.

[33] See General Administration of Customs *Announcement No. 69 of 2016 (Announcement on Issues Related to Outbound Processing)* (《关于出境加工业务有关问题的公告》).

[34] The General Administration of Customs of the People's Republic of China, Xiamen Customs Promotes "Outbound Processing" and "the Belt and Road Initiative" Capacity Cooperation (《厦门海关助推"出境加工"力促"一带一路"产能合作》), http://www.customs.gov.cn/customs/302249/302425/1922745/index.html (accessed on 3 February 2020).

Publication and Administration of Trade Regulations

The relevant articles of TFA are Articles 1, 3 and 4. As far as Article 1 of TFA "Publication and Accessibility of Information" is concerned, since China's accession to the WTO in 2001, the Ministry of Commerce, Customs, Quality Inspection and other agencies responsible for cross-border trade management have provided on the Internet a large amount of information related to import and export trade including legislation, import and export management, taxes, classification, trade license, etc. China Customs mainly carries out information disclosure according to the "*Regulations of the People's Republic of China on the Disclosure of Government Information*" (《中华人民共和国政府信息公开条例》) and "*the Measures of the People's Republic of China on the Disclosure of Government Information by Customs*" (《中华人民共和国海关政府信息公开办法》) promulgated by State Council. China's State General Administration of Quality Supervision, Inspection and Quarantine has formulated and implemented the "*Guidelines for the Disclosure of Government Information by the General Administration of Quality Supervision, Inspection and Quarantine (AQSIQ)*" (《质检总局政府信息公开指南》). In August 2016, the General Administration of Customs updated the "*Guidelines for the Disclosure of Government Information by the General Administration of Customs*" (《海关总署政府信息公开指南》).

Although China has fully implemented the requirements of this clause, the business sector still has higher expectations for the disclosure and accessibility of government information related to cross-border trade. Due to the following deficiencies in information disclosure, there is room for improvement. (a) For import and export and transit processes involved in import and export and transit, there are no concise and intuitive procedural guidance and forms released on the customs website; no specific import, export and transit procedures (including procedures at ports, airports and other entry points) and required forms and documents on the inspection and quarantine portal website, and the information is plenty but scattered which needs integration. (b) The General Administration of Customs of China has an English version of the published information on its official website, but the content is scarce. The website of AQSIQ is available in English, but almost all the English version of nature of laws and regulations is offered only in the form of catalogues while the content links are all in Chinese.

As far as Article 3 of TFA "Advance Rulings" is concerned, China has already formulated laws and regulations on advance rulings. As stipulated in Article 43 of the Customs Law, the Customs may make administrative decisions such as commodity classification in advance on the goods to be imported or exported according to the written application submitted by foreign trade operators. The same administrative ruling on commodity classification shall apply to the import or export of the same goods. The Customs shall make public the administrative ruling on the classification of commodities. Article 9 of the "*Interim Measures of the People's Republic of China on the Administration of Administrative Rulings of the Customs*" (《中华人民共和国海关行政裁定管理暂行办法》) stipulates that the applicant may request the Customs to keep confidential information provided to the Customs for applying for an administrative ruling if it involves commercial secrets. Except as required by judicial procedures, the Customs shall not disclose it without the consent of the applicant. The applicant's request for confidentiality of the information provided shall be submitted to the customs in writing and shall specify the contents that need to be kept confidential.[35]

[35] In addition to the Customs Law, laws and regulations related to the advance ruling include the following: Advance ruling: *Decree No. 92 of the General Administration of Customs "Interim Measures of the People's Republic of China on the Administration of Customs Administrative Ruling"* (海关总署令第 92 号《中华人民共和国海关行政裁定管理暂行办法》); *Advance Classification: Decree No. 158 of the General Administration of Customs "Administrative Provisions of the Customs of the People's Republic of China on Classification of Import and Export Commodities"* (海关总署令第158 号《中华人民共和国海关进出口货物商品归类管理规定》); Advance Examination Price: Article 10 *Decree No. 124 of the General Administration of Customs "Administrative Measures of the Customs of the People's Republic of China on Taxation of Import and Export Goods"* (海关总署令第 124 号《中华人民共和国海关进出口货物征税管理办法》) (taxpayers may apply to the Customs for pre-classification of import and export goods, pre-examination of prices or predetermination of origin in accordance with relevant regulations before the actual import and export of goods. The Customs shall notify the taxpayers in writing after verification and confirmation, and shall approve the actual import and export of the goods); Advance Determination of Origin: Article 12 of *State Council Decree No. 416 "Regulations of the People's Republic of China on Origin of Import and Export Goods"* (国务院令第 416 号《中华人民共和国进出口货物原产地条例》) (before the import of goods, the consignee of the goods to be imported or other parties directly related to the goods to be imported may apply in writing to the Customs for an advance determination decision on the origin of the goods to be imported if there are legitimate reasons). In addition, in 2011 and 2012, the General Administration of Customs respectively made regulations on price pre-examination and origin pre-determination for each directly affiliated Customs by means of notification, including: a. *Interim Provisions on the Administration of Price Advance Audit*

Nevertheless, the current relevant laws and regulations are not complete in themselves and are not fully implemented. A few cases of advance rulings found through public channels show that local customs has sporadically implemented the system of pre-determination of origin and pre-examination of import prices. If the Customs refuses to make an advance ruling, some provisions stipulate that the reason for refusal must be provided, while other provisions do not mention it. China Customs' advance ruling system has stipulated the validity period of some rulings, while others have not. The cancellation of the advance ruling decision must be notified to the parties concerned. China Customs has made clear requirements in the advance ruling regulations, but the rules on the pre-determination of origin are not clear. Although China's administrative reconsideration system has been fully implemented, no specific case has been found for the reconsideration of the customs advance ruling system due to its insufficient implementation. Generally speaking, although China has already formulated laws and regulations on advance ruling, the relevant regulations have not been fully completed and fully implemented. China should further improve the implementation of the requirements of Article 3 of TFA.

As far as Article 4 of TFA "Procedures for Appeal or Review" is concerned, the terms of the appeal or review procedures have been well implemented by the relevant departments in China. China has established a relatively complete legal system for administrative litigation and administrative reconsideration, mainly including the *Administrative Procedure Law of the People's Republic of China* (《中华人民共和国行政诉讼法》) and the *Administrative Reconsideration Law of the People's Republic of China*

of Imported Goods No. 419 [2011] of the State Administration of Taxation (署税发〔2011〕419 号《进口货物价格预审核管理暂行规定》), which makes corresponding provisions for enterprises to propose price advance audit; b. *Notice of the General Administration of Customs on Issuing the Interim Provisions on the Determination of Origin of Imported Goods, No. 129 [2012] of the Administration of Taxation* (署税发〔2012〕129 号《海关总署关于印发 < 进口货物原产地预确定暂行规定 > 的通知》). Most of the Customs directly under Beijing, Shanghai, Guangzhou and Qingdao have formulated specific operational management systems applicable to the advance examination of the prices of imported goods within their respective customs scope in accordance with circular No. 419 [2011] of the customs administration. Some directly affiliated customs such as Shanghai, Haikou, Jiangmen and Fuzhou have formulated specific implementation and management systems applicable to the advance determination of origin within their respective customs scope in accordance with circular No. 129 [2012] of the customs administration.

(《中华人民共和国行政复议法》). Based on the *Administrative Reconsideration Law*, China Customs formulated and promulgated the *Administrative Reconsideration Measures for Customs* (《海关行政复议办法》) and *the General Administration of Quality Supervision, Inspection and Quarantine of China formulated and promulgated the Administrative Reconsideration Measures for Entry-Exit Inspection and Quarantine* (《出入境检验检疫行政复议办法》). Generally speaking, China's provisions on procedures for appeal or review meet the requirements of Article 4 of TFA.

New Model to Promote Trade Facilitation

In addition to actively fulfilling its commitments on implementing the measures in Category A of TFA, China has also actively explored new models to promote trade facilitation between China and other countries (especially the BRI countries). For example, in November 2015, under the joint witness of President Xi Jinping and Prime Minister Lee Hsien Loong, China and Singapore formally signed a cooperation agreement to set up a "China-Singapore (Chongqing) Demonstration Initiative on Strategic Connectivity"[36] in Chongqing. The project takes "modern connectivity and modern service economy" as its theme, with financial services, aviation industry, transportation logistics and information and communication technology as its key areas of cooperation, and gradually expands to other areas to facilitate the "South Passage" trade in goods, to promote the development of trade in service and to realise the organic combination of tangible real economy and intangible virtual industry. Under the framework of the Demonstration Initiative, the project connects provinces and cities (regions) in western China, as well as Singapore and other ASEAN countries through regional linkage and international cooperation. The objectives are to promote trade and cooperation between regions in western China and ASEAN countries, to promote innovation of new model and practice of international multimodal transportation and to explore the new pattern of logistics driven industries

[36] This is the third project of cooperation between the Chinese government and the Singapore government. The first project is "Suzhou Industrial Park" (1994) and the second is "Sino—Singapore Tianjing Eco-city" (2007).

aggregation. As of 18 May 2018, China-Singapore connectivity projects have signed 116 projects with a total value of $ 20.76 billion.[37]

Challenges and the Way Forward

According to the "flexibility requirements" of the TFA, China has accepted 94.5% of TFA entities as Category A clauses based on its current affordability and about 5.5% of Category B clauses that need to be implemented after the transition period. On 6 June 2017, China submitted to the TFA Committee the 'Notice of Commitment of Clauses in Categories under the TFA' and proposed that, with the exception of Article 10.9 which was implemented in November 2016, the indicative implementation dates of the remaining Category B clauses are 22 February 2020.[38] As mentioned above, in practice, China has implemented Article 10.4 "single window" requirement of TFA in advance.

In general, the higher the percentage of Category A notices submitted in the WTO 'Clauses in Categories' notice, the higher the degree of implementation of the TFA. Of the 65 BRI countries including East Asia, ASEAN, South Asia, West Asia, Central Asia, CIS, and Central and Eastern Europe, 51 WTO members submitted "Clauses in Categories" notices, of which 50% were Category A notices. 14 countries' percentage of Category notices are below 50% and 8 countries are below 25%. As a WTO member, Yemen has not made any commitment notice. Thirteen other countries are not yet members of the WTO, so there is no way to implement TFA according to commitments (see Table 1). Therefore, due to their own capabilities, some BRI countries have not been able to fulfil their TFA obligations or implement trade facilitation in a short period of time. This is the challenge and obstacle that needs to be dealt with in China's promotion of the OBOR.

As mentioned above, in the process of fulfilling its TFA commitments, China has continuously sought trade facilitation cooperation with BRI countries to promote trade facilitation. In the process of OBOR rule of

[37] The data come from "China-Singapore (Chongqing) Strategic Connectivity Demonstration Project Management Bureau". The Bureau has now been renamed Chongqing China-Singapore Demonstration Project Administration.

[38] China's Notification of Category Commitments under the TFA, G/TFA/N/CHN/1, 6 June 2017.

Table 1 BRI countries and their TFA commitments

Regions	*Countries*	*Approve TFA or not*	*Category A (%)*	*Category B (%)*	*Category C (%)*	*No notice (%)*
East Asia	China	YES	94.5	5.5	0.0	0.0
	Mongolia	YES	23.5	36.1	40.3	0.1
ASEAN	Singapore	YES	100	0.0	0.0	0.0
	Indonesia	YES	88.7	11.3	0.0	0.0
	Malaysia	YES	94.1	5.9	0.0	0.0
	Thailand	YES	91.6	8.4	0.0	0.0
	Vietnam	YES	26.5	48.7	24.8	0.0
	Philippines	YES	93.3	5.0	1.7	0.0
	Cambodia	YES	60.9	19.3	19.7	0.1
	Myanmar	YES	5.5	9.2	85.3	0.0
	Lao People's Democratic Republic	YES	21.0	11.8	67.2	0.0
	Brunei Darussalam	YES	91.6	8.4	0.0	0.0
South Asia	India	YES	72.3	27.7	0.0	0.0
	Pakistan	YES	25.6	42.9	31.5	0.0
	Sri Lanka	YES	29	1.7	69.3	0.0
	Bangladesh	YES	34.5	38.2	27.3	0.0
	Nepal	YES	2.1	12.2	85.7	0.0
	Maldives	YES	16.4	36.1	47.5	0.0
	Bhutan (WTO observer)	NO	/	/	/	/
	Afghanistan	YES	11.3	31.1	57.6	0.0
West Asia	United Arab Emirates	YES	97.1	2.9	0.0	0.0
	Kuwait	YES	59.2	0.0	0.0	40.8
	Turkey	YES	100	0.0	0.0	0.0
	Qatar	YES	92.9	0.0	0.0	7.1
	Oman	YES	97.5	2.5	0.0	0.0
	Lebanese Republic (WTO observer)	NO	/	/	/	/
	Saudi Arabia	YES	100	0.0	0.0	0.0
	Bahrain	YES	61.3	30.3	8.4	0.0
	Israel	YES	100	0.0	0.0	0.0
	Yemen	NO	/	/	/	/

(continued)

Table 1 (continued)

Regions	*Countries*	*Approve TFA or not*	*Category A (%)*	*Category B (%)*	*Category C (%)*	*No notice (%)*
	Egypt	YES	23.1	2.5	74.4	0.0
	Iran (WTO observer)	NO	/	/	/	/
	Jordan	YES	81.5	8.8	9.7	0.0
	Syria (WTO observer)	NO	/	/	/	/
	Palestine (non-WTO member)	NO	/	/	/	/
	Greece	YES	100	0.0	0.0	0.0
	Iraq (WTO observer)	NO	/	/	/	/
	Cyprus	YES	100	0.0	0.0	0.0
Central Asia	Kazakhstan	YES	44.5	47.9	7.6	0.0
	Kyrgyz Republic	YES	16	17.6	66.4	0.0
	Turkmenistan (non-WTO member)	NO	/	/	/	/
	Tajikistan	YES	55.9	21.8	22.3	0.0
	Uzbekistan (WTO observer)	NO	/	/	/	/
CIS	Russia	YES	100	0.0	0.0	0.0
	Ukraine	YES	31.5	35.3	33.2	0.0
	Belarus (WTO observer)	NO	/	/	/	/
	Georgia	YES	92.4	0.0	7.6	0.0
	Azerbaijan (WTO observer)	NO	/	/	/	/
	Armenia	YES	50.8	41.6	7.6	0.0
	Moldova	YES	57.6	19.7	22.7	0.0
Central and Eastern Europe	Poland	YES	100	0.0	0.0	0.0
	Albania	YES	75.6	21	3.4	0.0
	Estonia	YES	100	0.0	0.0	0.0
	Lithuania	YES	100	0.0	0.0	0.0
	Slovenia	YES	100	0.0	0.0	0.0
	Bulgaria	YES	100	0.0	0.0	0.0
	Czech Republic	YES	100	0.0	0.0	0.0

(continued)

Table 1 (continued)

Regions	*Countries*	*Approve TFA or not*	*Category A (%)*	*Category B (%)*	*Category C (%)*	*No notice (%)*
	Hungary	YES	100	0.0	0.0	0.0
	Macedonia (non-WTO member)	NO	/	/	/	/
	Serbia (WTO observer)	NO	/	/	/	/
	Romania	YES	100	0.0	0.0	0.0
	Croatia	YES	100	0.0	0.0	0.0
	Latvia	YES	100	0.0	0.0	0.0
	Bosnia (WTO observer)	NO	/	/	/	/
	Montenegro	YES	87.0	8.4	4.6	0.0
	Slovak Republic	YES	100	0.0	0.0	0.0

Data sources http://ydyl.people.com.cn/n1/2017/0420/c411837-29225243.html; https://www.wto.org/english/thewto_e/whatis_e/tif_e/org6_e.htm; https://tfadatabase.org/notifications/implementation

law construction, China needs to continue to make efforts in the following aspects.

First, continue to promote the parallel implementation of BRI and TFA in the form of "soft law". From 14 to 15 May 2017, the first OBOR International Cooperation Summit (BRF) was successfully held in Beijing. From 25 to 28 April 2019, the second BRF was successfully held again. Accordingly, the BRF Advisory Committee and Liaison Office were established. As a new platform for BRI coordination, BRF has made its debut as a new force for China to promote the parallel implementation of BRI and TFA. BRI is a China-initiated century project to build a community with a shared future for mankind. At the same time, the implementation of TFA is also an attempt to implement the "common but differentiated" principle under the WTO system. The implementation of BRI and TFA involves the common interests of all countries and regions in the world and should take into account the particularities of different levels of economic development. The WTO is an existing platform for coordinating trade and economic policies of various countries and regions. It is irreplaceable. The rules of international law, including TFA, have the "hard law" features of treaty obligations, and even the "flexibility provisions" are optional treaty obligations. The BRF itself is not the major venue for treaty negotiation, but it provides diplomatic opportunities for consultation, discussion and coordination. It is more flexible, allowing leaders and practitioners of various countries to speak freely, to seek consensus in a harmonious atmosphere and to reach common cooperation intentions and eventually, agreements. BRF will greatly facilitate the better implementation of international economic and trade rules, including TFA. This is not only in the interests of China but also the common pursuit of relevant countries and regions. This is also a win-win cooperation goal of promoting the implementation of TFA from the perspective of BRI (Zhang 2017: 9).

Second, strengthen cooperation mechanisms for regional trade facilitation. The OBOR is not a regional concept in itself. The "region" here refers to the existing regional arrangements involving BRI countries, including not only areas formed in economic cooperation, such as ASEAN, EU and Eurasian Economic Union, but also natural areas formed by geographical environment, such as Southeast Asia, South Asia, West Asia and North Africa, and Central and Eastern Europe. Based on the several natural areas where the BRI countries are currently located, almost all regions have formed certain economic cooperation arrangements. The OBOR regional cooperation for trade facilitation focuses on strengthening and upgrading existing rules and expanding regional cooperation on trade facilitation issues. China needs to arrange and engage in active dialogues and cooperation with various regions. OBOR trade facilitation is not a new approach of China. China has clearly stated in the 'Initiative on Promoting Unimpeded Trade Cooperation along the Belt and Road' that it will maintain the WTO-based multilateral trading system and will strengthen the docking and cooperation between OBOR and other initiatives and plans; therefore, the promotion of OBOR trade facilitation will be based on the TFA (Liu and Wang 2019: 46).

Third, initiate bilateral negotiations to promote trade facilitation. Although bilateral trade facilitation negotiations will fragment multilateral and regional arrangements, they are more flexible than regional negotiations. One-on-one negotiations further clarify the conditions of both parties and prompt parties to pay more attention to each other's actual situation when it comes to arranging the terms of the agreements, which improves the enforceability of the agreements. As for the BRI countries that have not entered the aforementioned regional arrangements, they can be classified according to specific circumstances. The classification criteria should be based on the international trade organisations and agreements in which countries are currently participating. Based on whether they can join the TTA and/or the WTO, the BRI countries may be classified into four categories, that is, countries that have both joined the WTO and the TFA; countries that only join the WTO but not the TFA; countries that only do based on the TFA without joining the WTO; countries that have neither joined the WTO nor the TTA. Then, China should seek bilateral negotiations with countries in different categories. TFA is the latest accomplishment of multilateral trade facilitation negotiation. In the bilateral trade facilitation cooperation between China and the BRI countries, China should steadfastly safeguard the multilateral results of trade facilitation and its fundamental requirement on countries in trade facilitation should be TFA-based (Liu and Wang 2019: 47).

Fourth, enhance the level of unilateral trade facilitation. In addition to seeking regional and bilateral cooperation mechanisms, China should also actively promote the pilot programs of domestic free trade zones.[39] China's free trade pilot zone is a new model for China to explore domestic regional economic cooperation. The construction of the free trade pilot zone must comply with international rules and include reform and innovation so that the degree of unilateral trade facilitation can be continuously improved. To this end, China should increase the risk testing of the newly established free trade pilot zone on the basis of the existing free trade pilot zone trials to ensure the replication and distribution of successful experiences. At the same time, based on the adherence to the

[39] By January 2020, China has established 18 free trade pilot zones in total, including China (Shanghai) Pilot Free Trade Zone (established on September 27, 2013); China (Guangdong) Pilot Free Trade Zone, China (Tianjin) Pilot Free Trade Zone, China (Fujian) Pilot Free Trade Zone (established on April 20, 2015); China (Liaoning) Pilot Free Trade Zone, China (Zhejiang) Pilot Free Trade Zone, China (Henan) Pilot Free Trade Zone, China (Hubei) Pilot Free Trade Zone, China (Chongqing) Pilot Free Trade Zone, China (Sichuan) Pilot Free Trade Zone, China (Shaanxi) Pilot Free Trade Zone (established on March 31, 2017) and China (Shandong) Pilot Free Trade Zone, China (Jiangsu) Pilot Free Trade Zone, China (Guangxi) Free Trade Zone Trade Pilot Zone, China (Hebei) Pilot Free Trade Zone, China (Yunnan) Pilot Free Trade Zone, China (Heilongjiang) Pilot Free Trade Zone (established on August 2, 2019). In addition, on April 14, 2018, the State Council issued the "National Guideline on Supporting Hainan's Comprehensive Deepening of Reform and Opening Up" which clarified that Hainan will initially establish a free trade port in 2025.

principle of "first line deregulation and second line control", the supervision procedures have been continuously simplified to improve the supervision efficiency (Liu and Wang 2019: 47). The improvement of China's unilateral trade facilitation level is the basic prerequisite for China to provide technical supports and capacity building for the trade facilitation in some BRI countries.

Concluding Remarks

In the OBOR construction, the rule of law is in an irreplaceable and important position. It serves as a guarantee and support for areas such as policy coordination, connectivity of infrastructure, unimpeded trade, financial integration and so on. Building a rule-oriented, open, inclusive, democratic and transparent path to the rule of law is an important means to ensure the long-term, stable and healthy development of the OBOR. In October 2019, Chinese President Xi Jinping pointed out in a letter to the International Forum on the Rule of Law in China held in Guangzhou that the promotion of the OBOR joint construction requires the protection of the rule of law. China is willing to work with other countries to create a good environment for the rule of law, to build a fair, reasonable and transparent international economic and trade rules and regulations system, and to promote the joint efforts in the OBOR high-quality development, so that people of all countries can receive more benefits. China hopes that all countries, with a focus on the theme of "deepening international cooperation in the Chinese rule of law and serving the joint construction of the OBOR", will strengthen exchanges, promote consensus and actively develop and improve relevant legal systems, so that the rule of law can give its full play in the OBOR joint construction.[40] Given that the OBOR international cooperation mainly happens in the field of trade and investment, the construction of the OBOR rule of law also happens mainly in the rule of law cooperation of these fields. In the field of trade, there is a bi-directional relationship between the OBOR rule of law construction and the implementation of TFA. On the one hand, the OBOR rule of law construction can promote the implementation of the Trade TFA; on the other hand, the implementation

[40] Xi Jinping sent a letter to congratulate the opening of the International Forum on the Rule of Law in China (2019), http://politics.people.com.cn/n1/2019/1111/c1024-31447022.html (accessed on 3 February 2020).

of the TFA can, in turn, promote the OBOR rule of law construction. The OBOR was initiated by China. The complementarity and interaction of the above-mentioned bi-directional relations not only urge China to actively fulfil its trade facilitation commitments, promote domestic trade facilitation reforms, but also motivate China to proactively play the role of a giant country, to strengthen cooperation with the BRI countries and to promote these countries to implement the TFA. However, given the institutional arrangements of TFA itself and the status quo of the BRI countries who are non-WTO members, a lot of BRI countries have limited or refused to give their commitment to trade facilitation measures. Therefore, it is difficult to fully implement trade facilitation in the BRI countries in short notice. And there is a gap between the low level of trade facilitation implementation now and the level required by the OBOR construction, which brings challenges to China. In the era of the OBOR initiative, China needs to advocate the OBOR rule of law construction and cooperation, and to improve trade facilitation in the BRI countries through "soft laws" and "hard laws" like treaties, thus improving the level of rule of law in these countries.

References

Feng, Zongxian and Li, Gang (2015), "Construction of 'One Belt and One Road' and the Advancement Path to the Economic Cooperation in Peripheral Areas", in *Journal of Xi'an Jiaotong University (Social Sciences)*, 35(6), 1–9.

Gu, Yang (2018), "China Customs Actively Serve the OBOR Construction", in *Economic Daily*, August 23, Version 3.

Han, Xiuli (2018), "Revisiting the Implementation of BRI Initiative from the Perspective of International Rule of Law", in *International Business Research*, 39(6), 17–27.

Liu, Bing and Wang, Han (2019), "A Study on the Actual Conditions, Evaluations and Development Paths of International Trade Facilitation Legal Mechanism under the Belt and Road Context", in *Social Sciences in Ningxia*, 38(1), 40–48.

Liu, Jingdong (2017), "Research on the Construction of OBOR Rule of Law System", in *Tribune of Political Science and Law*, 35(5), 125–135.

Liu, Jingdong and Wang, Lulu (2018), "Research on the Approaches of OBOR Initiative Constructing International law", in *Academic Forum*, 41(6), 13–23.

Meng, Zhuming (2019), "Single Window of International Trade Continuously Optimizes Business Environment", in *China's Foreign Trade*, 64(10), 48–51.

Sheng, Bin (2016), "The Assessment on the TFA and Its Influence on China", in *China Trade*, 21(1), 4–13.

Wang, Gang (2017), "On the Legal Issues and the Establishment of Legal Mechanism in 'the Belt and Road' Construction", in *Law Science Magazine*, 38(2), 30–36.

Zeng, Wenge (2018), "Research on the Construction and Improvement of 'the Belt and Road' Trade Facilitation Rules System in Land Trade", in *Law Science Magazine*, 39(11), 16–22.

Zhang, Jianping and Fan, Ziyan (2016), "The Status of Trade and Investment Facilitation in OBOR Countries and the Need for Related Measures", in *Journal of China National School of Administration*, 20(1), 23–29.

Zhang, Naigen (2017), "Issues on the Implementation of the TFA from the Perspective of the Belt and Road Initiative", in *Journal of Customs and Trade*, 38(5), 1–9, 49.

Zhou, Yuexue (2017), "China's Trade Facilitation Measures and Legal Reforms under 'The Belt and Road' Initiative: International Legal Obligations and References", in *Special Zone Economy*, 34(5), 9–12.

Zhu, Caihua and Li, Nuo (2016), "The Trend of International Investment Policies Development and the Establishment of the 'One Belt and One Road' Cooperation Treaty Network", in *International Trade*, 35(9), 58–65.

Rule of Law Gaps and the Chinese Belt and Road Initiative: Legal Certainty for International Businesses?

Henrik Andersen

Introduction: Rule of Law and the Belt and Road?

The Chinese Belt and Road Initiative (BRI) increasingly gains support and involvement of states, international organisations, businesses and citizens. Although the BRI is an inclusive project where its stakeholders through soft and hard law instruments are part of forming its mild shapes with China in the centre, the question is whether the vague institutional and constitutional design of the BRI creates rule of law gaps to the detriment of international businesses and international trade. However, the BRI has some overall principles that include compliance with the UN Charter and international law, and the BRI must abide by market rules in the allocation of resources where businesses have a primary role.[1] In

[1] "Vision and Actions on Jointly Building Silk Road Economic Belt and Twenty-First Century Maritime Silk Road", 2015/03/28, Issued by the National Development and Reform Commission, Ministry of Foreign Affairs and Ministry of Commerce of the People's Republic of China, with State Council authorization (March 2015), Part II: Principles.

H. Andersen (✉)
CBS Law, Copenhagen Business School, Frederiksberg, Denmark
e-mail: ha.law@cbs.dk

G. Martinico and X. WU (eds.), *A Legal Analysis of the Belt and Road Initiative*, https://doi.org/10.1007/978-3-030-46000-6_6

order to attract investment, it is essential for businesses to lower transaction costs associated with rule of law gaps. The chapter discusses rule of law challenges and opportunities for the BRI from the perspective of businesses.

First, the chapter introduces the concept of the rule of law and its relevance for businesses. The rule of law is a contested concept and it is necessary to make some normative choices in defining the functions of the rule of law. In addition, the rule of law on international level has some challenges with specific rule of law gaps. Nevertheless, as the BRI is not clearly institutionalised, it leaves room for the BRI to engage in these rule of law gaps and to attempt to close them. Second, the chapter addresses the rule of law elements of transparency, access to justice and equality in the light of the BRI principles. The chapter discusses areas where the BRI can improve on its rule of law dimension to benefit businesses.

The Rule of Law and Its Substantive Limits in a Multilevel Context

For the BRI, the development of rule of law principles is essential to have a well-functioning market that attracts investments and that guarantees human rights as part of the economic development (Nordic Trust Fund/World Bank 2012). The rule of law is a public good protecting citizens, businesses and public institutions of society by guaranteeing that the expectations created by law and contracts can be met and enforced by the necessary institutions, and that these expectations do not fall victim of retrospective laws or arbitrary decisions by governmental agencies. A violation of rule of law principles leads to *legal uncertainty* and higher risks of investments.

Overall Definition of the Rule of Law

In the literature, the rule of law has been defined in various contexts and with different content. An often-cited definition of the rule of law is provided by Hayek:

> Stripped of all technicalities [rule of law] means that government in all its actions is bound by rules fixed and announced beforehand – rules which make it possible to foresee with fair certainty how the authority will use its

coercive powers in given circumstances and to plan one's individual affairs on the basis of such knowledge. (Hayek 2007 [1944])

Hayek's definition fits a business perspective. In order to reduce transaction costs of the market, businesses need to 'foresee with fair certainty' the laws and the administration of these laws that can have an impact on their conduct on the market. However, in a current climate where world governance is not only related to government intervention, but where businesses have a huge impact on global politics and global life, a wider definition should, besides government, mention business accountability and any institution holding formal and informal power over the law creation and the administration of the law and contracts.[2] In respect of the BRI, which at this point does not have clear institutional frames, businesses are part of forming the soft institutional structures.

Furthermore, even soft law frameworks, in spite of not being directly binding law, can be subject to rule of law requirements in order to provide the necessary certainty that reduces transaction costs for the market participants. Soft law instruments can contain a 'hard' dimension. For example, although EU Commission guidelines are not binding EU law, they nevertheless impose legal requirements on the Commission to follow its own guidelines based on principles of equality and legitimate expectations.[3] Even though the BRI at this point lacks clear institutional frameworks and largely is based on a soft approach by the Chinese government, it should not release it from rule of law requirements if the soft frameworks and norms create legitimate expectations for the stakeholders.

Rule of Law and Its Elements: Substantive or Formal?

There is no consensus among scholars about the content of the rule of law. In its narrowest form, the rule of law is formal and value-neutral whereas a substantive rule law is value-oriented and provides judgement over the laws and practices by the governing institutions. Raz is a proponent of a formal version. According to Raz, the rule of law is disconnected

[2] See UN Secretary-General's definition below that has a wider range of subjects of the rule of law.

[3] See, for example, Joined Cases C-189/02 P, C-202/02 P, C-205/02 P to C-208/02 P and C-213/02 P, Dansk Rørindustri and Others v Commission [2005] ECLI:EU:C:2005:408 paras. 209–211.

from democracy and human rights. Raz suggests a non-exhaustive list of 8 precepts of the rule of law, which can vary in degree. They are:

- All laws should be prospective, open and clear.
- Laws should be relatively stable.
- The making of particular laws (particular legal orders) should be guided by open, stable, clear and general rules.
- The independence of the judiciary must be guaranteed.
- The principles of natural justice must be observed.
- The courts should have review powers over the implementation of the other principles.
- The courts should be easily accessible.
- The discretion of the government agencies should not be allowed to pervert the law (Raz 2009).

The formal version promotes the aim of legal certainty and provides the infrastructure that is necessary for market participants to anticipate the rules and their administration by the government branches before entering into market transactions. However, it does not give much guidance to the lawmakers about the law itself apart from the transparency requirements. In contrast to a formal rule of law, a substantive rule of law will provide judgement over the content of law. Not all law can be accepted regardless of its enactment in conformity with procedural rules of the constitution. That will often be a rule of law requiring a system following a minimum level of democratic principles and/or human rights associated with a liberal system.[4] For example, Rawls suggests:

> [O]ne legal order is more justly administered than another if it more perfectly fulfils the precepts of the rule of law. It will provide a more secure basis for liberty and a more effective means for organizing cooperative schemes. (Rawls 1999: 53)

Even though Rawls' rule of law seems to imply that various political systems, even those without a strong liberal basis, can have a rule of law system, the strength of the rule of law is measured by its ability to protect liberty (Radin 1989). One argument in favour of the formal version of

[4] See for a general discussion of a formal and a substantive rule of law (Craig 1997).

the rule of law in respect of the BRI is that it does not seem to impose a strong requirement on a specific type of political system, nor on the level of human rights. There are apparent differences between China and the EU concerning both the political systems and the extent of civil and political rights. However, in the view of this writer, the rule of law cannot be free of values as it serves *legal certainty* in the constitutional and legal order. Even a formal version must have certain inherent values in order to provide an infrastructure to keep law supreme. For example, the rule of law will impose constraints on the political system in order to function. The exercise of a political system cannot be accepted if it conflicts with the fundamental requirements to uphold the rule of law and its guarantees to the citizens. The separation of powers is an institutional guarantee against government overstepping its powers. That makes the rule of law a challenge in an authoritarian regime unless the regime provides a transparent mechanism to limit the exercise of government and a reliable system to keep government accountable for its actions. Otherwise, there is the risk that citizens and businesses cannot anticipate their rights and obligations under the regime. The rule of law cannot accept a law or action that restricts the fundamental political and civil rights of citizens to uphold the rule of law.[5]

Citizens, businesses and public institutions must know in advance their rights and obligations in all aspects of society,[6] and, in particular individuals, their basic rights and freedoms.[7] Thus, there must be *transparency and predictability* in laws, governmental administration of law and the methodological approach adopted by the courts. Furthermore, there must be transparency in the political processes, where lawmaking

[5] This is not to suggest that the content of political and civil rights cannot vary between political systems. For example, the freedom of expression is not an absolute right but it is necessary with that right in order to have a rule of law system as citizens and businesses need to be able to express themselves against a law or action from government if it potentially violates the necessary principles to uphold the rule of law.

[6] That does not imply that there is no space for a political dimension. However, even the political dimension must comply with the constitutional limits of society.

[7] The European Court of Human Rights has also developed a practice where businesses to some extent have certain basic rights and freedoms which are protected by the European Convention on Human Rights. See, for example, case law from concerning fair trial, *Dombo Beheer B.V. v Netherlands*, ECHR (1993), Series A, 274; EHRR (1994) 213; or right to privacy, *Société Colas Est and others v France*, Case No. 37971/97 ECHR 2002-III.

goes through clear procedures, and where the constitutional rights and natural justice of the individuals are protected.

The rule of law contains *access to justice*. Justice can only be served by independent and impartial institutions, like constitutional and regular courts, that can review decisions from government. They ensure the functionality of the particular constitutional and legal system and must guarantee the supremacy of law by its checks on the government. It is highly problematic when states attempt to oust the courts from reviewing governmental administration of the law.[8] Furthermore, the independent and impartial institutions protect the market participants by interpreting contracts and settle issues between businesses, as well as issues between citizens and businesses.

Finally, the rule of law requires *equality* between the members and institutions of society. No one can be above the law, and the government cannot have a special status in a case against an individual. That is not to suggest that power distribution should be equal. Rather, it is to guarantee that the government or the businesses are not favoured over the citizens in accessing justice and in protecting their rights under the law.

Thus, according to this writer, the rule of law incorporates the elements proposed by Raz but it does not escape a normative function as it provides judgement over constitutions, laws, contracts and their administration that do not meet the essential rule of law requirements, including the minimum level of political and civil rights. For example, it will reject laws or practices if they make obstacles for an individual's access to the courts against the government, or a system allowing priority of businesses over the citizen or over governmental institutions. For example, it rejects a political system with corrupt practices that conflict with the transparency requirement and/or the requirement of equality. The BRI should take these elements into account when forming the Belt and Road policies to ensure the legal certainty.

[8] For example, in the context of UK constitutional and public law, which has supremacy of parliament as a basic constitutional principle, it is deeply concerning when parliament attempts to reduce the access of reviews by courts of decisions by governmental institutions through ouster clauses. The courts are reluctant to apply such clauses and interpret them narrowly. See, for example, *Anisminic Ltd v Foreign Compensation Commission* [1969] 2 AC 147. See also the Danish Supreme Court's narrow approach to the customary rule of Danish constitutional law about 'endelighedsbestemmelser' [ouster clauses], which can be accepted if there in the administrative system is an independent and impartial review board with court-like features, U 1997.1157 H.

Businesses and the Rule of Law

As mentioned above, Hayek's definition of the rule of law is relevant from a business perspective. It works for an economic system based on the market. Literature in economics has, besides markets, institutions and governance, including the rule of law, as focal areas of research. The strength of the rule of law is essential for business conduct and operation as it may decrease the transaction costs. Transaction costs are the costs of using the market, like the costs of information, including the costs of legal uncertainty. Transaction costs can also be monitoring costs when a business needs to ensure that a supplier complies with its human rights, labour and/or environmental standards. In a system with a strong rule of law, it can be expected that government ensures that suppliers comply with such standards, whereas in systems with a weak rule of law, the government might not have the resources or incentive to monitor the suppliers, or the system might be infected with corrupt practices. A weak rule of law adds to the transaction costs for the businesses. There are, of course, businesses thriving in systems with a weak rule of law if they are asset strippers or criminals, who navigate in a system with corrupt practices, leaving market inefficient and unattractive for legitimate investors. Businesses need a strong rule of law to protect investments through the contractual rights and obligations, and to protect property rights (Hoff and Stiglitz 2004).

Economic literature divides the rule of law and its impact on economics into 4 categories: (1) *Rule of law and security of persons*, personal insecurity in civil wars or in systems with high crime rates has a negative economic impact. (2) *Rule of law and contract and property rights*, strong property rights protection and contract enforcement correlate with better long-run economic performance. (3) *Rule of law and institutional balance*, judicial independence is necessary to secure contract and property rights. There is correlation between institutional checks on governments and economic growth. (4) *Rule of law and corruption*, corruption leads to increase in prices as lack of confidence in courts raises the costs of dispute resolutions as the disputing parties must use alternative, private enforcement mechanisms. Furthermore, rent-seeking behaviour by participants in corrupt societies raises costs for consumers and producers, and policy distortions cause barriers to long-run growth by protection or creation of monopolies (Haggard and Tiede 2011: 674–675).

The question is how the BRI will contribute to a rule of law that can decrease the transaction costs of the businesses. It requires that the policies of the Belt and Road facilitate peace and security in high-risk areas and areas with high crime rates, including areas where there are humanitarian problems and areas with grave human rights violations. Such problems have a negative effect on economics. In addition, the BRI must ensure that investments and property rights are protected. That implies that corrupt practices must be eliminated along the Belt and Road. Otherwise, businesses might be discouraged to, for example, invest in tender preparation for Belt and Road projects if it is likely that corrupt agents award the criminal suppliers. Another problem can be corrupt agents accepting market abuse or accepting unhealthy working conditions in violation of the law, which will put legitimate businesses, who comply with market rules and with workers' rights, in an unfair competitive environment. The rule of law infrastructure and its necessary institutions must be in place. The BRI must provide legal certainty to businesses so they can calculate the risks of investments and have expectations of their returns. The BRI must facilitate access to justice in order to signal to businesses that their rights and legitimate expectations can be protected, and it must provide equality under the law, which undeniably requires a system with no corruption.

Where law and its infrastructure does not provide the necessary tools to uphold the rule of law and legal certainty, more and more businesses get involved with Corporate Social Responsibility (CSR). The CSR development has a soft law character. However, as they create legitimate expectations in, for example, contracts, and may be seen as a marketing tool, they are closely related to contract and marketing laws. CSR is now increasingly getting regulated. The EU Commission has defined CSR as '*the responsibility of enterprises for their impacts on society*'.[9] According to Roland Bénabou and Jean Tirole, CSR is:

> about sacrificing profits in the social interest. For there to be a sacrifice, the firm must go beyond its legal and contractual obligations, on a voluntary basis. (Bénabou and Tirole 2010: 2)

[9] Communication from the Commission to the European Parliament, the Council, the European Economic and Social Committee and the Committee of the Regions—*A Renewed EU Strategy 2011-14 for Corporate Social Responsibility*, Brussels, 25.10.2011, COM(2011) 681 final, at 6.

According to Roland Bénabou and Jean Tirole, the motivations for CSR are (1) government failure, including jurisdictional issues and high transaction costs, and (2) promotion of another set of values than the lawmakers (Bénabou and Tirole 2010).

The UN Global Compact, which contains 10 principles, which companies can sign up to comply with, makes reference to both human rights and the environment. Thus, businesses can have an important role to play in carrying out protective efforts where international law does not provide the necessary rules or where there is institutional weakness in protecting these rights. The use of CSR may reflect the rule of law problems with a weak protection of human rights and environmental standards at international and national level or the need to fill in the gaps of international and national law.

Although businesses might fill in the gaps of international law through CSR, and the market might to some extent be able to punish companies for immoral or unethical conduct, the market itself has its limits. The lack of information and general transparency in businesses' monitoring of supply chain compliance with contract and ethical standards makes it a challenge for the outsider to ensure that a product is produced in accordance with human rights and environmental standards. The monitoring of suppliers' compliance with businesses' CSR, in particular in states with weak rule of law and with high level of corruption, increases the transaction costs. That opens up the possibility for the BRI to take the lead in implementing policies that reduce the transaction costs of businesses by requiring stronger rule of law protection of the participating states and other relevant stakeholders.

Rule of Law and International Law

The BRI must comply with the rules and principles of international law. It is within that legal space that the BRI can make its soft and hard laws, as well as having influence on the development of international law, including filling in the gaps. In this respect, it is worth to consider the rule of law aspects of international law. Although Lauterpacht regarded international law as a complete system (Lauterpacht 2011 [1933]), a position this writer appreciates, international law is characterised by its multiplicity of international organisations with different degrees of autonomy, authority and jurisdictional scope. A rule of law on international level must necessarily be seen in the light of the various contributors to the constitutional, institutional, political and legal elements underlying the sub-rule of laws that emerge within the respective organisations and sectors of law. International law has not provided 'the one' authoritative definition of the rule of law. Nevertheless, there is reference to 'rule of law' or its elements in a number of legal and political instruments at international level. The Charter of the UN provides in the Preamble that the UN is determined: 'to establish conditions under which justice and respect for the obligations arising from treaties and other sources of international law can be maintained'. Regardless of a formal or substantive definition of the rule of law, the function of international law relies as a minimum on the expectation that states comply with their international obligations. The international rule of law can only function with the positive participation of the stakeholders at international level. Furthermore, in 2004, the UN Secretary-General stated:

> The "rule of law" is a concept at the very heart of the Organization's mission. It refers to a principle of governance in which all persons, institutions and entities, public and private, including the State itself, are accountable to laws that are publicly promulgated, equally enforced and independently adjudicated, and which are consistent with international human rights norms and standards. It requires, as well, measures to ensure adherence to the principles of supremacy of law, equality before the law, accountability to the law, fairness in the application of the law, separation of powers, participation in decision-making, legal certainty, avoidance of arbitrariness and procedural and legal transparency. (UN Secretary-General Kofi Annan 2004: 4)

This version of rule of law has substantial traits, as it seems to include human rights as part of the rule of law. As mentioned above, this writer takes the position that certain human rights are inherent in the rule of law elements to make it function. Human rights have an abstract protection in the UN Charter, but are further defined in the Universal Declaration of Human Rights, and are more specifically formulated in the binding International Covenant on Civil and Political Rights (ICCPR) and International Covenant on Economic, Social and Cultural Rights (ICESCR). However, the conventions are not directly binding on states that have not ratified them. For example, China has not ratified the ICCPR. It does not rule out an indirect commitment through other means than the covenants. They may have influence on the interpretation of treaties as the Vienna Convention on the Law of Treaties (VCLT) provides that human rights principles should form part of the interpretative context.

Even though a rule of law in the context of the UN may include human rights, at least on an abstract level, the question is whether it can result in conflict with other international organisations. For example, in the WTO, there is no express reference to the rule of law or human rights in the treaties. Nevertheless, the WTO Appellate Body (AB) has emphasised that law prevails over economic considerations,[10] and former members of the AB have made reference to the rule of law as essential in the WTO legal system (Bacchus 2003; Hillman 2011 [2012]). Furthermore, it can be argued that the rule of law requirements concerning transparency, access to justice and equality has a certain degree of development and maturity in the WTO (Andersen 2019b). The question is whether the rule of law developed in the WTO includes a human rights dimension in line with the one proposed by the UN Secretary-General. In WTO cases, states have averted to make reference to human rights. The only WTO case directly referring to human rights, *US—Procurement*,[11] never reached panel stage.[12] However, a panel referred recently to the European Convention of Human Rights in support of its legal argument—but not as a direct legal basis for its legal argument.[13] Thus, the abstract reference to human rights in the UN Charter and the VCLT should inform the WTO system, but the extent of human rights is more difficult to define.[14]

[10] *EC—Fasteners (China)*, WT/DS397/AB/R, adopted by the DSB on 28 July 2011, para. 367.

[11] *US—Procurement*, WT/DS88 and WT/DS95, Authority for panel lapsed on 11 February 2000.

[12] The case concerned the Burma Law of Massachusetts, which implied a rejection of procurement of products from companies involved in business in Burma. The reason underlying the rejection was the human rights problems in Burma. The contested Burma Law was found by the US Supreme Court to be inconsistent with the US Constitution; see *Crosby v National Foreign Trade Council*, 530 U.S. 363 (2000).

[13] *Thailand—Cigarettes (Article 21.5—Philippines)*, WT/DS371/RW, issued on 12 November 2018, currently pending appeal, para. 7.583.

[14] The role of human rights in WTO law is highly debated in literature. See in respect of legal pluralism (Krisch 2012; Koskenniemi and Leino 2002) and in respect of constitutional pluralism (Avbelj and Komárek 2008; Walker 2002; Petersmann 2012; Andersen 2015).

Even though the rule of law exists on international level, and has in the UN been defined with some substantial elements, the international dimension has rule of law gaps. The doctrine of the rule of law emerged in the nation systems to ensure that the government could be under legal and constitutional constraints in order to protect the individual against arbitrary decisions by government. Thus, the context is a vertical power relation between government and the individual. The relationship between states has more a horizontal character under the traditional assumption that states are equal and cannot be bound by law beyond their consent or practice. The statist nature of the international system of law implies in particular two potential rule of law gaps:

- The connection between international law and national law, i.e. the access for the individual to apply international law if it gives the individual legal expectations in the national systems.
- The overlaps and scope of laws and regulations from different providers of international law, like the one mentioned above about human rights and WTO law (Andersen 2019a).

The rule of law gaps concerning citizen access to international justice and the overlapping jurisdictions is easier handled regionally than domestically if it is assumed that constitutional, legal and political cultures are closer connected on regional level than international level. For example, the EU has attempted to overcome these rule of law gaps by:

- establishing the rule of law as a legally binding norm of EU law towards both the member states and the EU institutions,
- providing an institutional structure between national courts and the Court of Justice of the EU allowing direct effect and applicability of EU law to the benefit of individuals,
- claiming primacy in the conflict between national law and EU law and
- providing legislative institutions that can balance the various sectors of law, like human rights, trade, labour, environment, financial law, etc.

Even though the EU can serve as inspiration for the broader international system of law, the EU consists of states which to a reasonable degree have some shared views on the concept of law, whereas international law consists of states with wide differences in the legal cultures. Nevertheless, there are various international law instruments to promote *legal certainty* and support *predictability and transparency* in the international order. The principle of *jus cogens* prevails over any treaty or practice related to the BRI. Furthermore, the VCLT provides rules on treaty making, application, termination and reference to *jus cogens*; and the UN Charter provides rules legitimatising the supranational character of UN Council Resolutions and its mandate. Nevertheless, the overlaps and potential conflicts between the different—and potentially competing—judiciaries cause legal uncertainty. Suggestions for applying principles of private international law, like *forum non conveniens* or *lis abili pendens*, lack legal authority (Shany 2003). Furthermore, the application of principles of private international law to overlap between different jurisdictions is limited as international courts may not have the mandate to reject a case that falls within its jurisdiction. That is regardless of a more appropriate forum elsewhere. In addition, there can be problems if an international court handles a case, which is also handled by another court in another jurisdiction. For example, in the case of the WTO, the Dispute Settlement Understanding provides that the Dispute Settlement Body is the most appropriate forum to handle a trade case (Marceau 2015). The respective jurisdictions have their own constitutional basis and treaties to apply. Even though two jurisdictions may be involved in an issue concerning the same facts, their treaty basis is different. For example, in the *Swordfish cases*, between Chile and the EU, Chile rejected Spanish vessels from entering port in order to protect the conservation of swordfish. The EU made a case under WTO law with reference to the rules of transit and prohibition of quantitative restrictions, whereas Chile made a case in the International Tribunal for the Law of the Sea (ITLOS) against the EU under UNCLOS for violating its obligations to protect and conserve swordfish. The parties settled the issue in an agreement, and thus, the case was not settled by the WTO panel or the ITLOS (Orellana 2002). Otherwise, the result could have been that the WTO panel with basis in GATT 1994 had found that Chile violated its WTO obligations while the ITLOS with basis in UNCLOS could have found that the EU violated its obligations. That would effectively cause legal uncertainty for WTO and UNCLOS members.[15]

[15] Although the outcome of the cases will never be known, it is worth mentioning that WTO law—and case law—has moved towards a stronger protection of exhaustible

The question is whether the BRI through soft and hard laws can find solutions to such overlaps, when they occur in Belt and Road projects.

The rule of law protects the *access to justice* delivered by an impartial and independent institution. There are a number of international courts and tribunals offering such access, and they are required under treaties to be independent and impartial. For example, the International Court of Justice (ICJ) must have independent judges,[16] the same applies for the ITLOS,[17] the International Criminal Court[18] and in the WTO, panels and AB.[19] However, one challenge is that international law has generally *states* as subjects and do not provide *locus standi* for citizens and businesses. There are some exceptions to it in, for example, regional human rights treaties and their courts. In addition, the International Centre for Settlement of Investment Disputes (ICSID) provides access for individuals to make claims against states. Otherwise, it is a question of national courts letting international law penetrate into the domestic order.

Finally, the requirement that *all are equal* under the law also applies on international level although in a weaker version. A basic assumption of traditional theories of international law is that states are equal. However, even though that, for example, WTO law is open for all the members to use the Dispute Settlement Body, the question is whether *equality* really exists between them. There is the divide between resourceful and less resourceful countries having a bearing on the use of the system. For example, in *Canada—Pharmaceutical Patents*,[20] Malaysia stated to the DSB that it had an interest in the case and would have liked to participate as a third party. However, due to limited resources, it was too costly

resources compared to the GATT case law, and there is clear justification under WTO law to protect swordfish, in particular as WTO case law is likely to include environmental treaties in support of a legal argument of protection of exhaustible resources, including UNCLOS, cf. *US—Shrimps*, WT/DS58/AB/R, adopted by the DSB on 6 November 1998.

[16] Art. 2 of the Statute of the ICJ.

[17] Art. 2 of the Statute of the ITLOS.

[18] Preamble and Art. 40 of the Rome Statute of the International Criminal Court.

[19] Art. 8.2 and Art. 17 of the Dispute Settlement Understanding (DSU), and Rule 2 of the Working Procedures for Appellate Review.

[20] *Canada—Pharmaceutical Patents*, WT/DS114/R, adopted on 7 April 2000.

for Malaysia to participate.[21] Also in the case of the ICJ, it can only handle disputes where the states have recognised its jurisdiction, which can be by special agreement or by declaration recognising the ICJ's judgements as compulsory.[22] Furthermore, the International Criminal Court has no jurisdiction in cases of crimes committed by nationals from the United States, China, India and Russia.[23] Thus, the equality on international level must be understood in the context of the respective international organisations, courts, etc., and based on the states that have ratified the specific treaties recognising the jurisdiction of the respective courts or tribunals.

The BRI works within these rule of law constraints—and gaps—on international level. The question is whether the BRI can improve the rule of law conditions of international law.

The BRI and the Rule of Law

Although it has been argued that the rule of law exists on international level, and that the rule of law is essential in lowering transaction costs for businesses, the question is whether it can be justified to compare rule of law elements with the BRI. After all, the BRI is at this point an initiative to, inter alia, facilitate trade along the Belt and Road. The constitutional and institutional structures of the Belt and Road will take shape as the initiative evolves. Nevertheless, the unclear scope of institutional structures and of a constitutional dimension can have a deterring effect on trade and investment. Businesses engaged in trade and investments may be subject to conflicting rules, different requirements, various bilateral and multilateral treaties, and unclear scope of governmental interference into market transactions and with no legal guidance on how to approach and solve these issues. However, the BRI is based on some overall principles that provide some clarity. The following part will discuss the principles of the BRI in relation to the rule of law.

[21] Dispute Settlement Body, 7 April 2000, Minutes of Meeting, WT/DSB/M/78, circulated on 12 May 2000, para. 68.

[22] Art. 36 of the Statute of the ICJ.

[23] See Art. 12 of the Rome Statute.

Principles of the BRI

In March 2015, the Chinese National Development and Reform Commission, the Ministry of Foreign Affairs and the Ministry of Commerce of the People's Republic of China (PRC) released a joint paper concerning the 'Vision and Actions on Jointly Building Silk Road Economic Belt and 21st Century Maritime Silk Road' outlining the overall aims and visions of the BRI. According to the joint paper, the BRI is a result of slow growth in the world economy, uneven global development and financial crises. It takes into account economic globalisation and the multi-polar world, cultural diversity and the higher level of IT application. The aims are to promote orderly and free flow of economic factors, a highly efficient allocation of resources and deep integration of markets. It aims at encouraging the implied countries to 'achieve economic policy coordination and carry out broader and more in-depth regional cooperation of higher standards; and jointly creating an open, inclusive and balanced regional economic cooperation architecture that benefits all'.[24]

The core principles of the BRI are to:

- Be in line with the purposes and principles of the UN Charter.
- Uphold the Five Principles of Peaceful Coexistence.
- Be open for cooperation for countries and international and regional organisations.
- Be inclusive and in harmony with tolerance among civilisations and in respect of the respective countries' development.
- Support dialogue between different civilisations where common ground is to be sought in order to be in peace for common prosperity.
- Abide market rules in the allocation of resources where enterprises have a primary role and where governments 'perform their due functions'.
- Seek mutual benefits for all parties involved.[25]

[24] "Vision and Actions on Jointly Building Silk Road Economic Belt and Twenty-First Century Maritime Silk Road", 2015/03/28, Issued by the National Development and Reform Commission, Ministry of Foreign Affairs and Ministry of Commerce of the People's Republic of China, with State Council authorization (March 2015), Part I: Background.

[25] Ibid., at Part II: Principles.

The BRI policies are based on these principles. The question is whether they are compatible with the rule of law dimensions of transparency, access to justice and equality to provide legal certainty for businesses along the Belt and Road, and whether the BRI can strengthen the rule of law at international level.

Transparency

As market economics is part of the principles of the BRI, it can be argued that it must imply adherence to the rule of law elements. As mentioned above, the rule of law is essential in a market economy. That implies that the BRI should stress transparency and predictability in its soft and hard laws governing the Belt and Road. At this stage, it is not particularly clear how the BRI policies will be implemented, apart from some guidance from the established institutions, like the Asian Infrastructure Investment Bank (AIIB). The BRI will cross into already established regional and international legal, economic and political regimes. For example, the AIIB takes some of the same functions as the World Bank (Wan 2016: 58).

However, the BRI does not seek to replace already established international trading systems (Cohen 2015: 3). The BRI projects must comply with the existing legal frameworks, which it crosses into. That seems also to follow from the main principles of the BRI, as the BRI must comply with the principles and purposes of the UN Charter. That implies that BRI projects must comply with 'principles of justice and international law' to adjust and settle issues that could breach international peace. Although this phrase is related to matters about international peace; trade, human rights and environmental protection can all be linked to peace.[26] Thus,

[26]See about the environment; the International Union for Conservation of Nature (IUCN) Commission on Environmental, Economic and Social Policy, https://www.iucn.org/commissions/commission-environmental-economic-and-social-policy/our-work/environment-and-peace (retrieved on 18 January 2020). See about human rights and international peace the recognition in the Preamble of the Universal Declaration of Human Rights: 'Whereas recognition of the inherent dignity and of the equal and inalienable rights of all members of the human family is the foundation of freedom, justice and peace in the world'. In addition, even though weak trading conditions do not directly threaten peace, it puts stress on the national system which eventually may result in conflict. Trade can have a mitigating effect on conflict (United Nations and World Bank 2018, xxi, 279).

it is expected that the BRI projects comply with international law in general. In respect of trade, the WTO rule of law developments will be the minimum rule of law expectations for international businesses (Andersen 2019b). However, the BRI can strengthen that by introducing stronger rule of law requirements in multilateral and bilateral trade treaties between Belt and Road states.

Furthermore, BRI projects should in accordance with Article 1.3 of the UN Charter seek to 'achieve international co-operation in solving international problems of an economic, social, cultural, or humanitarian character, and in promoting and encouraging respect for human rights and for fundamental freedoms for all without distinction as to race, sex, language, or religion'. China has so far not been very informative about the role of human rights in Belt and Road projects. The question is whether China's strategy risks undermining human rights in the Belt and Road projects. In particular, in situations where China has made fewer human rights commitments under international treaty law compared to, for example, the standards developed in the EU by the Court of Justice and in the EU Charter of Fundamental Rights. The problem for European businesses is that there will not be an even playing field if they compete with businesses along the Belt and Road that do not meet and guarantee the same human rights protection under their national laws, including core principles of the International Labour Organization (ILO). It is also an indirect penetration of lower human rights and labour standards into the European markets. Because of these differences between EU standards and China, the EU has indirectly required China to commit further to the core conventions of the ILO in the antidumping policies towards China. That will briefly be addressed below.[27]

Nevertheless, the BRI is not completely absent human rights dimensions. The AIIB has requirements of social inclusion, which according to its Environmental and Social Framework means to encompass 'policies to promote equity of opportunity and non-discrimination, by improving the

[27] China has not ratified the *Forced Labour Convention*, 1930 (No. 29); *Freedom of Association and Protection of the Right to Organise Convention*, 1948 (No. 87); *Right to Organise and Collective Bargaining Convention*, 1949 (No. 98); and the *Abolition of Forced Labour Convention*, 1957 (No. 105). The 4 core conventions ratified by China are *Equal Remuneration Convention*, 1951 (No. 100); *Discrimination (Employment and Occupation) Convention*, 1958 (No. 111); *Minimum Age Convention*, 1973 (No. 138); and *Worst Forms of Child Labour Convention*, 1999 (No. 182).

access of poor, disadvantaged and disabled people to education, health, social protection, housing, environmental quality, infrastructure, affordable energy, water and sanitation, employment, financial services and productive assets. It also embraces action to remove barriers against vulnerable groups, who are often excluded from the development process, and to ensure that their voices can be heard'.[28] Although it is welcoming that projects will be assessed against that backdrop, it is not clear how these overall requirements will be carried out. In addition, the AIIB needs to a wider extent provide transparency in how it assesses and monitors projects.

On the environmental side, the Chinese government has made an ecological and environmental cooperation plan for the BRI. It connects the BRI with the 2030 Agenda for Sustainable Development of the UN:

> The 2030 Agenda for Sustainable Development of the United Nations aims to jointly improve the welfare of all mankind and clearly specifies the targets of green development and environmental protection, mapping the road to sustainable development and international development cooperation in the next decades. The cooperation on eco-environmental protection under the framework of the Belt and Road Initiative will inject an effective impetus to accomplishment of environmental targets in the Agenda in countries along the routes.

In this respect, the legal framework for the conservation and sustainable use of the ocean and its resources will be based on the United Nations Convention on the Law of the Sea (UNCLOS). Furthermore, the cooperation plan also includes compliance with environmental conventions:

> Promote cooperation for compliance with environmental conventions. We will help relevant countries along the Belt and Road to fulfil commitments under multilateral environmental agreements (MEAs), such as Convention on Biological Diversity and Stockholm Convention on Persistent Organic

[28] AIIB Environmental and Social Framework, para. 8, available at: https://www.aiib.org/en/policies-strategies/framework-agreements/environmental-social-framework.html (retrieved on 29 January 2020).

> Pollutants, by building up cooperation mechanisms for MEA implementation and enabling technological exchange and South-South cooperation.[29]

That implies a green-oriented philosophy of the Belt and Road where the BRI shall 'improve green competitiveness, covering policy coordination, facilities connectivity, unimpeded trade, financial integration and people-to-people bonds'.[30] In addition, the cooperation plan promotes cooperation with multinational enterprises, including business commitments to the green philosophy, creation of win-win situations for economic development and environmental protection. Furthermore, it will expand import and export of environmental goods and services, which is in line with China's negotiations of the Environmental Goods Agreement in the WTO.[31]

The BRI seems to develop some legal certainty in respect of its environmental legal approach, and at this point uses the existing rules under the WTO in respect of trade. However, more work should be done concerning the human rights dimension. For example, an importer of products related to BRI projects must assess the whole supply chain, if the suppliers are under less obligations to human rights compliance than the importing business. As mentioned above, businesses adopt CSR policies where they monitor suppliers' compliance with human rights standards, but that indicates a rule of law problem and increases the transaction costs.

Access to Justice

The BRI opens up for disputes at a range of different levels: between employees and their employers, between businesses concerning contractual issues, between public institutions and businesses in respect of government procurement, competition law, etc., between public or private bodies against businesses concerning environmental issues, between states concerning trade issues, etc. Some issues will be addressed by national

[29] The Belt and Road Ecological and Environmental Cooperation Plan, Ministry of Ecology and Environment, the People's Republic of China, http://english.mee.gov.cn/Resources/Policies/policies/Frameworkp1/201706/t20170628_416869.shtml (retrieved on 28 January 2020).

[30] Ibid.

[31] Ibid.

courts, for example, in cases concerning private international law, whereas others must be addressed by specialised courts/tribunals in multilateral and bilateral trade agreements. The business industry offers solutions to handling of Belt and Road disputes. The International Chamber of Commerce (ICC) suggests its International Court of Arbitration to settle disputes along the Belt and Road, and it has established a Belt and Road Commission 'to promote and develop ICC's existing services to support Belt and Road disputes'.[32]

The Supreme People's Court of China (SPC) is also highly involved in the BRI. For example, it has established the China International Commercial Court, and in its recent policy initiatives, it suggests cooperation between courts in criminal matters to keep a *clean* Belt and Road and non-tolerance towards corruption. In addition, the SPC has in its policy documents towards lower courts emphasised the active application of international conventions, which are binding on China.[33] The work of the SPC is most welcoming as it both addresses issues of accessing justice and finds common denominators between various dispute institutions along the Belt and Road. However, it is of concern if it is not clearly formulated to the Belt and Road stakeholders, the constitutional divide between the Chinese courts and the government. For example, it is not clear the extent to which China can intervene in the work of the judiciaries as in the recent Hong Kong High Court case about the unconstitutionality of the mask ban.[34] The problem in that case is that in an appeal, the Appeal Court will be under political pressure undermining the rule of law. Although China has the right to reinterpret the Basic Law of Hong Kong, any reinterpretation must be taken with care, and more importantly, there must not be interference in the judicial process if the case is pending. The result is that international businesses lose confidence in the Chinese judicial system fearing that legislator or government can undermine the rule of law (Taplin and Wong 2019).

[32] The ICC website: https://iccwbo.org/dispute-resolution-services/belt-road-dispute-resolution/belt-and-road-commission/ (retrieved on 2 January 2020).

[33] See for more information: Susan Finder, Supreme People's Court Monitor: https://supremepeoplescourtmonitor.com/tag/belt-road/ (retrieved on 29 January 2020).

[34] KWOK WING HANG AND OTHERS v. CHIEF EXECUTIVE IN COUNCIL AND ANOTHER, HCAL 2945/2019 [2019] HKCFI 2820, judgement of 18 November 2019.

Cases concerning WTO law must be addressed in the WTO dispute settlement system unless the parties can find a mutually agreeable solution to the issue before bringing the case.[35] As mentioned above, only states have *locus standi* in the WTO. An alternative dispute solution option is to apply arbitration if the parties agree to it, and if all the WTO members are notified about it.[36] Currently, several states apply that option due to the US attempts to undermine the AB by blocking for new members to the AB. Another opportunity is if some WTO members make preferential trade agreements, which generally are exempted from WTO law. That is relevant for the trade in goods and in services along the Belt and Road. However, China has made a number of bilateral trade agreements with Belt and Road states containing clauses about dispute settlement. These clauses are not clear and various stakeholders of these bilateral agreements find them unreliable (Li 2019).

For businesses involved with Belt and Road investments and trade, it is essential that there are reliable forums for dispute settlement and that there is easy access to them. There must not be any doubt about their impartiality and independence, and that they can work without any influence from any government. The BRI needs to address these aspects more thoroughly and must provide clarity in case of competing institutions to avoid a conflict between laws addressing the same issue.

Equality

Whether the application of the BRI principles will improve the rule of law needs still to be tested. The reference to the Five Principles of Peaceful Coexistence may require that the Belt and Road institutions and government follow an international rule of law. According to former Vice-Minister for Foreign Affairs of China, Liu Zhenmin[37]:

> "The international rule of law is the common pursuit of mankind and an important priority of the international community. Adherence to the core values of the Five Principles of Peaceful Coexistence will provide us

[35] Art. 3.7 of the DSU.

[36] Art. 25 of the DSU.

[37] Liu Zhenmin is now Under-Secretary-General of the United Nations Department of Economic and Social Affairs.

> with valuable guidance for the establishment of international rule of law." (Zhenmin 2014: 479)

According to Liu Zhenmin, the Five Principles of Peaceful Coexistence contain 4 core values: the concept of sovereignty, the concept of peace, the concept of win-win progress and the concept of justice. Related to the latter, Liu Zhenmin states:

> "The inclusion of the word "mutual" or the prefix "co-" in the Five Principles reflects the unity of rights, obligations and responsibilities. Countries should engage in international relations in accordance with international law. No country shall place itself above international law, apply international law selectively, or adopt double standards in the application of international law." (Zhenmin 2014: 479)

The implication is that the Five Principles of Peaceful Coexistence will guide the international community towards an international rule of law where 'countries should participate in international lawmaking on an equal footing, to reflect rights, obligations and responsibilities of all countries in a comprehensive, balanced and fair manner, and accommodate the interests of individual countries and the common interests of the international community' (Zhenmin 2014: 480).

That understanding of the Five Principles of Peaceful Coexistence—in combination with adherence to the UN Charter—demonstrates a willingness of equality in the progression of the BRI, at least between states where equality is a basic premise for creating win-win situations (Zhenmin 2014: 479).

However, in spite of these principles and the strong connection to equality, the EU has taken reservations about the BRI, which was briefly addressed above. The EU concern is that the Belt and Road will facilitate trade of Chinese overcapacity of goods into Europe. In the EU antidumping policies towards China, China does not get the traditional market economy treatment. Instead, Chinese producers are subject to the 'distorted economy' approach, which is disadvantageous for Chinese producers compared to producers from other states. Some reasons behind the EU approach are that there is no equality for EU producers or investors to the Chinese markets compared to the access of Chinese goods and investments into Europe. As also mentioned above, in the EU antidumping regulations, the EU has indirect requirements on China concerning the ILO core conventions and environmental law as different standards affect the competition on the global market.[38] The BRI has taken a green profile by making international environmental law a priority but the ILO core principles seem not at this point to be of same concern as the environment and the climate.

Thus, equality has a multilevel dimension. That can be between states and their rights and obligations under international law, between a business and a government, between businesses and citizens or between businesses concerning contract, labour law, or consumer law, as well as between businesses in getting market access under international economic law. If the international system cannot guarantee equality between market participants due to different degrees of market access or different human rights commitments, the BRI should improve on closing that rule of law gap.

Concluding Remarks

The BRI has potential for contributing to the international rule of law if there is the political will. China is in the lead and should take that responsibility to improve on the rule of law. However, the rule of law is a contested concept, and even if there is a political will to improve on the rule of law conditions along the Belt and Road, it might be a rule of law in a narrow sense. To reduce the transaction costs of the businesses, there is the need of stronger human rights and environmental protection to make an even playing field, and the need of strengthening the legal infrastructure along the Belt and Road. The question is whether China has the interest in improving on all these aspects of the rule of law. There seems to be a focus on environment and climate, which is a good starting point, but will there also be improvement in respect of human rights?

There is also need of improving the access to justice. At this point, the various dispute settlement institutions on international level can cause rule of law gaps by overlapping jurisdictions addressing the same issues.

[38] See European Parliament resolution of 16 December 2015 on EU–China relations (2015/2003(INI)), para. 16, Council of the European Union, Council conclusions: EU Strategy on China, Brussels, 18 July 2016, (OR. en) 11252/16, Appendix 1, para. 11, and European Commission, Commission Staff Working Document on Significant Distortions in the Economy of the People's Republic of China for the Purposes of Trade Defence Investigations, Brussels, 20.12.2017, SWD(2017) 483 final/2.

There have been established specific courts and arbitration centres with focus on the Belt and Road. These are important contributions to the rule of law. However, there is need of further guarantees, in particular from the courts established in China, to ensure the independence of the courts, including no interference by the government. Finally, the equality under the trade laws concerning market access for businesses needs also to be addressed. At this point, Chinese exporters of goods into the EU are disadvantaged by the EU antidumping rules towards China, while EU producers are disadvantaged by China's fewer human rights and ILO commitments in their competition with Chinese producers.

References

Andersen, Henrik (2015), "Protection of Non-Trade Values in WTO Appellate Body Jurisprudence: Exceptions, Economic Arguments, and Eluding Questions", in *Journal of International Economic Law*, 18(2), 383–405.

Andersen, Henrik (2019a), "India—Solar Cells and Mexico—Taxes on Soft Drinks: Multilevel Rule of Law Challenges in the Interpretation of Art. XX (d) of GATT 1994 in WTO Case Law", in *Indian Journal of International Economic Law*, 10, 60–103.

Andersen, Henrik (2019b), "Rule of Law Developments by Judiciaries in the EU and the WTO: A Comparative Approach in a Multilevel Setting", *Copenhagen Business School, CBS LAW Research Paper* No. 19–38, available at SSRN: https://ssrn.com/abstract=3492638.

Avbelj, Matej and Komárek, Jan (2008), "Four Visions of Constitutional Pluralism", in *European Constitutional Law Review*, 4(3), 524–527.

Bacchus, James (2003), "Groping Towards Grotius: The WTO and the International Rule of Law", in *Harvard International Law Journal*, 44(2), 533.

Bénabou, Roland and Tirole, Jean (2010), "Individual and Corporate Social Responsibility", in *Economica*, 77(305), 1–19.

Cohen, David (2015), "China's 'Second Opening': Grand Ambitions but a Long Road Ahead", in *One Belt, One Road: China's Great Leap Outward*, European Council on Foreign Relations, London, June 2015.

Craig, Paul (1997), "Formal and Substantive Conceptions of the Rule of Law: An Analytical Framework", in Bellamy, Richard (ed.), *The Rule of Law and the Separation of Powers*, Sweet & Maxwell Stevens Journals, London, 467–487.

Haggard, Stephan and Tiede, Lydia (2011), "The Rule of Law and Economic Growth: Where Are We?", in *World Development*, 39(5), 673–685.

Hayek, Friedrich August, (2007 [1944]), *Road to Serfdorm*, Caldwell, Bruce (ed.), The Definitive ed., The University of Chicago Press, Chicago.

Hillman, Jennifer (2011 [2012]), *AB Annual Report* (2011), WT/AB/17, 13 June 2012 (12–3113).

Hoff, Karla and Stiglitz, Joseph (2004), "After the Big Bang?—Obstacles to the Emergence of the Rule of Law in Post-Communist Societies", in *The American Economic Review*, 94(3), 753–763.

Koskenniemi, Martti and Leino, Päivi (2002), "Fragmentation of International Law?—Postmodern Anxieties", in *Leiden Journal of International Law*, 15(3), 553–579.

Krisch, Nico (2012), "The Case for Pluralism in Postnational Law", in de Búrca, Gráinne and Weiler, Joseph H. H. (eds.), *The Worlds of European Constitutionalism*, Cambridge University Press, Cambridge, 203–261.

Lauterpacht, Hersch (2011 [1933]), *The Function of Law in the International Community*, Oxford University Press, Oxford.

Li, Lao (2019), "The Legal Challenge and Legal Safeguards for the Belt and Road Initiative", in *Global Trade and Customs Journal*, 14(5), 211.

Marceau, Gabrielle (2015), "The Primacy of the WTO Dispute Settlement System", in *Questions of International Law*, 23, 3–13.

Nordic Trust Fund/World Bank (2012), "Human Rights and Economics: Tensions and Positive Relationships", prepared by GHK Consulting Ltd.

Orellana, Marcos A. (2002), "The Swordfish Dispute Between the EU and Chile at the ITLOS and the WTO", in *Nordic Journal of International Law*, 71(1), 55–81.

Petersmann, Ernst-Ulrich (2012), *International Economic Law in the 21st Century—Constitutional Pluralism and Multilevel Governance of Interdependent Public Goods*, Hart Publishing, Oxford.

Radin, Margaret (1989), "Reconsidering the Rule of Law", in *Boston University Law Review*, 69(4), 781–819.

Rawls, John (1999), *A Theory of Justice*, Revised ed., The Belknap Press of Harvard University Press, Cambridge, MA.

Raz, Joseph (2009), *The Authority of Law: Essays on Law and Morality*, 2nd ed., Oxford University Press, Oxford.

Shany, Yuval (2003), *The Competing Jurisdictions of International Courts and Tribunals*, Oxford University Press, Oxford.

Taplin, Nathaniel and Wong, Jacky (2019), "Undermining Hong Kong Courts Is Bad for Business", *Wall Street Journal*, November 19.

Tuori, Kaarlo (2011), *Ratio and Voluntas—The Tension Between Reason and Will in Law*, Ashgate, Farnham.

United Nations and World Bank (2018), *Pathways for Peace: Inclusive Approaches to Preventing Violent Conflict*, World Bank, Washington, DC. https://doi.org/10.1596/978-1-4648-1162-3.

United Nations Secretary-General Kofi Annan (2004), "Report of the Secretary-General, the Rule of Law and Transitional Justice in Conflict and Post-Conflict Societies", United Nations Security Council, S/2004/616, 23 August 2004.

Walker, Neil (2002), "The Idea of Constitutional Pluralism", in *The Modern Law Review*, 65(3), 317–359.

Wan, Ming (2016), *The Asian Infrastructure Investment Bank: The Construction of Power and the Struggle for the East Asian International Order*, Palgrave Macmillan, New York.

Zhenmin, Liu (2014), "Editorial Comment: Following the Five Principles of Peaceful Coexistence and Jointly Building a Community of Common Destiny", in *Chinese Journal of International Law*, 13(3), 477–480.

Comparative Law Reflections on the Use of Soft Law in the Belt and Road Initiative

Giuseppe Martinico

Introduction

The aim of this chapter is to look at the role played by soft law measures in the design and implementation of the Belt and Road Initiative (hereinafter BRI). Soft law has acquired a growing relevance as scholars have stressed: 'BRI-related soft law documents arise through a myriad of forms and involve a large number of parties. In terms of form, these instruments are generally found to be cooperation agreements, including joint communiques, joint statements, agreements, a MOA, MOUs, a letter of intent, initiatives and consensuses'.[1] Starting from a systematisation of the literature on soft law, I shall try to classify this jungle of measures and explain the reasons for their massive use within the BRI. I shall pay special attention to the Memorandum of Understanding (MoU) between

[1] 'To sum up, soft law is preferred to treaties in China's BRI approach. Although existing treaties remain relevant, the BRI does not have many formal international law instruments. There is no BRI-wide treaty or similar international law instrument establishing the BRI. The BRI neither has a constituting treaty with all BRI states (a BRI-wide treaty) nor formal membership protocols. China, as such, does not appear to have a strong intention to bring in BRI-wide hard law obligations at this stage' (H. Wang 2019: 43).

G. Martinico (✉)
DIRPOLIS Institute (Institute of Law, Politics and Development), Sant'Anna School of Advanced Studies, Pisa, Pisa, Italy
e-mail: giuseppe.martinico@santannapisa.it

G. Martinico and X. WU (eds.), *A Legal Analysis of the Belt and Road Initiative*, https://doi.org/10.1007/978-3-030-46000-6_7

China and Italy that represents, in my view, an emblematic example of this trend.

Indeed, flexibility is one of the pillars of the BRI, and this already represents an explanation of this massive use of soft law instruments. However, flexibility means different things when applied to the BRI, having both a normative and institutional dimension (H. Wang 2019: 31) as we will see. Another reason why soft law instruments are vital in this area is due to the 'partnership-based relational approach' promoted by the Initiative:

> Being "relational" means the cooperative framework for the BRI is not based on a treaty-based institutional design. Rather, it utilizes a variety of means, most of which are rather abstract and even ambiguous, with the view to building confidence and developing good relations through volunteer cooperation and non-binding promises. The "partnership" dimension in the BRI indicates that the bilateral cooperation between China and individual BRI countries is always oriented toward building partnership, for which the BRI does not impose a uniform model applying to all countries. Rather, China seemingly seeks a model of "One Country One Approach" (yiguo yice). That is, China's bilateral cooperation with each and every BRI country can adopt a different model, as long as it is mutually acceptable solution through friendly bilateral negotiations.[2]

[2] 'Obviously, the structures and provisions of the two arrangements are very similar. However, if the China-Philippines MoU is representative of China's BRI cooperation with a developing country while the China–New Zealand MoA represents BRI arrangement with a developed country, several interesting points of differences can be observed. First, there is clearly a "development" dimension in the China-Philippines MoU, in which China offers assistance to Philippines' development. Understandably, China–New Zealand MoA does not need such development-based assistance, but it constantly stresses the importance of the private sector and market economy. Second, in cooperation principles, the China–New Zealand MoA mentions the need to follow "international good practice, market orientation and professional Principles", which does not exist in the China-Philippines MoU as the latter seems to emphasize adherence to national rules and regulations. Third, in areas of cooperation, the China-Philippines MoU specifically encourages the use of local currencies in bilateral trade and investment, while the China–New Zealand MoA specifically mentions regulatory harmonization. Fourth, both arrangements provide that they only embody the "common will" or "common aspiration" of the state actors involved, but the China–New Zealand MoA does not contain a "legal status" clause to emphasize that none of the provisions in the text is binding. Further, with respect to amendment, though both arrangements require mutual consent for amending the text, the China-Philippines MoU uses "shall" while the China–New Zealand MoA uses "will", arguably indicating a stronger consensus requirement, which is symbolic in nature, in the MoU for changing anything that is already agreed upon between the Participants' (J. Wang 2019).

This variety does not exclude fruitful comparison between different Memoranda of Understanding but explains why it is possible to find some differences between those concluded between China and developing countries and those concluded instead between China and developed countries as suggested by scholars (J. Wang 2019). Apart from these differences, the MoU seems to follow a common scheme which then refers to other acts (statements, policy documents), triggering a sort of cascade system, where the MoU is understood as part of a legally hybrid jungle in the sense described by Trubek, Cottrell and Nance.[3]

From a methodological point of view, this proliferation of measures should not be studied adopting a formalistic approach but relying on a pragmatic view. This is due to the fact that 'the BRI is a holistic exercise: China promotes the BRI through all possible means and coordinated efforts' (H. Wang 2019: 32).

As Snyder pointed out in his seminal studies, soft law should not be seen as legally irrelevant. As in other legal fields, it may acquire juridical importance. This point has been stressed by Wang in the field of the BRI as well:

> While these BRI-specific soft law documents are not binding, they nonetheless should not be ignored. China currently prefers to avoid engaging through treaties, with measurable compliance requirements, in favour of less formal, but more flexible, arrangements. BRI-specific documents usually call for voluntary forms of cooperation, or statements of future intent, instead of imposing hard law treaty obligations backed by enforcement mechanisms. For example, the MOA and MOUs under the BRI are nonbinding documents. However, they are nonetheless essential to BRI implementation. (H. Wang 2019: 42)

Starting from these considerations, I shall try in this chapter to explore the possible role to be played by soft law within the scope of the BRI.

[3] 'We immediately recognize that the question is not necessarily one of hard versus soft law: there is also the issue of the possible interaction between these two approaches to governance and thus of "hybrid" constellations in which both hard and soft processes operate in the same domain and affect the same actors' (Trubek et al. 2005).

Soft Law: A Map of the Literature

Soft law is a very ambiguous concept given the difficult location of this category in the classic hierarchy of sources. These have been defined by Snyder as 'measures which are not legally binding but which nevertheless have practical and even legal effects' (Snyder 2010). Scholars have identified the following features for this type of norms:

> [T]hey have been articulated in non-binding form according to traditional modes of law-making; (ii) they contain vague and imprecise terms; (iii) they emanate from bodies lacking international law-making authority; (iv) they are directed at non-state actors whose practice cannot constitute customary international law; (v) they lack any corresponding theory of responsibility; (vi) they are based solely upon voluntary adherence, or rely upon non-juridical means of enforcement. (Chinkin 2000: 28)

In other words, we are speaking of legally relevant norms that are sometimes included in non-binding acts, which differ from hard law due to the different prescriptive intensity and whose 'main differentiating features lie in the capacity of the norm to prescribe legally binding commitments, the clarity and precision of its terms, and its enforceability' (Stefan 2012: 9).

As Trubek, Cottrell and Nance have argued, soft law is a very general term that has been used to refer to a variety of processes (Trubek et al. 2005). Both soft law and hard law have been attacked by scholars and are sometimes seen as complementary and not mutually exclusive (Shaffer and Pollack 2010). As Abbott and Snidal recall, 'the choice between hard and soft law is not a binary one' (Abbott and Snidal 2000: 421–422) and this is also due to the variety of processes behind this formula. Generally, these are the advantages of soft law: 'lower contracting costs', 'lower sovereignty costs', 'coping with diversity', 'flexibility', 'simplicity and speed', 'participation and incrementalism' (Trubek et al. 2005). The ambiguity of soft law is frequently associated with that of governance, defined as 'political steering' (Treib et al. 2007). Frequently, soft law is identified as opposed to hard law since they would respond to opposite logics: 'legal bindingness versus soft law'; 'rigid versus flexible approach to implementation'; 'presence versus absence of sanctions'; 'material versus procedural regulation'; 'only public actors involved versus only private actors involved'; 'hierarchy versus market'; 'central versus dispersed locus of authority'; 'institutionalised versus non-institutionalised interactions'; 'fixed norms versus malleable norms' (Treib et al. 2007).

In international law, soft law is frequently employed since 'soft legalization is much easier to achieve than hard legalization, especially when the states concerned are not willing to be seen to have their sovereignty directly challenged' (J. Wang 2019). Recently, a proliferation of soft law instruments can also be found in the creation, enforcement, oversight and regulation of counterterrorism measures[4] or in international taxation law (Chaisse and Ji 2018) because of the advantages in terms of respect of pluralism that soft law guarantees. At the same time, '[h]owever, the ways in which soft law is adopted are not always legitimate or transparent. In this context, many have warned that the use of soft law in Courts might foster illegitimate ways of decision making and "backdoor legislation"' (Stefan 2012: 8). Soft law might also generate uncertainty and ambiguity and, generally speaking, marginalise courts or tribunals.

In EU law, soft legal instruments have acquired growing importance and this can be explained by the fact that they favour the preservation of legal diversity at the national level. For instance, in their works on welfare policies, Esping-Andersen (1990) and Ferrera (1998) have distinguished at least three or four worlds of welfare coexisting in Europe. This is one of the reasons for the difficulty of harmonisation in the field of social policies and partly explains why the European Union (EU) has more recently resorted to soft law instruments and the Open Method of Coordination (with questionable results in the majority of the cases: Hatzopoulos 2007), defined as 'an experimentalist approach to EU governance based on iterative benchmarking of national progress towards common European objectives and organized mutual learning' (Zeitlin 2005), based on the idea of complementarity to the national action and policies.[5]

Actually, the argument of the absence of a unique welfare system in Europe does not impede—per se—the existence of a common sense of solidarity at a supranational level. On the contrary, asymmetry, in this respect, is common even in other contexts (plurinational-federal systems) characterised, like the EU, by a high level of social (in terms of policies) and constitutional differentiation.

The Open Method of Coordination (Borràs and Jacobsson 2004: 188) is frequently associated with soft law, but some scholars have actually

[4] Report of the Special Rapporteur on the promotion and protection of human rights and fundamental freedoms while countering terrorism, 2019, available at: https://undocs.org/A/74/335.

[5] On the Open Method of Coordination, see Dawson (2011).

pointed out the existence of some differences between the two, especially in the light of the so-called supranational approach which galvanises the role of the Commission and the Court of Justice of the European Union. These two actors have traditionally had a central role in the integration process by favouring the progressive departure of EU law from the traditional public international law scheme. In Snyder's words: 'In fact, the use of soft law in the EU in recent years has increased to such an extent that some scholars ask whether or not the rule of law in the EU is being undermined' (Snyder 2010).

Not by coincidence, Senden wrote of norms with '(indirect) legal effects' and identified at least three categories of soft law: preparatory and informative instruments; interpretative and decisional instruments; and formal and informal steering instruments (Senden 2004: 219–220).

Soft law is also known at the national level, especially in those systems characterised by the coexistence of diverse legal cultures. This is the case in Canada, for instance, and in many other federal jurisdictions in which soft law has been used in combination with intergovernmental dynamics. These constitutional processes thus display similarities with the EU: the necessity to involve citizens and national parliaments in order to overcome the democratic deficit of the Union; the difficulty of finding 'a satisfactory and comprehensive constitutional settlement' (Kay 2005: 706); and the important role played by courts in reshaping the relation between centre and periphery. Moreover, both Canada and the EU have discovered the importance of alternative sources of constitutional update: intergovernmental agreements for Canada (see the importance of the Social Union Framework Agreement, SUFA, a major intergovernmental agreement governing social policy) and new governance products in the EU (de Búrca and Scott 2000). The importance of these alternative and non-legally binding sources of constitutional update produced another common feature: the asymmetry and flexibility that characterise the two constitutional experiences. This explains why Bruno Theret (2002), for instance, described Canada and the EU as two examples of multinational and asymmetrical federalism. In Canada, soft law measures have been employed to avoid judicialisation and the involvement of courts (this is the case of the Social Union Framework Agreement) as 'SUFA does not change the constitutional powers of any governments. Nor is it legally binding. If governments do not fulfil their obligations, there is no recourse to the courts' (Lazar 2000).

There is, however, a crucial structural difference which should be taken into account when comparing the role played by soft law in the EU and in the BRI, and it is connected to the institutional flexibility stressed by H. Wang (2019: 31). The BRI is not an international organisation, and it does not claim to represent an exhaustive and institutionally autonomous phenomenon. Its 'One Country One Approach' strategy is very far from the legal uniformity desidered, to a certain extent achieved and preserved by the Court of Justice of the EU in its legal system as shown by such decisions as Melloni[6] or Opinion 2/13[7]—in particular, the former, which has stressed the importance of preserving 'the primacy, unity and effectiveness of EU law',[8] while in Opinion 2/13, the Luxembourg Court emphasised the need to ensure 'consistency and uniformity in the interpretation of EU law'.[9] Indeed, primacy and direct effect are direct offsprings of the concept of autonomy of EU law and make EU law different from the rest of public international law. This is an important caveat that should be taken into account when comparing the role of soft law in jurisdictions other than EU law.

Indeed, in her book, Stefan (2012: 9) has investigated the role of judicialisation by analysing the case law of the Court of Justice in competition law and state aid. In general, scholars have also highlighted the relevance that traditional non-binding measures, such as recommendations, can play in EU law, as they can serve to specify the general duty of sincere cooperation stemming from the EU treaties (now Article 4.3 TEU). In the light of these considerations, Motzo suggested considering recommendations as non-immediately binding instruments (Motzo 1965: 1420). Similar considerations can be extended to soft law instruments.

[6] Court of Justice of the EU, Case C-399/11, Stefano Melloni v Ministerio Fiscal, ECLI:EU:C:2013:107.

[7] Court of Justice of the EU, Opinion 2/13, ECLI:EU:C:2014:2454.

[8] Court of Justice of the EU, Case C-399/11, Stefano Melloni v Ministerio Fiscal, ECLI:EU:C:2013:107, para. 60.

[9] Court of Justice of the EU, Opinion 2/13, ECLI:EU:C:2014:2454, para. 174.

The Memorandum of Understanding Between China and Italy

Italy and China entered into a MoU signed by President Xi Jinping and Prime Minister Giuseppe Conte on 23 March 2019. The conclusion of this agreement has always been surrounded by concerns as to the potential clash of this deal with Italy's duties stemming from its NATO and EU memberships. This point was apparently balanced by the references to international law obligations included in the MoU.

The language of the agreement is very vague, but this MoU has great political and symbolic importance because Italy is a G-7 and founding member of the EU. Indeed, the agreement has caused many concerns among the other EU member states. This agreement has been complemented by other agreements (nineteen, to my knowledge) concluded in specific sectors, such as culture, sport, energy, finance and infrastructure. Plus, the harbours of Trieste and Genova have concluded other agreements with the China Communications Construction Company (Y. Wang 2019). The MoU reflects the usual structure followed in these cases; it is a seven-page document divided into six paragraphs. The first paragraph is devoted to the 'Objectives and Guiding Principles of Cooperation' in which it is stated that the bilateral cooperation will be developed consistently with 'the purposes and principles of the UN Charter'. Compliance with national and international law is also recalled later in the same provision, when it is stated that '[i]n accordance with their respective domestic laws and regulations, consistent with their respective international obligations'. Paragraph II recalls the 'Areas of Cooperation', namely 'Policy dialogue', 'Transport, logistics and infrastructure', 'Unimpeded trade and investment', 'Financial cooperation', 'People-to-people connectivity' and 'Green development cooperation'. Apart from the 'Green development cooperation', the other areas respond to the priorities already listed in the 'Vision for Maritime Cooperation under the Belt and Road Initiative'.[10] Paragraph III is devoted to the 'Modes of Cooperation', where a non-hard list of ways to cooperate is identified ('high-level visits and discussions', 'development of pilot programs in key areas, economic

[10] Full text of the Vision for Maritime Cooperation under the Belt and Road Initiative, https://www.fmprc.gov.cn/mfa_eng/zxxx_662805/t1249618.shtml.

exchanges and cooperation, joint research, capacity building, personnel exchanges and training'), plus there is the mention of possible future agreements in other areas and of cooperation with (and in) third countries.

Paragraph IV, 'Cooperation Mechanisms', provides for a joint Italy–China Government Committee to monitor cooperation, while Paragraph V ('Settlement of Differences') confirms the preference for solutions other than legal ones in case of interpretative disagreement, as it states that 'the Parties will settle amicably differences in the interpretation of this Memorandum of Understanding through direct consultations'. Doubts have been cast over the consistency between Paragraphs IV and V:

> Paragraph V of the MoU (Settlement of Differences) reads indeed "The Parties will settle amicably differences in the interpretation of this Memorandum of Understanding through direct consultations". However, this is not true, because that claim is already neutralised at paragraphs IV and VI of the same MoU. Paragraph IV (Cooperation Mechanism) does in fact bind the parties to the "full use of existing bilateral mechanisms", which, of course, are not included in the declaration of intents, however, were already established by previous bilateral agreements, ratified and implemented in the domestic law of both the Italian Republic and the People's Republic of China. (I.L. 2019)

However, I think that a conforming interpretation is possible, although these provisions are undoubtedly ambiguous on purpose. Finally, Paragraph VI ('Applicable Law') confirms the soft law nature of this MoU and corresponds to similar clauses included in other Memoranda. Paragraph IV of this MoU reads:

> This Memorandum of Understanding does not constitute an international agreement which may lead to rights and obligations under international law. No provision of this Memorandum is to be understood and performed as a legal or financial obligation or commitment of the Parties. This Memorandum of Understanding will be interpreted in accordance with the legislations of the Parties and as well as applicable international law and, as for the Italian Party, with the obligations arising from its membership of the European Union.

It is possible to find similar provisions in other Memoranda, for instance, in the one signed between China and the Philippines.[11] What does it mean? Does this confine this kind of MoU to a mere propaganda dimension? And why do these Memoranda contain such ambiguous provisions? I shall try to contextualise in the light of the main structural features of the BRI in the next section of this chapter.

Soft Law in the Belt and Road Initiative

In the Chinese case, the preference for soft law can be also explained in the light of some cultural reasons, as suggested by international[12] and comparative law scholars:

> At times, soft law can trump hard law in instances where a court or arbitral tribunal recognizes something as international customary law that preempts the application of attributable domestic hard law (choice of law or conflicts of law). Such a dichotomy is also at work in domestic legal systems. This is especially true in China, which has a long history of informal customary law. Indeed, in China's case hard law (CCL, CISG, General Rules, administrative regulations) is insufficient to truly understand the role of law in Chinese society [...] Chinese cultural norms weigh in favor of mediation, compromise, and relationship preservation than it does to litigation. Second, rational judicial reasoning in the application of hard rules and principles is lacking in the Chinese judiciary because of its lack of skill and familiarity with the Western legal concepts found in the CCL [...] In China's case, cultural norms (Confucianism, guanxi, socialistic communal-collective ideals) are, in a sense, the law behind the law. The meaning attached to the hard rules of contract is heavily influenced by this normative background, which one scholar has characterized as the "normative richness of life in China". (Di Matteo 2018: 440–441)

When this cultural *humus* is coupled with what Heng called 'institutional flexibility' (i.e. the absence of a common structural frame), the outcome

[11] 'This Memorandum of Understanding does not create legally binding obligations for the Participants. It is an expression of their common aspiration to cooperate on the Belt and Road Initiative for the mutual benefits', Memorandum of Understanding between the Government of the Republic of Philippines and the Government of the People's Republic of China on Cooperation on the Belt and Road Initiative.

[12] 'Reflecting Chinese culture, China takes a flexible "middle-of-the-road" strategy in respect of the BRI, avoiding extremes or "radical" development' (H. Wang 2019: 53).

results in giving soft law a role completely different from that played, for instance, in the context of EU law. This explains why soft law has become 'trendy' in China[13]: an important 'Soft Law Centre' has been set up at the Peking University, where also an eminent scholar in the field, Francis Snyder, currently works.

The BRI has indeed no treaty-based institutional frame since it is 'an initiative for which there are no publicly-stated KPI, no overarching institutionalization, no formal membership protocols, no founding charters, and a timeline for development that is not measured in mere years, but decades' (Shepard 2017). Not by coincidence, Wang defined the BRI as 'a hub-and-spoke network, with China as the hub' while the 'spokes, therefore, are "software" (mechanisms and agreements) and "hardware" (e.g. devising economic corridors with BRI states) with different BRI states' (H. Wang 2019: 35). Seen from this perspective, the BRI does not claim to overcome or replace existing international organisation but, rather, tries to interact with (and perhaps take advantage of) other institutionalised subjects by presenting itself as complementary.

Against this background, soft law plays a twofold function:

> First, from the perspective of international relations, it helps alleviate the concerns of the BRI countries, especially China's neighbors, that China will use the BRI to 'assert regional leadership in Asia' economically, diplomatically and militarily. Not requiring the parties to make hard commitments under binding legal obligations will reduce the fear of the BRI countries that, given the power asymmetry between them and China, as well as, the uncertainty about China's intention and future, specific and binding commitments will make them vulnerable to Chinese dominance. (J. Wang 2019)

[13] 'In China today, soft laws far outnumber hard laws. With regard to their functions, according to Professors Haocai and Song, soft law remedies the structural deficiencies of hard law governance; it enhances the effectiveness of the rule of law, reduces the costs of the rule of law and social progress, creates a more responsive public governance and promotes the rule of law. In terms of their impact, without soft law to fill in the gaps and spaces, and enable flexibility and detail in the legal system, hard law could not function. Indeed, given the growth in size and complexity of Chinese society today, hard law is becoming "softer" because of its need to adjust to changing circumstances' (Clark 2013).

This also confirms the instrumentality of law in the spirit characterising the BRI, although two international commercial courts have been set up to deal with possible disputes about the BRI (J. Wang 2019).[14]

Here, the temporal factor matters, the BRI—if carried out—will keep China and its partners busy for years, and that is why institutional flexibility is an added value as priorities and agendas might change in the light of the contingencies. In this sense, both normative and institutional flexibility might provide the BRI with adaptiveness and pragmatism, two key elements for such a big enterprise that is supposed to involve many public and private subjects. Concerns in terms of transparency and ambiguity remain, but these are connected with the BRI per se, rather than with the use of soft law. Indeed, as we saw previously, soft law is above all a multi-function device or, better, it refers to a universe of measures and acts which may have legal relevance depending on the context in which they are employed. In a strong integrated system like that of the EU—provided with direct effect and primacy and with strong common institutions—soft law has acquired an interesting role before the courts (Stefan 2012). In the Canadian case, especially with regard to the SUFA, soft law has been employed to galvanise political mediation and consensus, thereby avoiding the involvement of judges. For different reasons, this seems the desired goal in the design of the BRI. However, in the case of the BRI, there are additional motives for scepticism, in spite of the reassurances of the Supreme People's Court, according to which 'the rule of law is an important safeguard for the BRI, in which the role of the judiciary is indispensable'.[15]

[14] Two for the Road: China's International Commercial Courts, 17 August 2018, http://simc.com.sg/blog/2018/08/17/two-road-chinas-international-commercial-courts/.

[15] 'Zuigao Renmin Fayuan Guanyu Renmin Fayuan wei "Yidai Yilu" Jianshe Tigong Sifa Fuwu he Baozhang de Ruogan Yijian' ("Several Opinions of the Supreme People's Court on the Judiciary's Provision of Judicial Services and Safeguard for the Belt and Road"), Fa Fa (2015) 9 Hao, 16 June 2015, quoted by J. Wang (2019).

References

Abbott, Kenneth W. and Snidal, Duncan (2000), "Hard and Soft Law in International Governance", in *International Organization*, 54(3), 421–456.

Borràs, Susana and Jacobsson, Kerstin (2004), "The Open Method of Co-Ordination and the New Governance Patterns in the EU", in *Journal of European Public Policy*, 11(2), 185–208.

Chaisse, Julien and Ji, Xueliang (2018), "'Soft Law' in International Law-Making—How Soft International Taxation Law Is Reshaping International Economic Governance", in *Asian Journal of WTO & International Health Law and Policy*, 13(2), 463–509.

Chinkin, Christine (2000), "Normative Development in the International Legal System", in Shelton, Dinah (ed.), *Commitment and Compliance: The Role of Non-Binding Norms in the International Legal System*, Oxford University Press, Oxford.

Clark, Eugene (2013), "China's 'Soft Law' a Major Factor for Success in Future", available at: http://www.china.org.cn/opinion/2013-10/17/content_30321578.htm.

Dawson, Mark (2011), *New Governance and the Transformation of European Law: Coordinating EU Social Law and Policy*, Cambridge University Press, Cambridge.

de Búrca, Gráinne and Scott, Joanne (eds.) (2000), *The Changing Constitution of the EU: From Uniformity to Flexibility*, Hart, Oxford.

Di Matteo, Larry (2018), "'Rule of Law' in China: The Confrontation of Formal Law with Cultural Norms", in *Cornell International Law Journal*, 51(2), 391–443.

Esping-Andersen, Gøsta (1990), *The Three Worlds of Welfare Capitalism*, Princeton University Press, Princeton.

Ferrera, Maurizio (1998), *Le trappole del welfare*, Il Mulino, Bologna.

Hatzopoulos, Vassilis (2007) "Why the Open Method of Coordination Is Bad for You: A Letter to the EU", in *European Law Journal*, 13(3), 309–342.

I.L. (2019), "The Trap of the Italian-Chinese Memorandum of Understanding", 18 May 2019, available at: https://www.lavoceditrieste.net/2019/05/18/the-trap-of-the-italian-chinese-memorandum-of-understanding/.

Kay, Richard S. (2005), "Book Review Essay: Canada's Constitutional Cul De Sac", in *American Review of Canadian Studies*, 35(4), 705–714.

Lazar, Harvey (2000), "The Social Union Framework Agreement: Lost Opportunity or New Beginning?" in *Institute of Intergovernmental Relations School of Policy Studies, Queen's University Working Paper*, available at: https://qspace.library.queensu.ca/handle/1974/14909.

Motzo, Giovanni (1965), "Commento Sub Art.189", in Quadri, Rolando, Monaco, Riccardo and Trabucchi, Alberto, *Commentario C.E.E*, Giuffrè, Milan, 1388–1422.

Senden, Linda (2004), *Soft Law in European Community Law*, Hart, Oxford.
Shaffer, Gregory C. and Pollack, Mark A. (2010), "Hard vs. Soft Law: Alternatives, Complements, and Antagonists in International Governance", in *Minnesota Law Review*, 94(3), 706–799.
Shepard, Wade (2017), "Why the Ambiguity of China's Belt and Road Initiative Is Perhaps Its Biggest Strength", in *Forbes*, 19 October 2017, available at: https://www.forbes.com/sites/wadeshepard/2017/10/19/whatchinas-belt-and-road-initiative-is-really-all-about/#72adce76e4de.
Snyder, Francis (2010), "Soft Law and Governance: Aspects of the European Union Experience in the European Union Experience", available at: https://papers.ssrn.com/sol3/papers.cfm?abstract_id=3101617.
Stefan, Oana (2012), *Soft Law in Court: Competition Law, State Aid and the Court of Justice of the European Union*, Kluwer Law International, The Hague.
Theret, Bruno (2002), "L'Union sociale canadienne dans le miroir des politiques sociales de l'Union européenne", available at: https://www.researchgate.net/publication/236341097_L'union_sociale_canadienne_dans_le_miroir_des_politiques_sociales_de_l'Union_europeenne.
Treib, Oliver, Bähr, Holger and Falkner, Gerda (2007), "Modes of Governance, Old and New: A Note Towards Conceptual Clarification", in *Journal of European Public Policy*, 14(1), 1–20.
Trubek, David M., Cottrell, Patrick and Nance, Mark (2005), "'Soft Law', 'Hard Law', and European Integration: Toward a Theory of Hybridity", available at: https://ideas.repec.org/p/erp/jeanmo/p0242.html.
Wang, Heng (2019), "China's Approach to the Belt and Road Initiative: Scope, Character and Sustainability", in *Journal of International Economic Law*, 22(1), 29–55.
Wang, Jiangyu (2019), "China's Governance Approach to the Belt and Road Initiative (BRI): Partnership, Relations, and Law", in *NUS Law Working Paper* No. 2019/005, available at: https://papers.ssrn.com/sol3/papers.cfm?abstract_id=3346427.
Wang, Yi (2019), "What Is the China-Italy MoU?", available at: https://www.oboreurope.com/en/what-is-the-china-italy-mou/.
Zeitlin, Jonathan (2005), "Social Europe and Experimentalist Governance: Towards a New Constitutional Compromise?" in *European Governance Papers (EUROGOV)*, available at: http://www.connex-network.org/eurogov/pdf/egp-connex-C-05-04.pdf.

The Importance of International Water Law to the Successful Implementation of the Belt and Road Initiative: Evidence from Central Asia

Imad Antoine Ibrahim

Introduction

The literature concerning transboundary water management is constantly growing, given the importance of water as a resource and the sensitivity of this topic (Biswas and Tortajada 2010; Tortajada 2010; Grigg 2011). Despite the increasing focus on this matter, the problems associated with the good governance of shared freshwaters have not disappeared. Transboundary water management remains a great challenge for many reasons, and it is one of the great challenges of the twenty-first century (Gupta and Pahl-Wostl 2013; Cosgrove and Loucks 2015). In fact, the main reason the governance of shared waters is highly complicated and sometimes controversial is the necessity to make compromises between states having various interests and needs. Such compromises are often hard to reach given the lack of trust among the different nations seeking to exploit shared waters (Yoffe and Ward 1999; Petersen-Perlman et al. 2017). This

I. A. Ibrahim (✉)
Sant'Anna School of Advanced Studies, Institute of Law, Politics and Development (Dirpolis), Pisa, Italy

gLAWcal—Global Law Initiative for Sustainable Development, Essex, UK

G. Martinico and X. WU (eds.), *A Legal Analysis of the Belt and Road Initiative*, https://doi.org/10.1007/978-3-030-46000-6_8

is where the international community intervened with the aim of solving this problem through the progressive codification of International Water Law (IWL) that was meant to regulate the use and exploitation of transboundary freshwaters (Dellapenna and Gupta 2009; McIntyre 2010a). Even then, and with the efforts of a wide range of actors, including international lawyers, diplomats and scientists, the problems did not seem to disappear. Indeed, the solutions to ensure transboundary water governance have already been stated countless times through the work of academics, scientists and practitioners. It is always the state's reluctance to pursue these solutions that constitutes the greatest obstacle (Tropp 2007; Gupta et al. 2013). The interplay between IWL, transboundary water governance and the state's role in this context has been seen everywhere around the globe where nations are sharing freshwater resources (Boisson de Chazournes 2013; Magsig 2015). Such interplay has also been noticed in Central Asia where states are unable for the time being to pursue meaningful negotiations for ensuring the good governance of transboundary waters (Chatalova et al. 2017; Zhupankhan et al. 2017). From a geopolitical perspective, this region is surrounded by powerful countries including China and Russia. China has important interests in Central Asia in the framework of the Belt and Road Initiative (BRI), considered as one of the flagship projects of Beijing (Schortgen 2018).

In this context, one would wonder whether China can play a role in pushing Central Asian countries to make compromises to ensure the good governance of transboundary freshwaters, given the Chinese economic interests in the region that also covers its natural resources. As such, the author is seeking to answer the following question: Could China push countries that are members of BRI to pursue cooperation over transboundary freshwaters on the basis of IWL? This article will highlight that the answer to this question depends on whether the countries members of BRI are sharing freshwater with China or not. For this reason, the author chose Central Asia as a region to examine this question using two selected case studies. The first concerns the water shared between China and Kazakhstan and the second concerns the entire Central Asian region where China is making huge investments. The article will highlight that, in the first case, the principles of IWL could be included within transboundary water agreements where such agreements provide the basis for the governance of shared freshwaters. In the second case, China can play the role of a responsible regional power pushing the different country members of BRI to reach a compromise upon which effective transboundary water agreements can be established.

Regarding the structure, this chapter will first analyse the topic of water management in the context of BRI and then proceed to examine the role of IWL. After that, the chapter will discuss the potential role IWL can play when China shares transboundary waters with countries that are members of BRI taking the shared resources between China and Kazakhstan as a case study. The author will then analyse the potential role IWL can play in the situation where the countries that are members of the BRI share transboundary freshwaters without having China as one of the parties. For this purpose, Central Asia was chosen as a case study, as the countries of this region are members of the BRI and simultaneously share freshwaters that are not shared with China. In conclusion, the author will highlight the importance of IWL to the implementation of BRI given China's foreign policy of adopting the role of a responsible power at the global and regional stages.

Water Management in the Context of BRI

Water is considered by China as a vital resource for the economic development of the country as it can be used for various purposes. Shared water is viewed as a source of profit and as a means of regional development where BRI plays an important role in ensuring the sort of regional development that would allow increasing political and economic influence in the country (Deng et al. 2016; Pham Do and Dinar 2017; Xie and Shaofeng 2018). Chinese interests in transboundary water resources are expected to further grow with BRI. This is the reason scholars are seeking to understand China's strategy in this regard, given that water is 'recognized as the world's greatest societal, economic, and perhaps security risk in the coming decade' (Zhang and Li 2018a: 706). China is seeking to benefit through BRI from the huge amount of mineral resources that currently exist across the regions, including freshwater resources (Dunford and Liu 2019). Through BRI, China is looking to further open the foreign markets to Chinese goods and services, is encouraging Chinese investments overseas in sectors such as infrastructure and is seeking access to natural resources such as water and energy. In this context, it has been noted that China has funded, built or is currently building numerous hydropower projects overseas (Urban et al. 2018). The sensitivity of water resources and China's ambitions in this regard affects the implementation of BRI.

The size and power of the country sharing the water with China affect its perception of BRI, the kind of compromises that need to be made by China to ensure the acceptance of its initiative, the likelihood of that country to join the BRI… All these factors will eventually affect the legal field (Williams 2019).

BRI is expected to affect natural resources management and the environment of the countries that are members of this Initiative because any Chinese investment may create advantages to certain nations or further water stress in other states (Zhang and Li 2018c). China's plans to invest in natural resources, including water resources, along with the country members of BRI may create new problems and conflicts between the water users located near the sources, particularly in rural areas (Sternberg et al. 2017). Therefore, China is seeking to embrace an active water diplomacy, given the awareness of the negative impact of transboundary water conflicts on the successful implementation of the Initiative. This is very relevant, particularly in the regions and countries that are experiencing huge water stress, such as Central Asia and South East Asia (Zhang and Li 2018c). Indeed, countries across BRI are increasingly facing issues related to water supply and safety where the negative impact of climate change is intensifying these threats (Li 2017). Numerous BRI projects have affected, and are currently impacting, transboundary water resources, in particular in South and Southeast Asia. Chinese companies are building hydropower projects in places like the Mekong, Indus and the Ganges (Williams 2019). In places like the Mekong where China shares water with five other states, the establishment of the Lancang-Mekong Cooperation (LMC) mechanism by China was linked to BRI (Williams 2018). Among the many words that are used by China in this context, one can notice the use of the concept of 'natural belt of the Mekong' which 'parallels that of the Belt and Road and naturalises the river as the arena for development under the Belt and Road' (Williams 2018: 12).

The policies adopted by China concerning transboundary freshwaters in the context of BRI have also been adopted regarding other BRI projects where major criticisms have likewise been made concerning issues such as environmental risks. Still, these matters are much more relevant in the case of transboundary water resources as numerous populations rely on these resources, the ecological damage cannot be reversed and any Chinese involvement in water governance will lead to Chinese control of this important resource, in particular in the region where China shares transboundary freshwaters (Williams 2019). According to Patrick Martens:

> The complex interplay of social, political, economic and environmental factors does raise questions about the sustainability of cooperation on B&R initiatives as well as highlighting the importance of China's abilities to address problems between participating countries. (Martens 2018: 90)

Despite the challenges faced in the context of water resources, BRI can also be used as a tool for fostering collaboration among the nations and reducing tensions (Duarte 2018). Water as a resource holds an important role to play in the success or failure of BRI where even Chinese investments at the local level, such as building 'water-, waste- and carbon-treatment plants near industrial areas', can provide the necessary means for its implementation (Rauf et al. 2018). Water security is extremely important, as any potential water insecurity is expected to heavily affect the implementation of BRI (Zhang et al. 2019). The success of the Initiative requires that China improve the management of transboundary freshwaters to ensure the development of great relations on the basis of mutual trust with its neighbours while building regional stability (Zhang and Li 2018b). It is in this context that scholars are wondering, 'How will the country's policy towards transboundary water issues be affected by its high-profile Belt and Road Initiative?' (Zhang and Li 2018b: 700). One answer to this question is that China will have to adjust its transboundary water policy to ensure good management of shared freshwaters in a manner that allows the implementation of joint economic development plans. Beijing must ensure the protection of the environment and the ecosystem services of shared freshwaters (Zhang and Li 2018b). Such adjustment must be based on an appropriate regulatory framework, which is the reason the following section will analyse the importance of IWL to the implementation of BRI.

The Role of International Water Law

The development and progressive codification of IWL were the result of decades of extensive effort, with international lawyers, scholars and Non-Governmental Organizations (NGOs) playing a major role. Such codification occurred in the context of the work first conducted by the International Law Association (ILA) and then by the International Law

Commission (ILC) that drafted the existing water conventions (Magsig 2015). Progress towards the adoption of international conventions was slow given the many decades it took for the adoption of these treaties, despite the need for a global regulatory framework. Indeed, at least 90% of the world population is residing in a state that shares freshwater with another nation, while the majority of these transboundary resources lack a framework for cooperation (Stoa 2014). The existing international water regime includes binding global conventions and non-binding legal instruments in which the emphasis is put on the principles of transboundary water management, such as the principle of equitable and reasonable utilisation and the obligation not to cause significant harm (Fry and Chong 2016). This field is interacting with other important legal fields, mainly international environmental law, international human rights law and international investment law. All these fields are relevant to IWL, as they directly or indirectly affect its development (McIntyre 2017). IWL has gained momentum at the international level in recent years, with international water conventions finally ratified by 2014 and a new non-binding legal instrument addressing transboundary aquifers adopted in 2008. All these developments took place after the adoption of the human right to water in 2010 (Zeitoun 2015).

International water conventions are framework conventions upon which states establish transboundary water agreements addressing specific shared freshwaters. States negotiate the provisions of these treaties, taking into consideration international water principles and rules established by the international community. States then base their cooperation over management, governance and exploitation of the shared freshwater upon these transboundary water conventions (Grzybowski et al. 2010).

> International water law is meant to establish a state's rights and obligations vis-à-vis other states with respect to transboundary water. Unlike national law, there can be no direct enforcement of IWL, but it can build norms about 'acceptable' state behaviour and guide bilateral or multilateral treaties (to which IWL is always subordinate). (Zeitoun 2015: 951)

This field has the main objective of preventing nations from taking unilateral measures on shared water resources, as this law is trying to establish equitable and reasonable utilisation of transboundary freshwaters based on cooperation (Tzatzaki and Tarlock 2015). The importance of IWL lies in the fact that it is very difficult to resolve water disputes by relying on domestic legislation and courts. In many cases, water laws are poorly written and, if they exist in the first place, there may be few enforcement mechanisms. In fact, weak or non-hegemon states are usually in a bad position in the absence of international rules and regulations as stronger states with better position, more power and technological potential benefit more from the shared resource (Petersen-Perlman et al. 2017). In that sense, it is a consent-based system in which the different parties agree through legal provisions on the sharing of transboundary freshwaters, with this consent representing the foundation as there is no way to force a state to comply with the provisions of any water agreement adopted (Woodhouse and Zeitoun 2008).

This is not to say that IWL has not been criticised. Indeed, this global regulatory framework has been subject to criticism from international water lawyers who are seeking to constantly improve this field (Tarlock 2010). Suggestions have been made in this regard concerning different aspects that require further development, improvement and so on (Magsig 2011). Indeed, IWL has to 'fairly define the rights of respective states to set the outer limits of the use of the resource' and 'respond to many challenges posed by global climate change, increasing water consumption and population growth, adaptive management institutions must be developed to sustain interstate cooperation' (Tarlock 2008: 716). The problem is whether the political will that is often absent will lead to a gap between what is written within the water agreements and the practical implementation of these conventions (Tarlock 2008). This lack of political will has affected the implementation of IWL as the different principles and provisions adopted to address the issue of transboundary water management have gone through countless different debates, interpretations and misinterpretations by the different countries in accordance with their interests and perceptions (Grey and Garrick 2013). International water lawyers have examined in detail the shortcomings of this field and have expressly stated that IWL needs to adapt to the rapid changes that are occurring to address the different challenges, such as water security (Wouters and Moynihan 2013). This is not to say that no positive developments have occurred or are currently taking place. IWL is constantly evolving and maturing to stimulate further cooperation among the states sharing freshwaters (McIntyre 2010b; Tarlock 2016). Indeed, IWL has seen significant change over the last century, with the law expanding to recognise the functions that water plays not only in meeting human needs but also in servicing critical ecosystem functions (Stephens 2011).

The above-mentioned legal analysis of IWL will interact with the legal approach adopted through the BRI, as the flexible and pragmatic approach adopted by Beijing provides room for the use of different legal means as long as these means prove to be adequate and enhance the implementation of BRI. Hence, the analysis conducted in this section should be read in conjunction with the legal analysis of BRI conducted within the chapters of this book entitled *The Use of Soft Law in the Belt and Road Initiative* and *The Belt and Road Initiative: A Legal Analysis* which highlight the soft law approach adopted by Beijing. The following sections will examine whether IWL provides an adequate regulatory framework for the management of transboundary freshwaters that are covered within the BRI taking Central Asia as a case study.

The Role of International Water Law in the Context of BRI: Evidence from Central Asia

Good transboundary water governance is vital for the success of BRI, particularly in regions that are suffering from water stress (Martens 2018). In Central Asia, 'the uneven spatial distribution and complex pattern of transboundary water resources with contrasting national water needs have created an intricate water dilemma' (Zhupankhan et al. 2017: 139), despite the foreign aid and development projects that are taking place, especially since the 1990s (Chatalova et al. 2017; Zhupankhan et al. 2017). In fact, the collapse of the Soviet Union led Central Asian countries to adopt new water laws representing 'a compromise between state-centric socialist system and the new trend in water law, which recognizes an increasing participation of the public in the management of water resources' (Menga 2018: 50–51). This is very important, as the principles of Soviet water law contradicted the main principles of IWL (equitable and reasonable utilisation, obligation not to cause significant harm, principle of cooperation) since water was considered as only owned by the state and as inalienable (Menga 2018). Despite the progress shown by the ratification of international water agreements, Central Asian state attitudes towards IWL are governed by each state's interests and concerns (Ziganshina 2012; Libert 2018).

The question of sharing waters between the countries in Central Asia is just one example of how transboundary water governance may complicate the implementation of BRI (Martens 2018). Central Asian countries are looking to benefit from BRI to ensure a high economic growth despite the challenges surrounding the implementation of the Initiative in the region that are related to water and energy security (Guo et al. 2016). The potential rapid economic growth of the region as a result of BRI may lead to new water problems, which is the reason 'countries or regions along the belt urgently need to carry out coordinative development and effective cooperation of water resources' with the objective of safeguarding water resources (Guo et al. 2016: 9). In this context, China must create 'a strategic framework for collaborative development of water resources with Central Asia' that is based on existing water cooperation mechanisms (Guo et al. 2016: 9). China has to also provide all the necessary support in terms of water management experience, know-how and finances to ensure good transboundary water management, taking into consideration the synergies between water and energy developments (Guo et al. 2016). In this context, there is hope that the decrease in water quality and river ecosystems that occurred in China as a result of the developments that happened will not take place within the BRI (Bian 2018). To determine whether IWL can indeed constitute an appropriate regulatory framework fostering the implementation of BRI, the following sections shall examine two case studies from Central Asia representing two situations: first, where China shares transboundary freshwaters; and second, where China does not share such waters.

The Case of Water Resources Shared Between China and Other Nations: China–Kazakhstan Shared Freshwaters as a Case Study

China and Kazakhstan share twenty-four rivers, with the Irtysh and the Lli Rivers (Ho 2017) the most important ones. There are close ties between China and Kazakhstan that have resulted in successful cooperation between both countries, even though water disputes still persist, in particular given China's ambition of diverting water from the shared rivers (Zhang and Li 2018a) and the water pollution that exists in many rivers such as the Lli River that goes through a heavily industrial zone in China (Kukeyeva et al. 2018). Different studies have shown the complicated challenges surrounding transboundary water management, which is the reason water conflicts between both countries are occurring despite cooperation. Still, in comparison with the rest of the countries with whom China shares freshwater resources, most cooperation efforts have occurred with Kazakhstan (Pueppke et al. 2018a, b). Cooperation with Kazakhstan is important for China for numerous reasons, mainly:

> enhancing domestic stability involving the Uighur minority in Xinjiang; strengthening Sino–Kazakh economic and energy cooperation; engaging in regional competition for influence and power in Central Asia between Russia, China and the United States; and **implementation of China's Belt and Road Initiative**. (Zhang and Li 2018a: 716)

It is in this context that legal developments have already occurred and are currently taking place, with cooperation between the two countries taking the form of water agreements and joint institutions (Ho 2017). This is very relevant, as China has historically rejected the signature of international water agreements, despite its support for many of their principles, such as the principle of equitable and reasonable utilisation and the obligation not to cause significant harm, with many of the principles included within domestic water laws in China. Yet, for reasons related to issues of sovereignty, dispute settlement systems and the binding nature of these conventions, China decided not to sign them (Wouters and Chen 2013; Fry and Chong 2016). There were delays in the implementation of China–Kazakhstan water agreements for many reasons, including the lack of experts from the side of Kazakhstan (Ho 2017). The relevance of the agreements that are being adopted is that each one of them constitutes 'a step up in institutionalized riparian cooperation between the two countries' (Ho 2017: 150). According to some Kazakh scholars, BRI represents a great opportunity for both parties to tackle the transboundary water problems given the importance of water resources to the development and implementation of BRI (Ho 2017).

The cooperation for the management of shared rivers between China and Kazakhstan began in 1965 with the conclusion of the agreement on Distribution and Use of Horgos River (Zonn et al. 2018). After the dissolution of the Soviet Union, Kazakhstan attempted to establish cooperation with the Chinese government beginning in 1992 with the draft of 'Proposals for Consultation on the Joint Use of Transboundary Rivers' that was sent to China and was not successful (Ho 2017). Yet, the water diversion projects that were conducted by China in the 1990s raised serious concerns in Kazakhstan to the point where diplomatic relations were in danger, thereby pushing China to conduct five rounds of discussion with Kazakhstan from 1998 to 2001 (Ho 2017), resulting in the signature of the Agreement between the Government of Kazakhstan and the Government of China on Cooperation in the Use and Protection of Transboundary Rivers which was signed in 2001 and entered into force in 2002 (Agreement 2001; Gao 2014). The Joint Kazakh-Chinese Commission on Use and Protection of Transboundary Rivers was established in 2003 for the implementation of the treaty, leading to the signature of several agreements related to 'emergency notifications, natural disaster monitoring and technical cooperation' (Kukeyeva et al. 2018: 7) and, by 2011, agreements related to environmental protection and water quality (Kukeyeva et al. 2018). The 2001 agreement was criticised for not addressing plenty of issues that are vital for the management of shared freshwaters, given that it was a framework agreement; in particular, Article 4 related to the rational use and protection of water resources was criticised because of its vagueness and the fact that it was one sentence long (Kukeyeva et al. 2018). The 2001 agreement has also been criticised for the lack of provisions related to monitoring and compliance as well as dispute settlement, while 'volume intakes by both sides are not specified and the agreement does not stipulate any rules for the specific treatment of the Ili and the Irtysh' (Ho 2017: 158). There is also no mechanism stipulating the manner of implementation for the principle of rational and equitable use in Article 4 (Ho 2017). Still, this agreement represents the main and first bilateral agreement signed between China and Kazakhstan for the management of transboundary water resources, in this case, the rivers shared by both countries (Gao 2014).

The parties to the agreement expressly mentioned in the Preamble that the agreement is subject to international law principles and norms (Gao 2014).[1] This agreement included explicitly and implicitly several international water principles within either the Preamble or the provisions of the treaty. The convention included the main principles of IWL, such as the principle of equitable and reasonable utilisation, the obligation of avoiding significant harm and the principle of cooperation (Gao 2014). Concerning the principle of equitable and reasonable utilisation, the parties declared in the Preamble their intention of 'equitably and rationally resolving issues between the two States in the use and protection of the water resources of transboundary rivers' (Agreement 2001: Preamble). The parties also implicitly mentioned this principle in Article 2 where

[1] The agreement is 'governed by generally accepted principles and norms of international law on the basis of the principles of mutual respect for independence, sovereignty, and territorial integrity, non-interference in each other's internal affairs, equality and mutual benefit, and peaceful co-existence, in a spirit of mutual understanding, mutual amenability, and friendly consultation'.

they have based the use and protection of transboundary rivers on the principle of equity and rationality. The obligation of avoiding significant harm was stated explicitly in Article 3, according to which 'The Parties shall undertake appropriate measures and shall make efforts to prevent or mitigate serious harm caused to a State Party as a result of flooding disasters and man-made accidents' (Agreement 2001: Article 3). The principle of cooperation was mentioned explicitly numerous times in the agreement, in the Preamble and provisions Two and Five, with Article 5 stating the areas in which the parties may cooperate.[2] The agreement also established joint committees for coordination and organisation purposes and included provisions related to information and data exchange.[3] Still, some provisions of this agreement are considered ambiguous, while even those that mirror the provisions of the international framework water conventions are tailored to the needs of the parties and the context of the region. For instance, the provisions on information and data exchange within the agreement have specific restrictions that take into consideration the parties' interests and the sensitivity of the data (Gao 2014).[4]

[2] According to Article 2 of the Agreement: 'In the use and protection of transboundary rivers, the Parties shall adhere to the principles of equity and rationality, as well as closely cooperate in a sincere, neighborly, and friendly manner'.

In Article 5, the Parties may cooperate in the following areas:

- 'agreeing the existence and placement of posts for monitoring and measuring the volume and quality of waters;
- research into unified methods of monitoring, measuring, analysis, and assessment;
- conducting analyses of and staffing related thereto of data generated from hydrological monitoring and measuring at the posts agreed by the Parties;
- conducting possible joint research into the prevention of or mitigation of the consequences of flooding, freezing, and other natural disasters;
- studying trends related to future changes in the volume and quality of water in transboundary rivers; and
- when necessary, conducting joint research and sharing lessons learned in the use and protection of transboundary rivers'.

[3] See, for instance, Article 8:

'The Parties shall create a Kazakhstan–China Joint Commission on the Use and Protection of Transboundary Rivers (the "Joint Commission"), which shall be responsible for the development of a Statute regulating its activities and for deciding issues relevant to the effectuation of this Agreement'.

[4] Article 7 of the agreement states the following: 'No provisions of this Agreement may under any circumstances serve as the basis for the provision by a Party of extraordinarily important information or data related to that State's defense or security'.

What is more, there are some provisions that are not easily found in transboundary water agreements but are highly important. For example, the parties have agreed in Article 13 that the amendment of this agreement is possible if the parties mutually agree, with such amendment formalised through separate protocols (Agreement 2001: Article 13). This is very important given that many elements change or emerge over the course of the years, such as climate change where the entire literature is trying to deal with how such changes must be dealt with through water agreements that are not flexible enough for change and cannot be amended or updated (McCaffrey 2003; Cooley and Gleick 2011; Magsig 2015). The analysis below shows that IWL affected the wording of the framework agreement that was adopted after the Convention on the Law of the Non-Navigational Uses of International Watercourses (Watercourses Convention [UNWC]). This global framework convention included the principles that were mentioned earlier in its Articles 5, 6, 7 and 8, while Article 9 covered the exchange of data and information and the establishment of joint institutions (UNWC 1997).

Hence, the principles of IWL have already been used in the agreements between China and other countries that share transboundary waters and are part of the BRI, such as in the case of the framework agreement between China and Kazakhstan on the basis of which numerous more specific agreements were adopted (Gao 2014). The principles of IWL can also be used elsewhere and in the context of every transboundary freshwater resource shared between China and other countries that are also parties to BRI, providing the necessary regulatory framework for the management of shared water resources that are subject to constant tension and which may constitute a potential obstacle towards the successful implementation of BRI. Such use does not put pressure upon China to sign or ratify international water conventions while simultaneously providing the necessary legal support for the adoption of water agreements.

As already mentioned, since the conclusion of the first agreement in 2001, China and Kazakhstan have signed numerous agreements (Ho 2017). These conventions have been criticised as they are being drafted in the context of a lack of signature on the part of China of any international water agreement, which may provide further support to any claim that may be made, especially by Kazakhstan. Another criticism is related to the bilateral approach adopted by China even in the case of rivers shared between both countries in addition to other countries such as Russia and

Kyrgyzstan, in particular, as according to many scholars bilateral cooperation did not yield the expected results (Mustafina 2014). It is in this context that new agreements are also being suggested related to issues such as environmental protection and pollution prevention (Ryabtsev 2011). Despite the existence of water agreements, Kazakhstan needs to start finding alternative sources to satisfy its water needs, given the increasing use of water from these rivers by China, or adapt by changing, for instance, its agricultural practices (Kukeyeva et al. 2018). In fact, both countries need to enhance and change their management practices of the rivers given that the amount of water within these basins is expected to change in the course of this century for many reasons, including climate change (Thevs et al. 2017). Concluding agreements on water resources is a big step, but such development does not solve the issues that already existed or future problems. This is why cooperation among all the nations within the framework of any agreement adopted is incremental to the success of the treaty (Zhou and Wang 2017).

The Case Where China Is Only Making Investments or Seeking to Invest: Central Asia as a Case Study

Until the 1920s and before the Soviet era, Central Asian water rights were based on Islamic law and urbanisation and industrialisation resulted in the evolvement of the rules annually due to different factors, mainly 'economic development, democratic transition and the awareness that water agreements are crucial for regional cooperation' (Barić 2016: 124). During the Soviet era, the Soviet model of water allocation focused on making fair deals in which downstream countries with a well-developed agriculture and industry (Kazakhstan, Uzbekistan and Turkmenistan) received plenty of water from upstream states (Kyrgyzstan and Tajikistan) in exchange for electricity, gas and coal. The state in this period had the responsibility of covering all the costs related to water infrastructures (Barić 2016). The post-Soviet era witnessed disputes among the countries sharing freshwaters given the need to cover the costs of water infrastructures built upstream. Upstream and downstream states had different ideas and interests regarding the manner of covering the costs of water infrastructures and the way they should be used, especially as the use of irrigated agriculture grew in the upstream states and they also started producing energy through hydropower (Barić 2016). Several agreements have been adopted between the Central Asian countries to tackle the issue of transboundary water resources management, including the Agreement on Cooperation in Joint Management, Use and Protection of Water Resources of Interstate Sources (Almaty Agreement 1992). The agreement has the following main principles:

> equality of rights to use and responsibility of the State for transboundary water resources; obligation to respect the agreed procedure and rules for the use and protection of transboundary water resources; obligation to avoid actions that would affect the interests of other Parties and would be able to harm them. (Barić 2016: 125)

It has the objective of creating a regional regulatory framework for water cooperation through the creation of an Interstate Commission for Water Coordination (ICWC) that is:

> authorised to determine water policy in the region, to elaborate key directions, taking into account all economic branches needs, integrated and rational use of water resources, and long-term regional water supply program and measures for implementation and to elaborate and approve annually water consumption quotas for each republic and the region as a whole. (Barić 2016: 126)

The agreement was signed by Kazakhstan, Kyrgyzstan and Uzbekistan; Tajikistan joined in 1999. The agreement focused on the provision of electricity and fuels in exchange for balancing the water flow, balancing this water and energy concerns. Still, since this agreement was a framework agreement, it lacked implementation mechanisms (Antipova et al. 2002). Other agreements followed, such as the Agreement on Joint Activities in Addressing the Aral Sea and the Zone Around the Sea Crisis, Improving the Environment and Ensuring the Social and Economic Development of the Aral Sea Region (1993); the Agreement on the Use of Water and Energy Resources of the Syr Darya Basin (1998); and the Framework Convention on Environmental Protection for Sustainable Development in Central Asia (2006) (Barić 2016). In fact, from 1995 to 1998, the governments of Kazakhstan, Kyrgyzstan and Uzbekistan signed intergovernmental agreements between them to regulate water and energy use, while bilateral agreements were signed between Kyrgyzstan and Uzbekistan (Antipova et al. 2002). According to Dinara Ziganshina, the language of water agreements in Central Asia 'can be generally characterised as ambitious, declaratory and imprecise and so may hamper both effective implementation of the parties' commitments and verification of compliance' (Ziganshina 2009: 103). For instance, the 1992 Almaty convention lacks compliance procedures despite Article 2 of the agreement stating that the regime will be observed,[5] while Article 5 of the Syr Darya Agreement[6] provides some procedures for compliance (Syr Darya Agreement 1998; Ziganshina 2009). Moreover, new institutions were created as a result of signing the 1992 agreement that are:

> the Interstate Coordinating Water Commission (ICWC), the sub-ordinate Amu Darya and Syr Darya Basin Management Authorities (BVOs), the Interstate Council on Problems of the Aral Sea Basin (ICAS), and the International Fund for the Aral Sea (IFAS). (Coskun 2004: 96)

The regime created by the five countries is a voluntary and spontaneous one aimed at regulating water allocation, the protection of shared freshwaters and avoiding water disputes (Coskun 2004). The legal regime that was created was criticised for imposing a planning system that is like the one established in the Soviet era where states will not be satisfied with the allocation of water or the economic benefits in the long term. Moreover, the established institutions have also failed to deal with water tensions due to a lack of transparency and narrow focus. In summary, the legal framework is inefficient because of 'weak political commitment and cooperation, and financial and legal constraints' (Coskun 2004: 96). Moreover, the policies and decisions made on the basis of self-interest as well as the lack of a hegemon that can push towards a regime formation have resulted in the absence of a regional water regime, while the absence of Afghanistan also weakens the probability of establishing such a regime (Coskun 2004).

The main problems facing Central Asian countries are 'water allocation controversies, competition between irrigation and hydropower, water quality deterioration, environmental degradation, loss of species and biodiversity and climate change' (Ziganshina 2009: 96). The principal issue is that upstream countries (Kyrgyzstan and Tajikistan) are looking to invest

[5] Article 2 of the 1992 Almaty Agreement states that 'The Parties are obliged to provide for strict observation of agreed order and the establishment of rules of water resources use and protection'.

[6] Article V of the Syr Darya Agreement states that, 'The Parties shall undertake essential measures which will ensure the fulfillment of their Agreement commitments to the other Parties using various forms of guarantees, such as lines of credit, security deposits, or other forms'.

in hydropower to satisfy their energy needs. This is the reason they release a lot of water during the winter to produce such energy, thereby causing flooding in the downstream states. In contrast, downstream states Kazakhstan, Turkmenistan and Uzbekistan are looking for more water to be released during the summer, not the winter, due to their reliance on water for irrigated agriculture. There is a lack of interstate cooperation due to the dominance of national interests and the inefficiency of the existing regulatory frameworks (Janusz-Pawletta and Gubaidullina 2015). Many Central Asian countries have either signed, ratified or support the Convention on the Protection and Use of Transboundary Watercourses and International Lakes (UNECE Water Convention) adopted in 1992, while few have become party to the UNWC. Moreover, they are also parties to other international treaties focused on transboundary water management (Ziganshina 2009). Uzbekistan is the only country that ratified the UNWC, while Kazakhstan, Turkmenistan and Uzbekistan ratified the 1992 UNECE Water Agreement by 2018 (Paisley 2018). The upstream countries Kyrgyzstan and Tajikistan are not willing to join any of the conventions which complicate the role of IWL in this regard. A good governance of transboundary freshwater requires the development of cooperation between states on the basis of IWL where the implementation of global water principles would guarantee regional stability. In that sense, the main principles of IWL, that is, the principle of equitable and reasonable utilisation; the obligation of not causing significant harm; and the principle of cooperation that currently have limited application in Central Asia, must be better implemented. The existing legal framework in Central Asia has not been sufficient to solve the existing conflicts but has prevented the worsening of the situation. Still, the existing framework requires updating and modernisation, specially the 1992 agreement that is considered outdated and lacks proper implementation (Janusz-Pawletta and Gubaidullina 2015). Moreover, the domestic laws of each Central Asian country associated with the management of transboundary freshwaters must be effective and implemented to ensure the application of transboundary water provisions (Burchi 2018).

Hence, a legal framework for Central Asia on the basis of IWL and principles mainly from the UNWC and UNECE water conventions are needed to foster transboundary water cooperation (Khamzayeva 2009). Indeed, international water agreements such as the UNWC have been seen as having the capability of supporting water agreements on the regional and basin level in places like Central Asia (Mbengue and Rudall

2018). The international community foresees two scenarios: the development of a new international water agreement including Afghanistan or the development of basin water agreements, such as for the Syr Darya and the Amu Darya (Paisley 2018). An international agreement in Central Asia would include:

- A framework agreement for the conservation and management of shared international waters and related resources throughout CA consistent with the Watercourses Convention, the UN ECE Convention and the Helsinki Rules while at the same time reflecting the unique history and special arid nature of the CA region;
- A procedure for preventing and resolving various conflicts that have historically arisen between CA states with regard to the use and management of shared international waters and related resources—for example, infrastructure development and climate change, which could necessitate changes in flow regime or water allocation;
- A procedure for compliance and enforcement of agreed upon obligations in a part of the world where non-performance of agreed upon obligations has long been a serious challenge (Paisley 2018: 20).

In this context, there is a need for making political compromises among the countries of Central Asia as well as navigating and balancing the different interests of these countries (Waśkiel 2018). Such compromise is vital given the energy shortage that is being experienced by Central Asian countries due to growing demands, the inadequacy of energy infrastructures that suffer from low capacity and poor reliability (Farah 2015). This energy shortage is combined with an increasing water need, uncertainties concerning the amount of water and the potential impact of climate change. In this context, China's plans to invest and use the shared water resources may prove to be a sufficient reason to have a hegemon that can push towards the establishment of a regional legal regime, in particular as stronger states have a chance to push weaker states into water agreements even though such arrangements may not be fair to these weaker states (Zhupankhan et al. 2017) and as China is seeking to play a very important role regarding water governance in Central Asia (Allouche 2007). Hence, China could play the role of a hegemon, but a neutral one pushing Central Asian countries to establish, ratify and implement a regional water convention or a specific basin water convention in which international water provisions and rules that are used by China can be implemented by Central Asian countries in the framework of water agreements. In that way, China could create trust among the different parties while having a neutral position that ensures successful implementation of its BRI.

Conclusion

Transboundary water resources hold a great importance for China because it shares numerous freshwaters with other countries. In the context of BRI, transboundary waters gained further importance, as the responsible and fair management of these shared resources represents a way to ensure the success of BRI. Moreover, the success of China in pushing nations that share freshwaters to manage their water in an appropriate manner is also a great strategy to guarantee that these countries embrace BRI, which covers natural resources including water. In this context, IWL offers an appropriate legal framework according to which transboundary water resources, whether shared between China and third countries or between nations members to BRI, can be effectively managed. Regions such as Central Asia can benefit greatly from the adoption of this strategy given its importance to the success of BRI. The two case studies that were examined in this article and which are focused on Central Asia highlighted how this strategy can be used in practice. This does not mean, however, that there are no obstacles facing the appropriate implementation of this suggestion, as the adoption of water agreements must be complemented with the political will to cooperate in good faith for the proper management of shared freshwaters. It is in this context that the foreign policy of China based on acting as a responsible regional and international power can prove to be extremely useful by adopting such a responsible approach, ensuring the good governance of water resources shared with third countries and transboundary waters of country members to BRI which also serves the Chinese interests.

References

Agreement (1992), Between the Republic of Kazakhstan, the Republic of Kyrgyzstan, the Republic of Uzbekistan, the Republic of Tajikistan and Turkmenistan on Cooperation in the Field of Joint Water Resources Management and Conservation of Interstate Sources.

Agreement (1998), On the Use of Water and Energy Resources of the Syr Darya Basin. Finalized in Bishkek, March 17, 1998.

Agreement (2001), Between the Government of the Republic of Kazakhstan and the Government of the People's Republic of China on Cooperation in the Use and Protection of Transboundary Rivers (Astana, September 12, 2001).

Allouche, Jeremy (2007), "The Governance of Central Asian Waters: National Interests Versus Regional Cooperation", in *Disarmament Forum*, 4(1), 45–55.

Antipova, Elena et al. (2002), "Optimization of Syr Darya Water and Energy Uses", in *Water International*, 27(4), 504–516.

Barić, Danijel Javorić (2016), "Water Agreements in Central Asia and Their Impact on Human Rights", in *Pravnik*, 50(1), 123–132.

Bian, Yongmin (2018), "The Role of Environmental Impact Assessment in the Governance of the Nu-Salween River: A Comparative Study of the Chinese and Myanmar Approaches", in Zhao, Yun (ed.), *International Governance and the Rule of Law in China Under the Belt and Road Initiative*, Cambridge University Press, New York, 218–242.

Biswas, Asit K. and Tortajada, Cecilia (2010), "Future Water Governance: Problems and Perspectives", in *International Journal of Water Resources Development*, 26(2), 129–139.

Boisson de Chazournes, Laurence (2013), *Fresh Water in International Law*, Oxford University Press, Oxford.

Burchi, Stefano (2018), "International and Domestic Water Law in Central Asia—Implementing International Law Obligations Regarding Transboundary Waters: The Role of Domestic Water Legislation", in *Central Asian Journal of Water Research*, 4(2), 59–68.

Chatalova, Lioudmila et al. (2017), "The Paradox of Water Management Projects in Central Asia: An Institutionalist Perspective", in *Water*, 9(4), 1–14.

Convention on the Law of the Non-Navigational Uses of International Watercourses (1997), Adopted by the General Assembly of the United Nations on 21 May 1997.

Cooley, Heather and Gleick, Peter H. (2011), "Climate-Proofing Transboundary Water Agreements", in *Hydrological Sciences Journal*, 56(4), 711–718.

Cosgrove, William J. and Loucks, Daniel P. (2015), "Water Management: Current and Future Challenges and Research Directions", in *Water Resources Research*, 51(6), 4823–4839.

Coskun, Bezen Balamir (2004), "Hydropolitics in Central Asia: Towards a Regional Water Regime?" in *The Interdisciplinary Journal of International Studies*, 2(2), 79–101.

Dellapenna, Joseph W. and Gupta, Joyeeta (2009), "The Evolution of Global Water Law," in Dellapenna, Joseph W. and Gupta, Joyeeta (eds.), *The Evolution of the Law and Politics of Water*, Springer, Dordrecht, 3–19.

Deng, Yixiang et al. (2016), "China's Water Environmental Management Towards Institutional Integration: A Review of Current Progress and Constraints vis-a-vis the European Experience", in *Journal of Cleaner Production*, 113(1), 285–298.

Duarte, Paulo (2018), "China in the Heartland: The Challenges and Opportunities of OBOR for Central Asia", in Laruelle, Marlene (ed.), *China's Belt and Road Initiative and Its Impact in Central Asia*, The George Washington University, Central Asia Program, Washington, DC, 11–20.

Dunford, Michael and Liu, Weidong (2019), "Chinese Perspectives on the Belt and Road Initiative", in *Cambridge Journal of Regions, Economy and Society*, 12(1), 145–167.

Farah, Paolo Davide (2015), "Energy Security, Water Resources, Environmental Concerns and Economic Development in Central Asia", in Farah, Paolo Davide and Rossi, Piercarlo (eds.), *Energy: Policy, Legal and Social-Economic Issues Under the Dimensions of Sustainability and Security*, Imperial College Press and World Scientific Publishing, Singapore, 179–193.

Fry, James D. and Chong, Agnes (2016), "International Water Law and China's Management of Its International Rivers," in *Boston College International and Comparative Law Review*, 39(2), 227–266.

Gao, Qi (2014), *A Procedural Framework for Transboundary Water Management in the Mekong River Basin: Shared Mekong for a Common Future*, Brill, Leiden and Boston.

Grigg, Neil S. (2011), "Water Governance: From Ideals to Effective Strategies", in *Water International*, 36(7), 799–811.

Grey, David and Garrick, Dustin (2013), "Water Security, Perceptions and Politics: The Context for International Watercourse Negotiations", in Boisson de Chazournes, Laurence, Leb, Christina and Tignino, Mara (eds.), *International Law and Freshwater: The Multiple Challenges*, Edward Elgar, Cheltenham, 37–47.

Grzybowski, Alex, McCaffrey, Stephen and Paisley, Richard (2010), "Beyond International Water Law: Successfully Negotiating Mutual Gains Agreements for International Watercourses", in *Pacific McGeorge Global Business & Development Law Journal*, 22(2), 139–154.

Guo, Lidan et al. (2016), "Evolution, Opportunity and Challenges of Transboundary Water and Energy Problems in Central Asia", in *SpringerPlus*, 5(1), 1–11.

Gupta, Joyeeta et al. (2013), "Policymakers' Reflections on Water Governance Issues", in *Ecology and Society*, 18(1), 1–8.

Gupta, Joyeeta and Pahl-Wostl, Claudia (2013), "Global Water Governance in the Context of Global and Multilevel Governance: Its Need, Form, and Challenges", in *Ecology and Society*, 18(4), 1–10.

Ho, Selina (2017), "China's Transboundary River Policies Towards Kazakhstan: Issue-Linkages and Incentives for Cooperation", in *Water International*, 42(2), 142–162.

Janusz-Pawletta, Barbara and Gubaidullina, Mara (2015), "Transboundary Water Management in Central Asia: Legal Framework to Strengthen Interstate Cooperation and Increase Regional Security", in *Cahiers d'Asie Centrale*, 20(25), 195–215.

Khamzayeva, Anar (2009), "Water Resources Management in Central Asia: Security Implications and Prospects for Regional Cooperation", in Khamzayeva, Anar et al. (eds.), *Water Resources Management in Central Asia: Regional and International Issues at Stake*, CIDOB, Barcelona, 9–32.

Kukeyeva, Fatima et al. (2018), "Is Ili/Irtysh Rivers: A 'Casualty' of Kazakhstan–China Relations", in *Academy of Strategic Management Journal*, 17(3), 1–12.

Li, Zhifei (2017), "The Non-Traditional Security Issues in Realizing the Belt and Road Initiative", in Jie, Zhang (ed.), *China's Belt and Road Initiatives and Its Neighboring Diplomacy*, World Scientific Publishing, Singapore, 249–270.

Libert, Bo (2018), "Application of the UNECE Environmental Conventions in Central Asia", in Zhiltsov, Sergey S. et al. (eds.), *Water Resources in Central Asia: International Context*, Springer, Dordrecht, 81–101.

Magsig, Bjørn-Oliver (2011), "Overcoming State-Centrism in International Water Law: 'Regional Common Concern' as the Normative Foundation of Water Security", in *Goettingen Journal of International Law*, 3(1), 317–344.

Magsig, Bjorn-Oliver (2015), *International Water Law and the Quest for Common Security*, Routledge, Abingdon.

Martens, Patrick (2018), "The Political Economy of Water Insecurity in Central Asia Given the Belt and Road Initiative", in *Central Asian Journal of Water Research*, 4(1), 79–94.

Mbengue, Makane Moise and Rudall, Jason (2018), "The Relationship Between the Convention, Existing and Future Fresh Water Agreements (Articles 3 and 4)", in Boisson de Chazournes, Laurence et al. (eds.), *The UN Convention on the Law of the Non-Navigational Uses of International Watercourses: A Commentary*, Oxford University Press, Oxford, 63–75.

McCaffrey, Stephen C. (2003), "The Need for Flexibility in Freshwater Treaty Regimes", in *Natural Resources Forum*, 27(2), 156–162.

McIntyre, Owen (2010a), "International Water Law: Concepts, Evolution and Development", in Earle, Anton and Ojendal, Joakim (eds.), *Transboundary Water Management: Principles and Practice*, Earthscan, London and Washington, DC, 59–72.

McIntyre, Owen (2010b), "The Proceduralisation and Growing Maturity of International Water Law: Case Concerning Pulp Mills on the River Uruguay (Argentina v Uruguay), International Court of Justice, 20 April 2010", in *Journal of Environmental Law*, 22(3), 475–497.

McIntyre, Owen (2017), "Substantive Rules of International Water Law", in Rieu-Clarke, Alistair, Allan, Andrew and Hendry, Sarah (eds.), *Routledge Handbook of Water Law and Policy*, Routledge, Abingdon, 234–246.

Menga, Filippo (2018), *Power and Water in Central Asia*, Routledge, Abingdon.

Mustafina, Assem (2014), "Transboundary Water Issues Between Kazakhstan and China", in *IOSR Journal of Humanities and Social Science*, 19(1), 91–94.

Paisley, Richard Kyle (2018), "International Watercourses, International Water Law and Central Asia", in *Central Asian Journal of Water Research*, 4(2), 1–26.

Petersen-Perlman, Jacob D., Veilleux, Jennifer C. and Wolf, Aaron T. (2017), "International Water Conflict and Cooperation: Challenges and Opportunities", in *Water International*, 42(2), 105–120.

Pham Do, Kim-Hang and Dinar, Ariel (2017), "Issue Linkage: A Mechanism for Managing Conflict, Applied to the Mekong Basin", in Dinar, Ariel and Tsur, Yacov (eds.), *Management of Transboundary Water Resources Under Scarcity: A Multidisciplinary Approach*, World Scientific Publishing, Singapore, 91–114.

Pueppke, Steven G., Zhang, Qingling and Nurtazin, Sabir T. (2018a), "Irrigation in the Ili River Basin of Central Asia: From Ditches to Dams and Diversion", in *Water*, 10(11), 1–24.

Pueppke, Steven G. et al. (2018b), "Central Asia's Ili River Ecosystem as a Wicked Problem: Unraveling Complex Interrelationships at the Interface of Water, Energy, and Food", in *Water*, 10(5), 1–21.

Rauf, Abdul et al. (2018), "Energy and Ecological Sustainability: Challenges and Panoramas in Belt and Road Initiative Countries," in *Sustainability*, 10(8), 1–21.

Ryabtsev, Anatoliy Dmitriyevich (2011), "Threats to Water Security in the Republic of Kazakhstan: The Transboundary Context and Possible Ways to Eliminate Them", in Madramootoo, Chandra and Dukhovny, Victor (eds.), *Water and Food Security in Central Asia*, Springer, Dordrecht, 69–75.

Schortgen, Francis (2018), "China and the Twenty-First-Century Silk Roads: A New Era of Global Economic Leadership?", in Zhang, Wenxian, Alon, Ilan and Lattemann, Christoph (eds.), *China's Belt and Road Initiative: Changing the Rules of Globalization*, Palgrave Macmillan, Cham, 17–33.

Stephens, Tim (2011), "Reimagining International Water Law", in *Maryland Law Review Endnotes*, 71(1), 20–40.

Sternberg, Troy, Ahearn, Ariell and McConnell, Fiona (2017), "Central Asian 'Characteristics' on China's New Silk Road: The Role of Landscape and the Politics of Infrastructure", in *Land*, 6(3), 1–16.

Stoa, Ryan (2014), "The United Nations Watercourses Convention on the Dawn of Entry into Force", in *Vanderbilt Journal of Transnational Law*, 47(5), 1321–1370.

Tarlock, A. Dan (2008), “Water Security, Fear Mitigation and International Water Law (Symposium)”, in *Hamline Law Review*, 31(3), 703–728.
Tarlock, A. Dan (2010), “Four Challenges for International Water Law”, in *Tulane Environmental Law Journal*, 23(2), 369–408.
Tarlock, A. Dan (2016), “Toward a More Robust International Water Law of Cooperation to Address Droughts and Ecosystem Conservation”, in *Georgetown Environmental Law Review*, 28(2), 261–290.
Thevs, Niels et al. (2017), “Water Consumption of Agriculture and Natural Ecosystems Along the Ili River in China and Kazakhstan”, in *Water*, 9(3), 1–15.
Tortajada, Cecilia (2010), “Water Governance: Some Critical Issues”, in *International Journal of Water Resources Development*, 26(2), 297–307.
Tropp, Håkan (2007), “Water Governance: Trends and Needs for New Capacity Development”, in *Water Policy*, 9(2), 19–30.
Tzatzaki, Vasiliki-Maria and Tarlock, A. Dan (2015), “International Water Law and Climate Disruption Adaptation”, in Tanzi, Attila et al. (eds.), *The UNECE Convention on the Protection and Use of Transboundary Watercourses and International Lakes*, Brill/Nijhoff, Leiden and Boston, 379–393.
Urban, Frauke, Siciliano, Giuseppina and Nordensvard, Johan (2018), “China’s Dam-Builders: Their Role in Transboundary River Management in South-East Asia”, in *International Journal of Water Resources Development*, 34(5), 747–770.
Waśkiel, Tomasz (2018), “The Water Resources Management in Central Asia—The Political and Economic Contradictions as a Source of Inefficiency”, in *Nowa Polityka Wschodnia*, 1(16), 85–100.
Williams, Jessica M. (2018), “Stagnant Rivers: Transboundary Water Security in South and Southeast Asia”, in *Water*, 10(12), 1–23.
Williams, Jessica M. (2019), “Emerging Costs of China’s Belt and Road Strategy for Transboundary Water in South and Southeast Asia”, in *International Journal of Energy and Water Resources*, 3(2), 81–92.
Woodhouse, Melvin and Zeitoun, Mark (2008), “Hydro-Hegemony and International Water Law: Grappling with the Gaps of Power and Law”, in *Water Policy*, 10(S2), 103–119.
Wouters, Patricia and Chen, Huiping (2013), “China’s ‘Soft-Path’ to Transboundary Water Cooperation Examined in the Light of Two UN Global Water Conventions—Exploring the ‘Chinese Way’”, in *Journal of Water Law*, 22(6), 229–247.
Wouters, Patricia and Moynihan, Ruby (2013), “Water Security—Legal Frameworks and the UN Watercourses Convention”, in Loures, Flavia Rocha and Rieu-Clarke, Alistair (eds.), *The UN Watercourses Convention in Force: Strengthening International Law for Transboundary Water Management*, Routledge, Abingdon, 336–351.

Xie, Lei and Shaofeng, Jia (2018), *China's International Transboundary Rivers: Politics, Security and Diplomacy of Shared Water Resources*, Routledge, Abingdon.

Yoffe, Shira B. and Ward, Brian S. (1999), "Water Resources and Indicators of Conflict: A Proposed Spatial Analysis", in *Water International*, 24(4), 377–384.

Zeitoun, Mark (2015), "The Relevance of International Water Law to Later-Developing Upstream States", in *Water International*, 40(7), 949–968.

Zhang, Hongzhou and Li, Mingjiang (2018a), "A Process-Based Framework to Examine China's Approach to Transboundary Water Management", in *International Journal of Water Resources Development*, 34(5), 705–731.

Zhang, Hongzhou and Li, Mingjiang (2018b), "Editorial", in *International Journal of Water Resources Development*, 34(5), 699–704.

Zhang, Hongzhou and Li, Mingjiang (2018c), "China and Global Water Governance: New Developments", in Zhang, Hongzhou and Li, Mingjiang (eds.), *China and Transboundary Water Politics in Asia*, Routledge, Abingdon, 219–236.

Zhang, Zhaofang et al. (2019), "Water Security Assessment of China's One Belt and One Road Region", in *Water*, 11(3), 1–23.

Zhupankhan, Aibek, Tussupova, Kamshat and Berndtsson, Ronny (2017), "Could Changing Power Relationships Lead to Better Water Sharing in Central Asia?", in *Water*, 9(2), 1–17.

Ziganshina, Dinara (2012), "International Water Law in Central Asia: The Nature of Substantive Norms and What Flows from It", in *Asian Journal of International Law*, 2(1), 169–192.

Ziganshina, Dinara (2009), "International Water Law in Central Asia: Commitments, Compliance and Beyond", in *The Journal of Water Law*, 20(2/3), 96–107.

Zhou, Zhanggui and Wang, Ruolin (2017), "Sino-Kazakh Transboundary Water Cooperation: History, Current Status and Future Priorities", in Zhang, Hongzhou and Li, Mingjiang (eds.), *China and Transboundary Water Politics in Asia*, Routledge, Abingdon, 197–215.

Zonn, Igor S. et al. (2018), "Water Transboundary Policy of Kazakhstan and China", in Zhiltsov, Sergey S. et al. (ed.), *Water Resources in Central Asia: International Context*, Springer, Dordrecht, 153–167.

On China's Strategy in Belt and Road International Intellectual Property Cooperation

Xiaoling Tian

Introduction

Based on Chinese President Xi Jinping's proposals in 2013 to improve international cooperation through the construction of a Silk Road Economic Belt and twenty-first century Maritime Silk Road, the Belt and Road (B&R) Initiative has been in effect for six years. By late July of 2019, the Chinese government had concluded 195 intergovernmental cooperation agreements with 136 countries and 30 international organisations. Statistics show that from 2013 to 2018, China's trade value with countries along B&R is 6 trillion US dollars ($), while direct investment is $90 billion (National Bureau of Statistics of China 2019). Meanwhile, the products, services, technologies and capitals from other B&R countries were exported to China, and the China made, China construction, Chinese brands and Chinese services gained great popularity in these countries. It is worth noting that the Intellectual Property (IP) cooperation in high-technology fields is the new bright spot of the Belt and Road Initiative (BRI). According to Shen Changyu, the Director of CNIPA

X. Tian (✉)
Southwest University of Political Science and Law, Chongqing, People's Republic of China
e-mail: tianxiaoling@swupl.edu.cn

G. Martinico and X. WU (eds.), *A Legal Analysis of the Belt and Road Initiative*, https://doi.org/10.1007/978-3-030-46000-6_9

(National Intellectual Property Administration of China), the Chinese government has long cooperated on IP with countries along the B&R routes. China has signed bilateral cooperation agreements with 28 out of 65 core countries involved in the Initiative. And it has developed a trilateral cooperation mechanism with its peers in Mongolia and Russia. At the same time, CNIPA has partnered with regional organisations, including the Cooperation Council for the Arab States of the Gulf, the Association of Southeast Asian Nations, and the Adviser Group, an alliance comprising four central European countries—the Czech Republic, Hungary, Poland and Slovakia. Data from the CNIPA showed that the number of patent applications from Chinese filers grew 16% to reach 5608 in B&R countries last year (2017). Filers from B&R countries applied for 4319 patents in China in 2017, up 16.8% year-on-year (Xinhua News Agency 2018).

More and more Chinese companies have exported their products with independent IPR and brought tangible benefits to the countries and regions along the B&R. The Inspur Group, for example, is one of the largest global data centre and cloud computing solutions provider in the world and owns numerous advanced technologies in the fields of cloud computing, mass forages, high-end servers and artificial intelligence. In recent years, the Inspur Group has held more than 500 training classes to thousands of technicians in Vietnam, Indonesia, Egypt, South Africa and other countries and regions in the BRI. According to Li Yang, a representative from National Institution for Finance and Development under the Chinese Academy of Social Sciences, the output of China's advanced technology provides more opportunities for some developing and least developed countries and regions involved in the BRI. This is in accordance with the Silk Road spirit, which is peaceful cooperation, openness and inclusiveness, mutual learning, mutual benefit and win-win (China IP News 2017).

Two Different Tendencies of International Intellectual Property Protection in the Post-Trips Era

When the Paris Convention for the Protection of Industrial Property and Berne Convention for the Protection of Literary and Artistic Works came into force in 1884 and 1886, international intellectual property protection mechanism was initially formed. When the Bureaux Internationaux Réunispour la protection de la Propriété Intellectuelle (BIRPI) was redesigned to the World Intellectual Property Organization (WIPO) in 1967 and became a specialised agency of the United Nations (UN), there was no executable and effective dispute settlement mechanism. At the urging of the United States and other developed countries, international intellectual property protection was brought into issues under discussion of Uruguay Round of the General Agreement on Tariffs and Trade (GATT). Out came the Agreement on Trade-Related Aspects of Intellectual Property Rights (TRIPS) and it established for the first time the minimum standards of IP protection instead of treating each other in the Principle of National Treatment. Members must implement domestic enforcement of substantive requirements of IP. The TRIPS Agreement provides the international enforcement of treaty obligations. As a result of negotiation between developed and developing countries, there are deep contradictions existing in the TRIPS Agreement. After the implementation of the TRIPS Agreement for more than 20 years, more and more developing countries tended to demand issues concerning development, poverty reduction and public health, while developed countries tended to raise IP protection standard to the TRIPS-plus standard. It appears 'fragmentation' in international IP protection embodied as 'Regional Trade Agreements' and 'Plurilateral Agreements'. The United States—Mexico—Canada Agreement was signed on 30 November 2018, which provided that the protection term for bio-pharmaceutical data is ten years and copyright protection term is the duration of the author's life plus 70 years. The term is the author's life plus 50 years in the TRIPS Agreement. Countries interested in the protection of high standards for Intellectual Property Rights (IPRs) realised that it was difficult to achieve the goal through multilateral mechanisms and thus began to seek new ways to move intellectual property negotiations from the WIPO and World Trade Organization (WTO) regimes to Free Trade Agreements (FTAs). The Anti-Counterfeiting Trade Agreement is an example of a higher IP protection standard compared with the TRIPS Agreement out of the WTO system. This has intensified the fragmentation of the international intellectual property legal system.

Legal and political philosophers have often debated the status and legitimacy of intellectual property. The conventional arguments that justify the grant of private property rights in land and tangible resources are often premised on the scarcity or limited availability of such resources and the impossibility of sharing. It seems especially important to justify the grant of exclusive rights over resources—idea and information—that are not scarce and can be replicated without direct detriment to the original possessor of the intangible, who continues to be able to use the idea or information (Bently et al. 2018). Intellectual property is not a pure legal system; rather, it involves the industrial policy and public interests of a country. It is normal for different countries to have different opinions on the protection of intellectual property based on national interests at different times. The main principle of the TRIPS Agreement is that all the WTO members must obey its minimum standards of IP protection, no matter rich or poor, big or small. It did not set aside time for developing countries to prepare. Yet, in the nineteenth century, those developed countries at the beginning of their development did not willingly engage in this kind of IP trading. An example is that from 1869 to 1912, there was no patent law in the Netherlands, and Swiss patent law did not protect chemistry patents in order to protect its local chemical industry (Drahos and Braithwaite 2003). Not to mention the United States did not provide copyright to foreigners, which made Charles Dickens return to England with his heartbroken after total failure of fighting against pirated copies. The United States and some European countries used loose and flexible institutions to meet the needs of their economic development then. Yet nowadays countries have no choice to do so. The TRIPS Agreement is deemed to erode the sovereignty of other countries. On the signing of the TRIPS Agreement, critics have pointed out that, in view of the hundreds of years it took for developed countries to develop their intellectual property protection system, one to two years transition period accepted by the American pharmaceutical companies is not generous for developing countries. For developing countries have to spend millions of dollars to build infrastructures of IPRs (patent and copyright administration, court, judges, etc.). The IP infrastructure was primarily serving the needs of the foreign right holders. Indeed, the legal system of developing countries cannot protect its people from even the most basic violent crimes (Drahos and Braithwaite 2003).

These profound contradictions are the root causes of the fragmentation of the international intellectual property protection system, although we can no longer change the TRIPS Agreement. It is wise to rethink how to use this instrument to benefit mankind instead of to create more conflicts.

Last year, the General Offices of the CCP Central Committee and State Council have jointly issued a directive calling for intensified protection of IPRs. The document says that China will make comprehensive use of the law, technology and social governance policies to step up IPR protection. According to the document, by 2022 China will strive to curb IPR infringement effectively, and largely overcome challenges, including high costs, low compensation and difficulties in providing evidence for safeguarding IPRs. By 2025, social satisfaction with IPR protection in China will reach and maintain a high level.

It is hard to believe that it is just over 30 years since the People's Republic of China's earliest enacted Trademark Law. Yet, according to the development situation of China, this ambition is reasonable. China and the United States signed the first phase economic and trade agreement (Economic and Trade Agreement between the Government of the United States of America and the Government of the People's Republic of China) on 16 January 2020. In Chapter 1, the two sides put it this way: China recognises the importance of establishing and implementing a comprehensive legal system of intellectual property protection and enforcement as it transforms from a major intellectual property consumer to a major intellectual property producer. Recently, Jiangsu Provincial Higher People's Court made a judgement of second instance that trademark (Class 9 for cellphones) of Xiaomi Technology Co., Ltd. is a well-known trademark. Thus, by using the Xiaomi Life logo in its electric rice cooker and induction cooker, Zhongshan Benteng Electric Appliance Co., Ltd. constitutes an infringement. The penalty was three times punitive damages applied; the total indemnity for economic losses of Xiaomi Technology Co., Ltd. was 50 million yuan. This shows the determination of Chinese judiciary to maintain an honest society and fair competition order.

Because of the painful lessons of the last 30 years concerning IP protection, China was forced to provide administrative protection for patented chemistry and American pharmaceuticals, even there were no such provisions of patent law in China during that period. Similarly, the DVD industry of China was nearly destroyed by 3C/6C of developed countries during the 1990s. The Chinese government could not forget the lessons and hardships. Do unto others as you would have them do unto you. B&R is a domestic and diplomatic affair as well. There is a long-standing theory of Mencius (372–289 BC) that said, 'Rule by force is not as good as governed by benevolence'. This reflects the value of traditional Chinese culture, and maybe the 'universal value' of human society.

When we look back at the history of the Doha Declaration, we saw the struggle between human rights of public health and IPRs, the struggle between developed countries and developing countries. Article 4 of the Doha Declaration provided that 'We agree that the TRIPS Agreement does not and should not prevent members from taking measures to protect public health. Accordingly, while reiterating our commitment to the TRIPS Agreement, we affirm that the Agreement can and should be interpreted and implemented in a manner supportive of WTO members' right to protect public health and, in particular, to promote access to medicines for all'. This compromise vividly illustrates Mencius' celebrated dictum mentioned before. As we have said, philosophers have not always found IPRs to be justified. It is more appropriate to say that intellectual property is a tool to promote economic development. In other words, the IP protection level should be determined by a country's industrial and economic development. Thus it is clear to make a choice between two different opinions on international intellectual property protection: (a) build a higher regional intellectual property protection system like the Trans-Pacific Partnership (TPP) and the Transatlantic Trade and Investment Partnership (TTIP) represented by the United States; (b) build a fairer intellectual property protection mode and a community of common future represented by most of developing countries.

The Current Situation of Intellectual Property Protection Level Among the Countries of B&R

As of December 2019, China has signed cooperation agreements with 143 countries along the B&R. Among them, there are only 7 developed countries and 99 developing countries. The remaining 37 are least developed countries. According to Shen Changyu, Director of CNIPA, most of the B&R countries are developing countries or countries in the transitional stage, which have great demand for the innovative development of their economies by making use of IP. Many of the countries have a long history and rich resources in relics and traditional knowledge. However, the awareness of IP among the public and its applications are still limited. As for per capita gross domestic product (GDP), there are 45 countries higher than China and 98 countries lower than China.

Some countries lack the legal system of intellectual property due to underdevelopment of science and technology. For example, there is no patent law in the Congo. Up until now, there are 25 countries which are not members of WTO. Although some countries established IP legal system, there is less IP ownership and fewer professional personnel engaged in the IP field. For example, the ownership of inventions and utility models of Cambodia is zero, and some other countries are less than 10. On the other hand, developing countries also harbour hope. Table 1 shows the 10 best-ranked economies by income group in the Global Innovation Index (GII) 2019 issued by WIPO, and the top-ranked in the innovation input and output sub-indices. Highlighted in bold font are countries along the B&R. We can see that, except for only five B&R countries in the high-income countries, most of the countries in the middle and low-income range ranked at the top of the innovation index are B&R countries, which indicates from one side that BRI is a dynamic and innovative organisation.

How to Build an IP-Friendly Ecosystem in the Countries Involved in the Belt and Road Initiative

Taking into full consideration the difference in development levels, cultures, innovation capacities and legal systems, it is hard and unnecessary to establish a unified and effective international IP cooperation mechanism. The best way is by consensus, to establish bilateral or multilateral agreements with corresponding countries and regions to reflect the trends of multi-polarity, economic globalisation, cultural diversity and IT-based developments. Besides that, I think it is better to take different strategies in copyright and trademark based on their different characteristics.

First, compared to copyright and patent, the justifications for the legal protection of trademarks received relatively little attention. One possible reason is that the negative impact of trademark rights is less obvious. For thousands of years, people have used brands to do their businesses. Passing-off is a dishonest behaviour no matter in developed countries or even in the least developed countries. It is a widespread consensus among businessmen that it is worth protecting signs and symbols insofar as they operate as indications of origin or as a guarantee of quality. So it is acceptable to take strong measures against counterfeiting in countries along B&R to build a good reputation of 'China-made'.

With the development of science and technology, more and more trade has transcended national boundaries, and trademark squatting has transcended national boundaries. For example, Tongrentang trademark was

Table 1 Best-ranked economies by income group (rank)[a]

Rank	*Global innovation index*	*Innovation input sub-index*	*Innovation output sub-index*
High-income economies (50 in total)			
1	Switzerland (1)	**Singapore (1)**	Switzerland (1)
2	Sweden (2)	Switzerland (2)	Netherlands (2)
3	United States (3)	United States (3)	Sweden (3)
4	Netherlands (4)	Sweden (4)	UK (4)
5	UK (5)	Denmark (5)	United States (6)
6	Finland (6)	UK (6)	Finland (7)
7	Denmark (7)	Finland (7)	**Israel (8)**
8	**Singapore (8)**	Hong Kong, China (8)	Germany (9)
9	Germany (9)	Canada (9)	Ireland (10)
10	**Israel (10)**	**Republic of Korea (10)**	**Luxembourg (11)**
Upper middle-income economies (34 in total)			
1	China (14)	China (26)	China (5)
2	**Malaysia (35)**	**Malaysia (34)**	**Bulgaria (38)**
3	**Bulgaria (40)**	**Russian Federation (41)**	**Malaysia (39)**
4	**Thailand (43)**	**Bulgaria (45)**	**Thailand (43)**
5	**Montenegro (45)**	**Thailand (47)**	**Montenegro (46)**
6	**Russian Federation (46)**	**Peru (48)**	**Iran (Islamic Republic of) (47)**
7	**Turkey (49)**	**Belarus (50)**	**Costa Rica (48)**
8	**Romania (50)**	**South Africa (51)**	**Turkey (49)**
9	**Costa Rica (55)**	**North Macedonia (52)**	**Armenia (50)**
10	Mexico (56)	**Romania (54)**	**Romania (53)**
Lower middle-income economies (26 in total)			
1	**Viet Nam (42)**	**Georgia (44)**	**Ukraine (36)**
2	**Ukraine (47)**	India (61)	**Viet Nam (37)**
3	**Georgia (48)**	**Viet Nam (63)**	**Philippines (42)**
4	India (52)	**Mongolia (73)**	**Mongolia (44)**
5	**Mongolia (53)**	**Tunisia (74)**	**Republic of Moldova (45)**
6	**Philippines (54)**	**Philippines (76)**	India (51)
7	**Republic of Moldova (58)**	**Kyrgyzstan (78)**	**Georgia (60)**
8	**Tunisia (70)**	**Republic of Moldova (81)**	**Kenya (64)**

(continued)

Table 1 (continued)

Rank	*Global innovation index*	*Innovation input sub-index*	*Innovation output sub-index*
9	**Morocco (74)**	**Ukraine (82)**	**Tunisia (65)**
10	**Kenya (77)**	**Morocco (83)**	**Morocco (66)**
Low-income economies (19 in total)			
1	**Rwanda (94)**	**Rwanda (65)**	**United Republic of Tanzania (73)**
2	**Senegal (96)**	**Nepal (93)**	**Ethiopia (80)**
3	**United Republic of Tanzania (97)**	**Uganda (96)**	**Senegal (81)**
4	**Tajikistan (100)**	**Senegal (103)**	**Tajikistan (83)**
5	**Uganda (102)**	**Tajikistan (107)**	**Mali (100)**
6	**Nepal (109)**	Burkina Faso (111)	**Uganda (107)**
7	**Ethiopia (111)**	**Benin (114)**	**Madagascar (109)**
8	**Mali (112)**	**United Republic of Tanzania (115)**	**Zimbabwe (110)**
9	Burkina Faso (117)	**Mozambique (118)**	Malawi (112)
10	Malawi (118)	Malawi (119)	**Mozambique (114)**

[a]Global innovation index 2019 Creating Healthy Lives—The Future of Medical Innovation from WIPO

squatted in Japan in 1989; Wang Zhihe trademark was squatted in Germany in 2006. After the China Trademark Office affirmed Tongrentang as a well-known trademark in China, the Japan Patent Office revoked the improperly registered trademark. On 23 April 2009, the Munich High Court made a final judgement on Wang Zhihe v. Okai, referring to trademark infringement and unfair competition: trademark of Wang Zhihe returned to the original owner.

Trademark squatting is contrary to the principle of good faith; honesty and credit are the highest business ethics. Recently the final judgement about MUJI made by China Beijing Higher People's Court sparked heated debates. The Court ascertained that the Japanese company infringed the Beijing company's trademark by using its trademark Wuyinliangpin, so ordered the Japanese company to immediately stop infringing, to issue a statement, to eliminate the influences and to compensate the Beijing company's economic loss, and so on, a total of more than 400,000 yuan (Beijing Higher People's Court 2018). The main ratio decidendi is that the Wuyinliangpin trademark is in category 24, and the application for registration on the cloth, bedspread and towel was filed in 2000. After opposition, administrative review, first instance and second instance trial and the retrial, the registration was approved by the judgement of the Supreme People's Court on 29 June 2012. The reason was that Japanese company provided evidence only on publicity, use and popularity of the MUJI trademark in Japan, Hong Kong SAR and other places before 6 April 2000, but it did not prove that its MUJI trademark is actually used in category 24 for towels and other goods and has a certain influence in mainland China. During this period, Chinese consumers' awareness of MUJI is quite different from before. This is one of the reasons why the case is controversial. Also, Wuyinliangpin is an artificial trademark, which is different from the expression habits in Chinese. It is hard to convince people that the similarity between Wuyinliangpin and MUJI is a coincidence. In my opinion, such a judgement can protect some domestic enterprises in the short term, but in the long run, it is not beneficial for establishing good faith in the market.

Trademark Dongfeng is another story. China Shanghai Diesel Engine Co., Ltd. (SDEC) is an owner of Trademark Dongfeng for category 7, such as diesel engines. The trademark was registered in 1962, and in 2000 was recognised as a well-known trademark in China. Dongfeng diesel engine entered into Indonesia market in the early 1960s. Indonesia PT ADI company registered Dongfeng trademark in Indonesia in 1987. The official language of Indonesia is Indonesian, but PT ADI company registered the trademark of Dongfeng in Chinese and pinyin, and Dongfeng is the main part, which is exactly the same as the trademark of Dongfeng in China. Its registration is obviously unreasonable, but the trademark is not only registered but also renewed in Indonesia. This illustrated vividly that trademark rights are trade-related rights. Legal interpretation seems to be influenced by the economic and trade situation. That is why whether the original equipment manufacturer (OEM)[1] constitutes an infringement against the exclusive right of the domestic trademark holder has been a controversial question for a long time. The Supreme People's Court of China has rendered a retrial judgement on 8 April 2018 in the high-profile 'Dongfeng' OEM case, in which the Court affirmed that the OEM act does not constitute trademark infringement. The main reason

[1] Original equipment manufacturer (OEM) refers to a circumstance in which a Chinese manufacturer accepts the entrustment of a foreign trademark holder or a foreign trademark user and processes products as required, attaching the trademark provided, and delivering all the products processed to the foreign trademark holder or the foreign trademark user.

is that the act of using a trademark that is not intended to distinguish the source will not confuse the source of the goods or services. Therefore, it does not constitute trademark infringement. At the same time, given that OEM is a common and legal form of international trade, unless there is contrary evidence showing that the domestic manufacturer did not fulfil its duty of reasonable care after accepting the entrustment, and its act of entrusted processing has caused material harm to the trademark rights of the domestic trademark holder, the act will not generally be affirmed as having infringed on the trademark rights of the domestic trademark holder. This kind of explanation is reasonable and acceptable.

Secondly, it is wise to apply relatively loose measures to copyright. Not everyone thinks that copyright is a good thing. 'Pirate Party' won seats in the European, Czech and Icelandic parliaments. Anti-copyright sentiment has also given rise to a religion, 'the missionary church of kopimism'. Because copyright law prohibits the unauthorised use of 'copies', it has the potential to inhibit people using cultural objects. Copyright would impede cultural dissemination in certain aspects. BRI not only pursues economic benefits, but also political interests, diplomatic interests and cultural interests. The Chinese culture has a long history, but the discourse power of the whole world is still in the hands of Western developed countries. To build a multi-polar world, it is necessary to expand the influence of Chinese culture, and the BRI is a good opportunity. The United States took advantage of China's Boxer Indemnity[2] to cultivate Chinese students. It was a very clever approach. Every student bore the seeds of American politics and culture and came back to China with roots and fruits. These elites had an important influence on China's later politics and economy. Chinese universities currently provide a number of scholarships to foreign students, so it has the same intent. About a third of the B&R countries have a higher GDP per capita than China, and also have a higher demand for cultural products and corresponding purchasing power. Southeast Asian countries are deeply influenced by Chinese culture and have a high acceptance of Chinese cultural products. Based on the fact that copyright hinders the spread of culture to some extent,

[2] In 1900, the G8 allied forces invaded China, and the Qing government signed a treaty with UK, United States, Germany, France, Russia, Italy and Austria in Beijing on 7 September 1901, in which the United States was entitled to 32 million taels of silver, or more than 24 million dollars. In 1908, the US congress agreed to return half of the money to China to help finance students studying in the United States.

we might as well evaluate the output of culture in combination with the output of products, not only as an economic account but also as a political and cultural account. The export of cultural products such as films, novels and music can not only make money but also promote Chinese culture. To build a multi-polar world, we should increase cultural exchanges with other countries. Take films as an example. In the Chinese film market, there cannot be only Hollywood or only Germany, France and Italy. A few Iranian films imported by China before are very good in terms of stories, ideas and actors' performances. Dangal, an Indian film, has been a box-office and word-of-mouth hit in China. Films and novels from different countries give Chinese audiences a taste of the world and deepen their understanding of other cultures. At the same time, Chinese films should also go abroad. Culture is a kind of soft power, whose export is better than economic exchange or aid in the long run.

Professor Li Chen pointed out that the focus of the copyright issue in the current network environment is not the recognition of rights, but the realisation of rights. The latter involves many factors such as the social concept and market environment, not a single legal issue (Chen 2013). So simply strengthening law enforcement will not produce an obvious effect. Looking at the approximately 27,000 Recording Industry of America Association (RIAA) legal cases brought against (peer-to-peer) P2P users between 2003 and 2008, a Pew Internet and American Life Project survey, conducted just after the first RIAA announcement, showed a 50% drop in the percentage of users acknowledging use of P2P services, from 29 to 14%. However, by 2005 this number had reverted to 24% (Hargreaves 2011). China is currently in the process of the third revision of the Copyright Law. Punitive damages have been included in the discussion and are very likely to pass. I do not agree with it. B&R intellectual property cooperation should not adopt high standards because of the uneven economic level of various countries. In my opinion, the protection of copyright (except software, because it is more technical than culture) should adopt a relatively loose strategy. What is more important is to force businessmen to innovate business models, so that all countries and strata can enjoy the benefits of copyright, from the heart, to form respect for copyright. This is a long-term solution.

He Zhimin, Vice Director of CNIPA, pointed out that with the development and promotion of China, the pattern of Intellectual Property in the world has changed from being dominated by Europe and the United States to that of Europe and the United States and East Asia.

It is hard to say whether or not they can exist simultaneously, but when it comes to international intellectual property rulemaking, China should make its own voice heard and contribute its own wisdom. B&R intellectual property cooperation is a living example. He Zhimin said that with the active implementation of the BRI in the field of intellectual property, B&R cooperation on intellectual property has achieved fruitful results, and more and more Chinese wisdom has been recognised by other countries. According to the agreement signed between CNIPA and the Ministry of Industry and Handicrafts of Cambodia, valid Chinese invention patents can be directly registered and entered into force in Cambodia. In 2018 alone, 34 Chinese patents were directly registered and entered into force in Cambodia. In addition, CNIPA signed an agreement with the Ministry of Science and Technology of Laos to recognise the results of the examination of Chinese invention patents, and continued to promote the facilitation of the acquisition of IPRs by Chinese applicants in B&R countries. In recent years, CNIPA has organised various forms of personnel training.

When attending the Belt and Road Forum 2017, Francis Gurry, WIPO's Director General, said that building a positive IPR ecosystem will help improve the IPR system among the B&R countries and create an innovative and sustainable development environment and make contributions to global IPR system construction. According to him, as a very practical cooperative model, BRI has provided an important strategic opportunity for developing countries and will play a positive role in globalisation.

References

Beijing Higher People's Court (2018), Final Judgment, "jing min zhong" No. 171.

Bently, Lionel et al. (2018), *Intellectual Property Law*, Fifth Edition, Oxford University Press, Oxford.

Chen, Li (2013), *Criticism of Basic Theories of Copyright*, Intellectual Property Press, Beijing.

China IP News (2017), "The Belt and Road Build a Road of Innovation", available at: http://english.cnipa.gov.cn/news/iprspecial/920388.htm.

Drahos, Peter and Braithwaite, John (2003), *Information Feudalism: Who Owns the Knowledge Economy?* Earthscan Publications, London, 2002 (Chinese translation published 2005).

Hargreaves, Ian (2011), *Digital Opportunity: A Review of Intellectual Property and Growth*, available at: https://assets.publishing.service.gov.uk/government/uploads/system/uploads/attachment_data/file/32563/ipreview-finalreport.pdf,8.30.

National Bureau of Statistics of China (2019), "Six Years of 'Belt and Road'!", available at: https://eng.yidaiyilu.gov.cn/qwyw/rdxw/105854.htm.

Xinhua News Agency (2018), "Intellectual Property Cooperation with Nations Participating in Belt and Road Initiative Continues to Expand", available at: https://eng.yidaiyilu.gov.cn/qwyw/rdxw/63273.htm.

China's Political Risk Insurance for Outward FDI Within the Context of Belt and Road Initiative

Xueyan WU

Introduction

Since the beginning of the twenty-first century, China's overseas investment has been greatly encouraged and supported by the country's 'Going Out' strategy. Outward foreign direct investment (hereinafter called FDI) has been continuously increasing since 2003. During the ten years from 2002 to 2012, the rate of growth of outward foreign investment was explosive, with an average annual growth rate of 41.6%.[1]

The Belt and Road Initiative (hereinafter called BRI) put forward in 2013 further accelerated the growth of the outward FDI, especially in the Belt and Road (hereinafter called B&R) region. In 2014, China's outward FDI and foreign direct investment in China were almost equal for the first time. In 2015, China's outward FDI leapt to second place in the world, surpassing the inward FDI in the same period, and marking

X. WU (✉)
School of Law, Chongqing University, Chongqing, China
e-mail: wuxueyan@cqu.edu.cn

[1] See 2012 Statistical Bulletin of China's Outward Foreign Direct Investment, issued by the MOFCOM, the National Bureau of Statistics (NBS) and the State Administration of Foreign Exchange (SAFE) in September 2013.

G. Martinico and X. WU (eds.), *A Legal Analysis of the Belt and Road Initiative*, https://doi.org/10.1007/978-3-030-46000-6_10

China's changing role from a host country of foreign investment to a major overseas investor as well.[2]

With the implementation of the BRI and the establishment of a new economic policy of comprehensive opening up, the investment of Chinese enterprises overseas has been expanding greatly. In 2018, China's foreign direct investment reached US $143.04 billion, covering 188 countries.[3]

As a major investor in many countries around the world, Chinese investors face more political risks in relation to the host countries than many other countries.[4]

A well-designed and well-operated political risk insurance system could greatly benefit the implementation of the B&R strategy. The second part of this article will describe the evolution of political risk insurance and its development in China. The third part will analyse the flaws and problems of China's political risk insurance system. The fourth part analyses BITs signed by China in connection with China's political risk insurance. The concluding part put forward some suggestions to improve China's political risk insurance system.

Political Risk Insurance and Its Development in China

There is no generally recognised definition of political risk in the academic circle. Typical examples of political risk are the risks that a government nationalise or expropriate the assets of the investor. Political risk is often related to nonmarket factors as macroeconomic and social policies or events related to political instability, including terrorism, riots, coups, civil war and insurrection (Kennedy 1988).

Political risk has a significant impact on overseas investment and it is difficult for foreign investors to prevent and control such risks. If they do not take risk transfer measures in advance, then if political upheaval

[2] See 2015 Statistical Bulletin of China's Outward Foreign Direct Investment, issued by the MOFCOM, the National Bureau of Statistics (NBS) and the State Administration of Foreign Exchange (SAFE) in September 2016.

[3] See 2018 Statistical Bulletin of China's Outward Foreign Direct Investment, issued by the MOFCOM, the National Bureau of Statistics (NBS) and the State Administration of Foreign Exchange (SAFE) in September 2019.

[4] I explain why china faces more political risks in next part.

occurs, huge losses could create an enormous impact on the regular operation of their enterprises, and may even lead to bankruptcy.

Political insurance is a useful tool to mitigate the losses caused by political risks. It refers to the insurance provided by the government of the capital-exporting country against the losses that the overseas investor may suffer due to the political risks associated with the host country. In essence, it is a 'national guarantee' provided by the national government for overseas investors. The political risk insurance policy is implemented by or entrusted to the government-sponsored agency. Political risk insurance is policy-oriented insurance, in which the state plays a leading role, and therefore profit is not its primary objective.

Political risks covered by political risk insurance mainly include the risk of currency inconvertibility, the risk of expropriation, and the risk of war, revolution, insurrection, etc. If a qualified investor has purchased political risk insurance, when the agreed risk occurs and losses are incurred, the government-sponsored agency pays the insurance premium to the investor according to the insurance contract and has the right to claim compensation from the host government on behalf of the investor.

The United States was the first country to provide political risk insurance for foreign investment. It started providing political risk insurance for investment in connection with the Marshall Plan in 1948. Initially, the political risk insurance was designed to protect against currency inconvertibility but broadened to include insurance for revolution and insurrection in 1950. In 1969, the US government passed the Foreign Assistance Act,[5] which set up a special policy insurance institution, namely the 'Overseas Private Investment Company' (OPIC). OPIC provides political risk insurance against losses mainly resulting from currency inconvertibility, expropriation, political violence, war, revolution and civil strife,[6] thus supporting US private investment in some 150 countries and areas around the world. Political risk insurance provided by OPIC is backed by the full faith and credit of the US Government.[7] Later,

[5] 22 U.S.C. § 2191(4)(b).

[6] 22 U.S.C.A. § 2194(1) (West Supp. 1988).

[7] On 5 October 2018, the US president signed the Better Utilization of Investments Leading to Development ('BUILD') Act into law, creating a new agency, the US International Development Finance Corporation ("IDFC"), to support private investment in developing countries. IDFC replaced OPIC and is supposed to provide much more funding and new kinds of support for American companies working in developing markets.

some OECD countries, such as Japan, France and Germany, followed suit and started to promote overseas investment and protect the interests of overseas investors by providing political risk insurance through their own export credit agencies or similar government-authorised agencies. Nowadays, political risk insurance has become a powerful tool for capital-exporting countries to support cross-border investment. It is used by a growing number of countries and plays an increasingly important role in international investment activities.

China's political risk insurance is provided by China Export and Credit Insurance Corporation (hereinafter called SINOSURE), which was established in December 2001. SINOSURE is the only policy-oriented insurance corporation designated and authorised by the Chinese government to provide political risk insurance for overseas investment with the backing of state finance. SINOSURE is a wholly state-owned enterprise and its main task is to provide short-term, medium-term and long-term credit insurance and political risk insurance for export, to promote the export of domestic products and services. SINOSURE launched its 'political risk insurance' business one year after its establishment, which provides risk guarantees for economic losses caused by specific political problems in the country where the investor invests. The credit period of this underwriting business is generally 1–15 years.[8]

Under SINOSURE, eligible investors come in three categories: (1) a legal entity incorporated in China (excluding Hong Kong, Macao and Taiwan); (2) a legal entity registered outside China (including Hong Kong, Macao and Taiwan) if it is controlled by a legal entity registered in China; and (3) domestic and foreign financial institutions providing financing for the overseas projects. SINOSURE political risk insurance generally covers expropriation, currency inconvertibility, war and political riot, and breach of contract.[9]

[8] Official website of SINOSURE, available at: http://www.sinosure.com.cn/en/Insurance/oii/index.shtml (accessed on 30 December 2019).

[9] SINOSURE's expropriation policy compensates investors if the 'host country deprives the ownership and management of an investment project or the use and control of the funds and assets of an investment project through nationalization, confiscation or compulsory acquisition'. SINOSURE's exchange restrictions policy compensates the investor if 'the host country hinders or restricts investors from the free exchange of currencies or raises the exchange cost and prevents outward remittance of currency from the country'. SINOSURE's war and political riot coverage includes 'war, revolution, riot, coup, civil war, rebellion, terrorist activity or other warlike operations occur in the host country, which

As the second largest investor in the world, a well-designed and well-operated political risk insurance is essential as China is facing more political risks than many other countries for various reasons, among which the following three are the most important.

Firstly, the main recipients of Chinese outward FDI have been developing countries. Since 2003, more than 80% of China's annual FDI has flowed into developing countries and emerging market countries such as Asia, Africa and Latin America. In 2013, China's outward FDI stock in developing countries reached US $1458.81 billion, accounting for more than 86.3% of China's total outward FDI. With the implementation of the B&R Initiative, the investments flow to the countries in the B&R region has significantly increased. In 2018, China's non-financial direct investment in the countries along the B&R region increased by 9% over the previous year. Most of the 65 countries in the B&R area are developing countries. Political risk is more likely to occur in areas with poor economic and political environments, especially in emerging markets or developing countries. Take the countries in the B&R region for example. Many countries in this area are beset with geopolitical, nationalistic, and/or religious conflicts, regional and local wars, bureaucracy and even terrorist attacks (Yin et al. 2018). The national risk assessment model made by SINOSURE analyses and evaluates the risk of countries in the B&R region from the perspective of political risk, economic risk, business environment risk and legal risk. The proportion of countries with high risk level is 84%, and the absolute risk level of the region is relatively high.[10]

Secondly, a considerable proportion of China's overseas investment is concentrated in more traditional industries, such as energy exploitation, mining, transportation and manufacturing. One the one hand, these industries are usually the lifeblood of each country's national economy. Therefore, the host country may be more cautious about the investment in these industries due to their high political sensitivity. On the other hand, investment in these industries often involves long-term projects, which are more vulnerable to policy changes. For example, during the

results in the investors' loss of assets or permanent inability to operate'. SINOSURE's breach of contract policy compensates the investor if 'the host government or any other entity approved by the insurer breaches or fails to perform that which has been agreed in the investment project contract and refuses to pay compensation'.

[10] See the Country Risk Analysis Report—The Countries along B&R (2015), compiled by SINOSURE.

long-term span of the investment, the host country may introduce new legislation or change a policy that affects the operation of the project that is being invested in.

Thirdly, China's rapid economic growth and the differences between China and many developed countries in ideology and social systems make certain countries worried. For this reason, Chinese investment is more likely to be a target of government intervention in some developed countries. In recent years, the United States and certain European countries have frequently set restrictions or obstacles to Chinese enterprises entering specific sectors such as the energy sector or high-tech industries. After Donald Trump was elected president of the United States, he launched a series of foreign economic policies aiming at 'America first'. Under the background of growing 'anti-globalisation' sentiments, these political actions undoubtedly increase uncertainty pertaining to the world's economic prospects. China and the United States have close economic and trade relations. In this wave of trade protectionism, Chinese investment will inevitably be affected and be more likely to suffer from government intervention.

The Flaws and Problems Associated with the Chinese Political Insurance System

Founded nearly two decades ago, SINOSURE has played an increasingly important role as China's overseas investment has soared over the past two decades. In 2018 alone, SINOSURE supported US $58.13 billion overseas investment, an increase of 18.9% from the previous year. It covered a range of sectors including minerals, oil and gas, electric power, transportation infrastructure, and manufacturing, and involved a total of 646 overseas investment projects in 84 countries and regions.[11] However, in the past two decades, with the massive increase in China's overseas investment, some flaws and problems with China's political insurance system have also been exposed.

The first problem is that the legislation for political risk insurance in China is lagging behind other developed countries. Although SINOSURE provides political risk insurance, it has not been authorised

[11] http://finance.sina.com.cn/money/insurance/bxdt/2019-02-12/doc-ihqfskcp4545991.shtml (accessed on 30 December 2019).

by law to do so. In a strict sense, the operation of SINOSURE lacks a formal legal basis. At present, the operation of China's political risk insurance system relies entirely on two documents issued by SINOSURE. One is '*An overview of political risk insurance*' and the other is the '*Notice on issues related to the establishment of a risk guarantee mechanism for key projects of overseas investment*'. These two documents are not laws and are too general and lack operability. The '*Notice of the State Council on the establishment of China's Export and Credit Insurance Cooperation*' released in 2001 expressed the intention to consider making a law covering overseas investment insurance when 'the time is ripe'. However, no law has yet been passed. Political risk insurance is a system that needs legislative support. It is not enough to set up several types of insurance only in the form of a Notice. This lack of legislation may cause problems such as the loss of stability and predictability. The two Notices only state the types of the risks covered by the political insurance, without mentioning underwriting conditions, rates, rights of subrogation and other issues. Investors can only know the insurance conditions, coverage, rates and terms through negotiation based on the *Notices*, which dramatically inhibits the enthusiasm of investors for purchasing insurance and restricts the development of the investment insurance business.

In addition, China's current legislation does not specify the legal status of SINOSURE or recognise its right of subrogation. If there is no investment protection agreement between China and the host country, SINOSURE's subrogation right will not be recognised after it indemnifies the loss of the insured. When disputes arise with the host country, it will be in a disadvantageous position. Thus, in order to maintain the stability and predictability of the political risk insurance policy, it is necessary to create national laws covering such insurance. Some developed countries have had successful experiences in this regard. For example, in contrast to China, the United States established its political risk insurance system through the Economic Cooperation Act of 1948 and enacted a special piece of legislation called the Foreign Assistance Act in 1961, which clarified the purposes and objectives of OPIC, its insurance coverage and application in law.

This 'legislation first' approach not only provides the legal basis for the establishment of OPIC, but also provides important guidance for the operation and development of OPIC. The UK also enacted the Export Guarantees and Overseas Investment Act in 1978 and then replaced it with the Export and Investment Guarantees Act in 1991, making detailed provisions concerning political risk insurance. In view of the unique nature and operating mechanism of political risk insurance, it is not suitable to include it in commercial insurance law by amending pre-existing insurance law. Given the mechanism of China's central legislative work, it is impossible to formulate an overseas investment law or political risk insurance law in the short term. Therefore, a *Political Risk Insurance Act* enacted by the State Council could be a possible option.

The second problem is that because SINOSURE is the only insurance agency that underwrites overseas investment in China, it is challenging to meet the vast and diverse demands of the various investments and investors. With the accelerated economic transformation in China and the implementation of the B&R strategy, the investment of Chinese enterprises overseas has been expanding greatly and is more diversified than ever before. Traditionally, an overwhelmingly large proportion of China's outward FDI flowed to the sectors of energy exploitation, mining, transportation and manufacturing. However, the investment is now widely distributed among a range of industries. In 2018, China's foreign direct investment covered eighteen major industries, among which leasing and business services, financing, manufacturing, and wholesale and retail industries accounted for more than 70% of the investment. Investment flowing to information transmission, scientific research and technical services, power production, culture and education and other fields also grew rapidly.[12]

Traditionally, China's main investors overseas were state-owned enterprises (SOEs). But with the growing strength of Chinese privately owned enterprises (POEs) and the implementation of the B&R Initiative, a bigger proportion of China's increasing outward FDI is coming from POEs. In 2018, the outward FDI by non-state-owned enterprises increased by 11.2% from the previous year, accounting for 62.3% of China's total outward FDI.[13] Compared to SOEs, Chinese POEs are 'more flexible, faster-growing, more diversified in terms of investment, and less affected by

[12] 2018 Statistical Bulletin of China's Outward Foreign Direct Investment, issued by the MOFCOM, the National Bureau of Statistics (NBS) and the State Administration of Foreign Exchange (SAFE) in September 2019.

[13] 2018 Statistical Bulletin of China's Outward Foreign Direct Investment, issued by the MOFCOM, the National Bureau of Statistics (NBS) and the State Administration of Foreign Exchange (SAFE) in September 2019.

possible stringent market access or political censorship in the host countries'.[14] However, as EY stated in its report[15]:

> Many POEs are smaller and lack a good credit basis for overseas financing and cross-border payments. POEs also have problems in strategy and management. For example, many lack long-term strategy development and risk awareness, an understanding of the investment environment and cultures of host countries, and experience of overseas investment.[16]

Compared with large-scale SOEs, the ability of POEs to resist risks, including political risks, is lower. Purchasing political insurance is one of the most direct and simple ways to avoid political risk. Unfortunately, POEs experience more difficulties in being able to get insured by SINOSURE, just as they experience more difficulties to get financial support from banks.

Allowing other qualified private insurance providers to carry out political risk insurance business could be a way to meet the diversified needs of the market. If private insurance providers were allowed to offer overseas insurance, it would provide an opportunity for certain investors who fail to meet the eligibility requirements of SINOSURE to get insured. Although SINOSURE has better facilities for covering currency inconvertibility risks than do private insurance providers, private insurance providers have their own advantages. For example, private insurance providers are more flexible than SINOSURE and are able to provide more tailored services according to the needs of the investors. In addition, it takes a long time for insurance applications to SINOSURE to get approved. The negotiation process with private insurance providers could take less time (Comeaux and Kinsella 1994).

Finally, allowing private insurance providers to provide investors with diversified insurance types and services could, to some extent, increase the bargaining power of investors. In the political risk insurance market, state-owned insurance agencies and private insurance providers could be complementary and cooperative, which would be conducive to the formation of an economic, scientific and efficient political risk insurance mechanism. For example, the possibility of SINOSURE and other private

[14] Outlook for China's Outward Foreign Direct Investment 2015, EY.

[15] Outlook for China's Outward Foreign Direct Investment 2015, EY.

[16] Outlook for China's Outward Foreign Direct Investment 2015, EY.

insurance providers jointly providing overseas insurance for qualified overseas investors could be explored.

The third problem with SINOSURE is its dual status as an insurance approver and insurance business operator. SINOSURE is a policy-oriented insurance provider financed by the state. It makes decisions about which projects are qualified for coverage, which is the exercising of a monitoring function as the policy-oriented agency. At the same time, SINOSURE is the insurance business operator. These dual identities make it likely to experience conflicts of interests and increase the possibility of corruption. It would be better to remove the authority of approval from SINOSURE. The Ministry of Commerce might be better placed to authorise applications for political risk insurance. The intervention of the Ministry of Government also consistent with the official nature of overseas investment insurance, which could reflect the country's guidance and regulation of overseas investment to a certain extent.

Bilateral Investment Treaties and Overseas Investment Insurance

Bilateral Investment Treaties (BITs) usually provide investors with a number of guarantees including fair and equitable treatment, protection against expropriations, free exchange and transfer of currency, and full protection against acts of political violence. The BIT's dispute resolution mechanism gives investors a course of action against host governments. With this in place, investors in the home countries need not rely on their governments to file claims against the government of the host state (Ginsburg 2013). Yet, research reveals that the vast majority of investors do not appear to take BITs into account when deciding on where to invest abroad. Investors typically only inquire about a BIT when disputes have already arisen (Ginsburg 2013). Political risk insurers tend to regard BITs as mere a signal of the host country's protective attitude towards foreign investors (Kerner 2009). Nevertheless, from the perspective of the home country of investment, BITs are helpful to mitigate the risks of its overseas investors and the overseas investment insurer (Sauvant and Sachs 2009). However, even though it is the second largest capital-exporting country, China has not signed BITs with all of the critical outward FDI destination countries. Although China has signed BITs with 105 countries, there are still many countries in the B&R that have not signed BITs with China. For example, China signed 34 BITs with African countries, but

20 African countries have not signed BITs with China, including some important countries in the B&R such as Angola and Zambia.[17]

In addition, many of the BITs signed by China decades ago do not correspond to China's current needs and interests. Of the 104 bilateral BITs in force signed by China, only 27 were signed between 2000 and 2018, and the remaining 77 were signed in the 1980s and 1990s.[18] During the 1980s–1990s, China's foreign investment policy and legislation focused on attracting foreign investment as the host country, while paying less attention to the protection of overseas investment. What China sought to include in these bilateral treaties embodied its policy orientation at the time. However, almost forty years have passed, China has already transformed from being a capital-importing country to the second largest capital-exporting country in the world. The dual status of China means that China not only needs to attract foreign direct investment but also needs to protect its overseas foreign investment.

Once it has indemnified the insured for its losses, the insurer has the subrogation right which allows it to 'step into the shoes' of the insured. This is one of the primary principles of an insurance company's business model. However, whether the insured's subrogation rights can be realised depends on whether the insurer's home country has a BIT with the host state of the overseas investment and whether a subrogation clause is included in the BIT or whether the insurer's home country authorises the insurer to subrogate the right of the insured (Ocran 1988). BITs with subrogation clauses allow the government-sponsored insurer to 'subrogate' insured investors' claims against host states, thereby providing a legal basis for the insurer, namely the government's insurance agency to recover losses from the host countries (Poulsen 2010). However, this is not the case with China for two reasons. On the one hand, China does not make its political risk insurance contingent on the adoption of BITs, in other words, SINOSURE does not make the existence of a BIT with the host country a necessary condition for the investor to get insured. This is called the 'unilateral mode' of political risk insurance. Under this model,

[17] A list of BITs signed by China with other countries, available at: http://tfs.mofcom.gov.cn/aarticle/Nocategory/201111/20111107819474.html (accessed on 30 December 2019).

[18] A list of BITs signed by China with other countries, available at: http://tfs.mofcom.gov.cn/aarticle/Nocategory/201111/20111107819474.html (accessed on 30 December 2019).

it is difficult for the subrogation right of SINOSURE to be recognised by the host country, and it cannot be recovered after paying the investors' losses, which increases the operational risk of SINOSURE itself. If the policyholder is also a state-owned enterprise, the loss is ultimately borne by the state, which makes buying insurance less meaningful. On the other hand, many BITs signed by China do not have a subrogation clause. For example, nearly a third of the countries in the B&R have not reached an agreement with China on the recognition of subrogation, which means that SINOSURE does not have the legal basis to recover losses from the host country after it indemnifies the losses of its clients.

Conclusion

With the implementation of the 'Going Out' strategy and the expansion and promotion of the B&R Initiative, China has already transformed from being a capital-importing country to also being the second largest capital-exporting country in the world. As a major investor, a large portion of Chinese outward FDI flows to developing countries, especially to countries in the B&R region, where political risk is high. China's dual status means that it not only needs to attract foreign direct investment but also needs to protect its overseas foreign investment. But China's changing role and the status of its overseas investment have not been adequately reflected in the relevant domestic laws and the BITs it has signed. China has not yet established a comprehensive legal system to protect its overseas investment from political risk. Its BITs also have insufficient legal protection against political risk. The time has come to reconstruct China's overseas investment insurance system and speed up the signing and revision of BITs with countries in the B&R region. In addition, in order to meet the diversified needs of various investors, especially the needs of POEs, and the growing demand for overseas investment insurance, private insurance providers should be encouraged to take an active part in the overseas investment insurance business. The improvement and reconstruction of the overseas investment insurance system would provide institutional guarantees for the safety, stability, transparency and predictability of Chinese investments in the B&R region and around the world.

References

Comeaux, Paul E. and Kinsella, N. Stephan (1994), "Reducing Political Risk in Developing Countries: Bilateral Investment Treaties, Stabilisation Clauses, and MIGA & OPIC Investment Insurance", in *The New York Law School Journal of International and Comparative Law*, 15(1), 1–39.

Ginsburg, Robert (2013), "Political Risk Insurance and Bilateral Investment Treaties: Making the Connection", in *The Journal of World Investment & Trade*, 14(6), 943–977.

Kennedy, Charles R., Jr. (1988), "Political Risk Management: A Portfolio Planning Model", in *Business Horizons*, 31(6), 26–33.

Kerner, Andrew (2009), "Why Should I Believe You? The Costs and Consequences of Bilateral Investment Treaties", in *International Studies Quarterly*, 53(1), 73–102.

Ocran, T.M. (1988), "International Investment Guarantee Agreements and Related Administrative Schemes", in *University of Pennsylvania Journal of International Business Law*, 10(3), 341–370.

Poulsen, Lauge N. Skovagaard (2010), "The Importance of BITs for Foreign Direct Investment and Political Risk Insurance: Revisiting the Evidence", in Karl P. Sauvant (ed.), *Yearbook on International Investment Law & Policy 2009/2010*, Oxford University Press, New York, 539–574.

Sauvant, Karl P. and Sachs, Lisa E. (eds.) (2009), *The Effect of Treaties on Foreign Direct Investment: Bilateral Investment Treaties, Double Taxation Treaties, and Investment Flows*, Oxford University Press, New York.

Yin, Meiqun et al. (2018), *Overseas Investment Risk in the Background of One Belt and One Road*, Economy & Management Publishing House, Beijing.

An Analysis of the Legal Issues of China's Overseas Investment in the Context of the 'Belt and Road' Initiative

Wenge Zeng

Introduction

The opening-up policy has become a fundamental long-term policy for the Chinese government in general and has actively promoted the international cooperation of the 'Belt and Road' Initiative (BRI) in particular (Ohashi 2018). At present, China has already signed 197 cooperation documents with 137 countries and 30 international organisations, including both developing and developed countries. Besides, there are a large number of companies and financial institutions from developed countries cooperating with China to explore the third-party market.[1] BRI shows China's determination to build an opening economy and its importance to China's global economic and political reach (Naughton 2020). In contrast to the opportunities that lie in the implementation of BRI (Feng and Liang 2019), we should also realise that BRI involves a set of countries that are different in terms of religion, culture, market system

[1] https://www.yidaiyilu.gov.cn/xwzx/gnxw/109858.htm (accessed on 21 December 2019).

W. Zeng (✉)
School of Law, Chongqing University, Chongqing, China
e-mail: zengwenge@126.com

G. Martinico and X. WU (eds.), *A Legal Analysis of the Belt and Road Initiative*, https://doi.org/10.1007/978-3-030-46000-6_11

and level of development, all of which pose a great challenge on China's ability to cope with the legal risks, coordinate relevant interests and integrate value conflicts in its overseas investment (also see Himaz 2019).

The Impact of BRI on China's Overseas Investment

In the aftermath of President Xi's proposal for BRI in 2013, the National Development and Reform Commission (NDRC), the Ministry of Commerce (MOFCOM) and the Ministry of Foreign Affairs (MOFFA) of China jointly issued the 'Vision and Action for Promoting the Joint Construction of the Silk Road Economic Belt and the 21st Century Maritime Silk Road' in 2015.[2] It commits to provide direct investment to countries and regions along the 'Belt and Road' mainly in the form of country-country cooperation. The first 'Belt and Road' international cooperation summit was held in Beijing in May 2017, in which China signed economic and trade cooperation agreements with 30 countries. At the opening ceremony of the 19th National Congress of the Communist Party of China (CPC) on 18 October 2017, President Xi pointed out in the report that 'we should focus on the development of the "Belt and Road", attach equal importance to bringing in foreign countries and going global, follow the principle of extensive consultation, joint contribution and shared benefits, strengthen openness and cooperation in innovation capacity, and form an open pattern of land and sea connectivity and mutual benefit between east and west'.[3]

According to the 2018 Statistical Bulletin of China's Outward Direct Investment, China's OFDI was US$ 143.04 billion, ranking second in the world.[4] It, to a large extent, indicates that China has taken a more positive posture in comprehensively enhancing its opening-up level and

[2] Document is available at: http://english.www.gov.cn/archive/publications/2017/06/20/content_281475691873460.htm (accessed on 21 December 2019).

[3] The report is available at: http://www.xinhuanet.com/english/download/Xi_Jinping's_report_at_19th_CPC_National_Congress.pdf (accessed on 21 December 2019).

[4] The 'Statistical Bulletin of China's Outward Direct Investment' was issued by the MOFCOM, the National Bureau of Statistics (NBS) and the State Administration of Foreign Exchange (SAFE) in September 2019. See http://english.mofcom.gov.cn/article/newsrelease/significantnews/201909/20190902901191.shtml (accessed on 21 December 2019).

strengthening its determination to expand cooperation with other countries (Mumtaz and Smith 2019). Besides, it also signifies that the relevant departments of the Chinese government will continue to actively guide the qualified Chinese enterprises to 'Go Out' and further optimise the structure and quality of China's overseas investment (Gu et al. 2016).

The Regulatory Framework of China's OFDI

For the protection of international investment, legal measures have been used either jointly or separately by the capital-importing country (host country) and the capital-exporting country (home country) (generally see Bungenberg et al. 2015). These measures can be divided into several categories, namely the foreign investment law (which is the guarantee provided by the domestic law of host countries), the overseas investment insurance law, the bilateral agreement (between the host country and the home country) and the multilateral treaty (signed by the majority of sovereign states). Thus, these measures can also be subsumed into domestic legislation and international legal regulation.

Domestic Legislation

China's domestic legislation on foreign investment involves, in short, three aspects of the investment in question, i.e. the regulation, protection and encouragement of foreign investment. While the regulatory legal norms mainly control foreign investment, the purpose of the protective legal norms is to provide certain protection for domestic investors, such as the establishment of overseas investment insurance laws. As to the legal norms concerning encouragement, they are mainly composed of the preferential measures for foreign investment.

Approval Procedure

China's OFDI is changing from an approval system to a registration and enterprise participation system (Tong 2012: 145). The administrative departments of China's central government are responsible for making formal policies, which can be divided into four levels. First, the highest decision-making body is the State Council (SC), which is responsible for the overall management of the Chinese government and the major decisions that affect the economy and society. The second level is mainly the MOFCOM and the SAFE, and these two institutions are involved in overseas investment management. In addition, for the NDRC has long played a key role in the approval of overseas investment, it thus can also be considered as one part of the second level. The third level is the functional department, namely the ministries responsible for finance, taxation and other aspects of this work. The role of these ministries is primarily to assist the core sectors in ensuring that these policies are compatible with other existing policies and in their promulgation and implementation. The fourth level includes the ministries of the sectors responsible for mining, agriculture and forestry.

In accordance with the requirements of the SC to further streamline the administration and delegate power,[5] the NDRC and the MOFCOM issued regulations in 2014 to simplify the supervision of China's (non-financial) foreign direct investment. The measures for the administration of the approval and archival filing of overseas investment projects, which came into effect on 8 May 2014, established a new management mechanism of 'filing first, approval second'. On 6 October 2014, the revised measures of the MOFCOM on the administration of overseas investment came into effect, which also adopted the management mechanism of 'filing first, approval second'. These measures also implemented the negative list management mode for the first time without considering the amount involved in overseas investment.

Non-financial Chinese enterprises may invest abroad with the approval of the MOFCOM, the NDRC or the relevant provincial authorities. Through the NDRC, China has invested more than \$300 million in natural resources or more than \$100 million in other areas, which is subject to further approval from the SC (Sauvant and Chen 2013: 18). However, except for sensitive issues, the filing system is currently adopted for any project. Domestic enterprises that involve sensitive countries, regions and industries shall, in addition to outward direct investment projects, report to the central office of the MOFCOM for approval. Enterprises set up abroad by other domestic enterprises shall be subject to record-keeping management.

[5] In fact, the governmental reform to streamline administration and delegate power has been underway for several years in China. See, for instance, http://english.www.gov.cn/premier/news/2018/07/19/content_281476228570636.htm (accessed on 22 December 2019).

In 2014, the new regulation restricted four types of investment, including investments endangering national sovereignty, security and social and public interests, violating Chinese laws and regulations, damaging the relationship between China and relevant countries (regions), and violating international treaties and agreements concluded or acceded to by our country exporting products and technologies prohibited by China. It signifies the implementation of the management of the 'negative list'. The new regulation also no longer requires the approval/filing of the development and reform departments as the preliminary procedure for applying for approval or filing with the commercial departments, which means that the two procedures should be processed in parallel to accelerate the approval process of overseas investment. Furthermore, according to the Notice on Further Simplifying and Improving the Foreign Exchange Management Policy for Direct Investment issued by the SAFE in February 2015, the approval of foreign exchange registration for OFDI has been cancelled since 13 June 2015, and the mode of 'bank handling and foreign supervision' takes its place.

Investment Promotion

The Chinese government supports OFDI through financial and fiscal measures, risk management, providing information, international support through foreign aid and international investment agreements.

Fiscal and Tax Policies

The Chinese government has already promulgated various fiscal policies.[6] The promulgation of these measures and the establishment of funds (banks) are strong guarantees provided by the government for Chinese enterprises to conduct foreign direct investment, contracted projects and labour service cooperation, and they provide smooth channels for enterprises to finance investment projects and contracted projects.

[6] Concerning the fiscal policies, the Chinese government promulgated, for instance, the 'Administrative Measures on Special Fund for Foreign Economic and Technological Cooperation' (2005), 'Measures for the Administration of International Market Developing Funds of Small and Medium-Sized Enterprises' (2010), 'Measures for the Administration of the Special Fund for Foreign Trade and Economic Development' (2014), 'Silk Road Fund' (2014).

For their part, the Export-Import Bank of China (EXIM) and other state-owned commercial banks offer low lending rates, rapid approval processes and flexible terms for OFDI projects. In February 2006, the China Development Bank (CDB) and the EXIM reached an agreement to extend special financial services, including a discount on loan interest rates, to mineral and forestry exploration projects. Other projects conducive to government cooperation and central state-owned enterprises and large enterprise groups with sufficient capital, technology, management experience and brand can be financed. Besides, the Chinese government also provides direct subsidies to eligible OFDI projects through special funds jointly established and managed by the Ministry of Finance (MOFFIN) and the MOFCOM. The eligible projects include activities such as building foreign research and development centres and machinery manufacturing facilities, investing in China's economic and trade zones overseas, and investing in natural resources (Sauvant and Chen 2013: 29).

In terms of tax support, the State Administration of Taxation (SAOFT) has also issued a series of tax relief policies to support China's 'Going Out' strategy (Maurin and Yeophantong 2013). One policy is tax treaties. The trade between countries is close, and agreements with legal effect are signed through a consultation based on the laws of each country. In the event of a conflict between a tax treaty and the domestic tax code, the companies choose the more favourable tax rate. At present, China's SAOFT has established a bilateral tax cooperation mechanism with more than 100 countries and regions and signed more than 100 tax agreements with more than 60 countries and regions along 'the Belt and Road', which has reduced the overseas withholding tax of Chinese financial institutions by 10 billion and reduced the tax burden. The signing of bilateral or multilateral tax agreements provides favourable conditions for the development of the Chinese enterprises that go abroad.

A second policy is the export tax rebate. To encourage enterprises to conduct international trade and foreign investment, the central government has carried out a series of export tax rebate policies. Until 2012, claims for export rebates were limited to exports subject to the value-added tax (VAT) and excise taxes. In 2012, the MOFFIN and the SAOFT issued a notice on the policies of the VAT and consumption tax on export goods and labour services. In addition, in 2014, the notice of the MOFFIN, the General Administration of Customs (GAOFC) and the SAOFT on the pilot export tax rebate policy for finance lease goods nationwide also stipulated that for the goods that finance a lease, financial leasing companies and their established project subsidiaries that lease to an overseas lessee in the form of a finance lease have a lease term of 5 years or more and actually leave the country after customs declaration, VAT and consumption tax refund policies are implemented. These documents have expanded the scope of applying for export tax rebates to benefit more foreign enterprises.

A third policy is the VAT. The business activity affected by the VAT on sales tax is more profound after the change of the VAT. The SAOFT is based on all the way 'area' construction to develop a series of policies regarding various industries in various fields related to VAT tax preferential policies, such as the difference in tax, tax exemption, investigation policy, and so forth, to support enterprises to better participate in 'belt and road area' construction and to help promote the 'neighbourhood country' all the way along the country's economic development.

Foreign Exchange Policy

The People's Bank of China (PBC) promulgated and immediately implemented the new foreign direct investment RMB settlement exchange rate policy. This policy enables Chinese enterprises to reduce their foreign exchange risks by directly using RMB for overseas investment under certain conditions. The condition is that the applicant must be a non-financial enterprise registered in a province that allows RMB cross-border trade settlement accounts; in addition, the host country must allow RMB outward direct investment account settlement (Sauvant and Chen 2013: 38).

According to the 'Regulations on Foreign Exchange Administration on Cross Border Guarantee and Securities' (2014), which was released by the SAFE, in addition to qualifying for 'inside' loans and to 'protect the borrowed', two types of cross-border guarantees need to be made after the contract is signed to guarantee the SAFE for the record registration and other forms of cross-border guarantees without approval or registration. The new rules also eliminate the early restrictions on the equity relationship between the guarantor and the principal (except for special cases such as overseas bond issuance) and the requirements on the proportion of assets and liabilities of the principal. Besides, the SAFE has not made any further changes to other rules related to foreign investment.

Risk Management

In the process of the BRI or globalisation, the China Export and Credit Insurance Corporation (SINOSURE) has undertaken very important tasks. From January 2013 to March 2017, the SINOSURE assumed a total of $444.2 billion. The export supported was $328.5 billion, and the investment supported was $115.69 billion, which accounted for 73% and 21% of the total export investment supported, respectively. That is, our export investments in the BRI countries are 73% and are very heavily insured. The main functions of the SINOSURE are risk prevention and financing expansion. Many Chinese institutions need to export credit insurance when they go global. Risk prevention is more important than risk insurance because most enterprises in China must be supported by credit in the expansion of enterprises. With this kind of risk prevention, this financing can be satisfied. Many companies value export credit insurance and, more importantly, providing them with a financing expansion. The loss compensation of export credit insurance has a distinctive feature. Unlike other insurance, China's credit insurance has the status of government recovery. In many bilateral agreements, the SINOSURE not only represents enterprises but also has a status of sovereign pursuit to a certain extent. Moreover, the recovery is centralised by the SINOSURE, which has higher benefits than a single enterprise. If a company cannot solve this problem well, it effectively closes the door to communication with most Chinese companies. SINOSURE's recovery is more efficient.

Chinese investments abroad are also likely to be protected through SINOSURE's various insurance products and services. Enterprises and financial institutions registered in the mainland and with the mainland as their main business premises may apply for investment insurance from the SINOSURE. The eligible projects include new OFDI projects and existing, expanding and changing projects. The SINOSURE has taken several measures to help enterprises cope with overseas risks. First, the SINOSURE actively responds to the needs of enterprise risk management and increases its support for export credit insurance, especially for small and micro-businesses, to effectively enhance their export confidence. From January to September 2019, the SINOSURE's credit assurance service supported more than 110,000 customers, among which the number of small and micro-enterprises accounted for more than 70%. Second, the SINOSURE provides full support to enterprises in exploring diversified international markets and offers assistance to export enterprises in jointly building 'the Belt and Road' and expanding emerging markets in terms of credit limit approval and credit investigation. Third, special measures should be introduced to accelerate the settlement of claims from the aspects of loss determination, compensation verification and strengthening professional guidance to compensate enterprises for foreign exchange losses in a timely manner, help export enterprises to control risks to the greatest extent, and effectively relieve the financial pressure of enterprises. The overall claim settlement efficiency of short-term export credit insurance has significantly improved.

Provision of Information

First, the MOFCOM provides information about overseas investment opportunities through its global commercial consulate. Equally important, the directory of countries and industries that guide overseas investment provides information on the priorities of 127 foreign destinations that attract FDI and lists the priorities of each host country (Sauvant and Chen 2013: 30). On this basis, the MOFCOM established in 2008 a global investment cooperation information service system that integrated information statistics, decision support and other services. In addition, the MOFCOM, the NDRC and the MOFFA jointly issued guidelines for international investment cooperation in OFDI countries, which 'lists current investment opportunities by country, industry, and project, seeking to facilitate OFDI flows' (Sauvant and Chen 2013: 31).

The SINOSURE publishes risk reports and overseas investment risk rating reports every year, which have been recognised in the industry to a certain extent. We have performed some work, and there is much room for improvement. The SINOSURE specifically studies the country risk of the 'Belt and Road'. On 11 October 2019, the Trust Insurance of China released the 2019 'National Risk Analysis Report' in Beijing and launched a global risk map and a globe that visually presents the panorama of national risks simultaneously.

International Legal Regulation

Bilateral Investment Treaties (BITs)

Both foreign investment and Chinese investments abroad are protected by a series of bilateral investment treaties signed by China and its major business partners (Cohen and Schneiderman 2017). As of 2019, China had signed 145 bilateral investment treaties. For investors, the advantages of such agreements generally include two aspects: substantive standards of investment protection (e.g. non-confiscation, national treatment, and fair and equitable treatment) and the possibility of directly resolving disputes with host countries through international arbitration.

Since the conclusion of the first BIT with Sweden in 1982, the protection content of China's BITs has undergone significant changes (Shan and Chen 2016). The first BITs were signed in the 1980s. In general, first-generation agreements offer lower levels of protection for investors. This agreement either does not contain any arbitration clause in the investing country or is limited to disputes over damages arising from forfeiture. The second-generation BITs, which began in the late 1990s, filled most of the gaps in the first-generation BITs, including arbitration provisions for all types of differences between investor countries, and are gradually aligning their substantive provisions with international standards. The third generation of bilateral investment treaties is the most recent type of agreement. A typical case is the China–Canada bilateral investment treaty concluded in 2012. This agreement attempts to strike a better balance between protecting the interests of investors and host countries. In one respect, the third-generation BITs have a lower level of protection for foreign investors, but its arbitration clause covers all types of investor country differences.

Most of China's BITs grant investments made by an investor of a contracting state in the territory of another state a number of guarantees, which typically include 'fair and equitable treatment', 'protection from expropriation', 'free transfer of means' and 'full protection and security'. Several unique features are that BITs allow an alternative dispute resolution mechanism, namely, that when investors' rights have been violated, they can rely on international arbitration, often under the auspices of the International Center for the Settlement of Investment Disputes (ICSID), rather than their own courts suing the host state. This process is known as investor-state dispute resolution.

In international investment, the collection of the host country is the problem of most concern for international investors. Moreover, expropriation or nationalisation is an important part of some countries' economic development plans, which has led to a long struggle in the field of international investment between developed and developing countries and between capital-exporting countries and capital-importing countries. At present, different countries have a different understanding of the concept, type and standard of compensation. Currently, the BITs signed by China generally stipulate that the authorities of one contracting party shall not nationalise, expropriate or take other measures of equal effect against the other party unless the measure is (1) for a public purpose, (2) in accordance with legal procedures, (3) non-discriminatory, and (4) accompanied by provisions for the payment of fair and reasonable compensation.

Multilateral Investment Treaties

The purpose of the Multilateral Investment Guarantee Agency (MIGA) is to provide guarantees, including co-insurance and renewable insurance, for the non-commercial risks of another member state that arise from overseas investment. These guarantees help investors protect the foreign direct investment from political and non-commercial risks in developing countries. China is one of the founding members of the MIGA. China is also the largest developing country among the members of the convention that enjoy rights and obligations. The purpose of the convention is to promote and encourage international capital flows, especially to developing countries. The MIGA covers investments such as equity, loans, shareholder loans and shareholder loan guarantees. The agency can also ensure investments such as management contracts, securitisation, bonds, leasing activities, franchise agreements and licensing agreements. The agency typically offers coverage for up to 15 years, with a 5-year extension depending on the nature and circumstances of the programme. In the event of an insured event, the MIGA may exercise the investor's right to the host country through subrogation to recover the costs associated with compensation. However, the agency's convention does not require member governments to treat foreign investment in any special way. As a multilateral institution, the MIGA also has the capacity to resolve potential disputes before they turn into insurance claims.

The purpose of the Convention on the Settlement of Investment Disputes between States and Nationals of Other States is to provide a corresponding mechanism for the settlement of investment disputes between countries and the nationals of other countries. For this purpose, ICSID has been established as a permanent institution. The ICSID is an international arbitration body that was established in 1966 to resolve legal disputes and mediate between international investors. The ICSID is part of the World Bank Group, is headquartered in Washington, D.C., and is funded in the United States. The ICSID is an independent multilateral specialised agency drafted by the executive director of the International Bank for Reconstruction and Development, and its convention is signed by member countries to encourage international flows of investment and reduce non-commercial risks. The ICSID itself does not conduct arbitration or mediation proceedings but provides institutional and procedural support to mediation committees, tribunals and other committees that address such matters. The centre has two sets of rules to determine how cases are initiated and handled, either under the ICSID conventions, regulations and rules or as additional facilities rules for the ICSID. To be dealt with in accordance with the ICSID convention, there must be a legal dispute between one state party of the centre and the nationals of another state.

The dispute must also be of a legal nature and directly related to investment. If a party to the dispute is not a state party or a national of a state party, the case may be addressed under the ICSID additional facilities rule. However, most cases are arbitrated under the ICSID convention. Recourse to ICSID mediation and arbitration is entirely voluntary. However, once the parties agree to arbitration under the ICSID convention, no party can unilaterally withdraw its consent. The ICSID secretariat may also administer dispute settlement procedures under other treaties and periodically assist tribunals or parties to disputes in arbitrating between investors and states under the arbitration regulations of the United Nations Commission on International Trade Law (UNCITRAL). The ICSID provides administrative and technical support to a number of international dispute settlement procedures through institutions such as the permanent court of arbitration in The Hague, the Netherlands, the international court of arbitration in London and the international chamber of commerce in Paris, France. Jurisdiction through the convention is involved in the concrete practice problem, and it is easy to cause an unfair phenomenon in our country in international treaties relating to jurisdiction problems when using a salvo clause that involves bilateral investment treaties signed when some special problems in our country do not agree with the ICSID jurisdiction and place. China's Ping An group vs. the Belgian government was rejected because this reason and led to the ICSID Ping An group litigation request.

Most agreements under the legal framework of the WTO directly or indirectly affect international capital flows to some extent. Countries along the route of the 'Belt and Road' may not have signed bilateral investment agreements with China, or they may not be members of the

ICSID; thus, they need to seek relevant WTO rules to resolve disputes on overseas investment. Therefore, in the process of the 'Belt and Road' construction, the role of relevant WTO rules cannot be ignored. Currently, the following three agreements concern overseas investment under the WTO framework. The purpose of the Agreement on Trade-Related Investment Measures (TRIMs) is to encourage investors to invest overseas and to make them aware of the fact that the agreement can enhance the security of overseas investment activities and thus facilitate the effective flow of capital around the world. The purpose of the General Agreement on Trade in Services (GATS) is to develop international trade in services. Because of the conclusion of GATS, overseas financial services investment develops rapidly in scale and quantity and is closely related to the overseas investment in the financial industry. The Agreement on Trade-Related Aspects of Intellectual Property Rights (TRIPs) is introduced and covers the exporter of capital and the capital between the demands for overseas investment that involve intellectual property disputes. TRIPS can be used to provide solutions, which is usually through the panel or the appellate body of the controversial proposal, and special circumstances can be unilateral or multilateral treaty economic sanctions to revenge.

Limitations in China's Overseas Investment Law

Under BRI, the domestic legal protection and response measures of overseas investment are seriously insufficient, and they cannot provide comprehensive protection and reduce the risk of overseas investment. At present, most of the legal protection of China's overseas investment is based on principles, and there are few protection measures related to detailed rules. In addition, China has signed a large number of multilateral treaties and bilateral agreements that, to a certain extent, lag behind and expose certain defects.

The Domestic Legal System of Overseas Investment Is Flawed

On the one hand, China's overseas investment started late but developed rapidly, and the legislative system will obviously lag behind. The development of the economy, the change in China's investment status and the changes in investment content have caused many existing laws and regulations to show omissions. The legislative content is not perfect. On the other hand, China's existing overseas investment is one-sided, and many investments are made from the perspective of various departments. A large portion of the domestic legislation aims to stipulate the government's supervision of foreign exchange and the approval of investment projects. This domestic legislation mainly focuses on the supervision of investors. Although the regulations have been revised to focus on government guidance and protection functions, these are insufficient compared to the real needs of foreign investment. The frequent risk is actually caused by the immaturity of the investment legal protection system. Therefore, perfecting China's foreign investment and forming complete legal protection has become the focus.

In the current situation, first, most of China's laws and regulations on adjusting overseas investment are dominated by departmental regulations and policy documents, which cannot form a complete legal system. Departmental regulations and policy documents are not rigorous in terms of procedures and content standards and are easily affected by major events. Second, the scope of protection is relatively narrow. Large state-owned enterprises are the main force of China's overseas investment activities, and corresponding protection measures and incentive policies are formulated for large state-owned enterprises, while the protection for private enterprises is relatively insufficient, and there are few relevant laws and regulations. Finally, China's regulatory system is not perfect, and there are many departments to manage overseas investment, which leads to decentralised functions and low efficiency.

Difficulties in the Application of International Treaties

At present, although China has acceded to the Convention on the Guarantee of Multilateral Investment Institutions and the Convention on the Settlement of Investment Disputes between States and Nationals of Other States, the application rate of these two conventions is not high. To date, Chinese investors have not only rarely used these conventions. The International Dispute Center has settled disputes, and few have insured against multilateral investment guarantee institutions. Precisely because of this, China's foreign investment practices have not played their due role in the practice of foreign investment. In addition, many bilateral treaties have fragmented the foreign investment legal system and increased the difficulty of applying the law. For China, most of the bilateral investment agreements were signed a long time ago, before 1996. These agreements lacked China's economic strength and were signed by capital importing countries. These treaties have been unable to protect China's current foreign investment. For the bilateral investment treaty, most of the provisions are based on principles, and the section that involves details lacks operability. Although the bilateral investment treaty signed in recent years has been improved, its operability cannot be determined without much practice. Besides, the compensation regulations of China's overseas investment losses are inconsistent with those of developed countries. The loss referred to in the bilateral investment treaty is the loss caused by the political risk of the capital exporter in the host country. Western developed countries adhere to the principle of adequate, efficient and timely compensation, whereas developing countries adhere to the principle of appropriate and reasonable compensation; different claims will lead to different compensation obligations.

China's Overseas Investment Insurance System Is Imperfect

From January to September 2019, the SINOSURE insured more than 450 billion dollars and paid more than 800 million dollars in compensation for customer support, with overall business risks under control. The underwriting data of the SINOSURE show that from the enterprise level, the largest risk that Chinese enterprises face in their foreign economic and trade activities is the default of overseas buyers, while the amount of losses caused by buyer rejection and bankruptcy has significantly increased. From the perspective of industry, the risk level of the light manufacturing, textile and electronic information industry is relatively high, and the rising trend of risk in the electronic information industry is the most significant. At the country level, bankruptcies in some industries have increased due to trade frictions between China and the United States, Brexit and European elections.[7]

Two fundamental problems exist in the current overseas investment insurance system (Pei and Zheng 2015: 42–53). The first problem is the lack of legislation, and overseas investment insurance is policy insurance.

[7] See the 'Country Risk Analysis Report 2019' at http://www3.weforum.org/docs/WEF_Global_Risks_Report_2019.pdf (assessed on 22 December 2019).

China's insurance law only adjusts commercial insurance that does not involve the overseas investment insurance system. The operation of the overseas investment insurance system of the SINOSURE depends entirely on the two documents of the 'overview of overseas investment insurance' and the 'notice on the establishment of a risk protection mechanism for key overseas investment projects'.[8] The former has only four contents (underwriting risk, compensation proportion, application conditions and business flow), which are too general and lack operability. The latter has only ten rules that cover three items, and it is only a guidance document.

Second, the operation mode of overseas investment insurance is unreasonable. From the institutional point of view, China's investment insurance is the 'application and protection in one' model. From the perspective of a bilateral investment agreement (BIT), China's investment insurance implements the 'unilateral mode', which is not based on the BIT signed by the host country and China. The lack of supervision in the former model is likely to breed corruption, which is not conducive to the healthy operation of the insurance mechanism. For the 'unilateral mode' without the BIT as the premise, China's subrogation right cannot be recognised by the host country, and it is difficult to recover after paying investors' losses. If the insurer is a state-owned enterprise and cannot recover from the host country, underwriting has lost practical significance.

Future Strategies and Trends

BRI is regional cooperation across Asia, Africa and Europe that involves 65 countries, which mainly includes emerging economies and developing countries, and it provides great development opportunities for China's overseas investment. Therefore, it is imperative to establish a perfect legal protection mechanism for overseas investment to help the construction of BRI (Chaisse and Górski 2018).

Improving Domestic Legislation

We should fill the gap in China's foreign investment protection laws and further improve the relevant laws and regulations of foreign investment. It is significant to establish special overseas investment protection laws

[8] See http://wzs.ndrc.gov.cn/zcfg/jwtzp/200804/t20080411_203668.html (accessed on 22 December 2019).

to systematise China's foreign investment protection laws. We must raise the level of relevant legislation. China's existing overseas investment is one-sided and more subject to policy constraints rather than legal regulation. Many of the policy perspectives are based on the interests of various departments. The legislation not only is scattered and ineffective but also has a single protective measure, which is highly prone to problems in the event of a dispute. Increasing the level of legal effectiveness can not only improve existing regulations but also transform existing administrative regulations into laws or formulate a new law to protect the interests of investors.

In addition, a special regulatory agency should be established for the current situation of overseas investment. Since many Western countries are very mature in establishing regulatory bodies, China can learn from the successful experience of these countries to establish institutions specifically for overseas investment, which will formulate development plans and relevant policies for overseas investment and conduct macroleadership and supervision on all overseas investment activities. Also, the establishment of a legal system for overseas investment in China must simplify the approval and handling of administrative procedures, establish special operating funds for key overseas investment projects supported by the state, provide preferential loan policies and guarantees for overseas investment enterprises that meet certain conditions, and establish a sound information service system.

Fulfilling the Effectiveness of International Treaties

Bilateral investment protection agreements and international investment conventions are used to protect foreign investment (Frenkel and Walter 2019). Although China has acceded to the Convention on the Settlement of Investment Disputes between States and Nationals of Other States and the Convention Establishing the Multilateral Investment Guarantee Agency, it is still unable to make better use of them. There may be two reasons for this. First, the risk awareness of Chinese investors is weak, and second, China is unfamiliar with these relevant regulations. The government should increase its awareness of these conventions and enhance its science and education for investors.

Bilateral investment treaties are the most important legal form to adjust and protect overseas investment activities worldwide (Wang 2019).

According to China's actual situation, it needs to be improved in the following two aspects. The first aspect is to change the focus of the BIT. It is necessary to negotiate on the basis of each party's required interests to achieve the equal rights and obligations of both parties, to clarify the protection of overseas investment, and to ensure that China's overseas investment activities are subject to risks. The second aspect is to refine the provisions of the agreement. The previous bilateral investment agreements were mostly based on principles, and the two sides did not have a unified understanding of the relevant provisions when they had disputes over overseas investment. Currently, we need to elaborate on the protection measures for overseas investment when signing the agreement, such as the scope of adjustment and the standard of treatment. Moreover, the dispute settlement mechanism of the treaty should be specific to make it more operational and practical, and the safety of China's overseas investment activities should be improved.

China should conclude different bilateral investment agreements according to different circumstances. For developing countries, the first choice is to sign bilateral investment agreements with countries that may have more economic contacts with China in the future. Second, because the legal protection mechanism for overseas investment in developing countries may not be perfect, it is necessary to raise the protection standard when signing bilateral investment treaties. Finally, it is necessary to sign relevant articles according to the political, social and economic situations of the other party.

Improving China's Overseas Investment Insurance System

The overseas investment insurance system is a systematic and standardised system, which needs legislative support. Therefore, we can learn from the experience of overseas investment insurance systems in developed countries and formulate special legislation of overseas investment insurance in China as soon as possible. There are two possible paths. One path is to formulate a special 'Overseas Investment Insurance Law of the People's Republic of China' or 'Regulations of the People's Republic of China on Overseas Investment Insurance'. The second path is to formulate a comprehensive overseas investment law of the People's Republic of China, and based on this law, a series of supporting regulations or judicial interpretations, including the overseas investment insurance law, would be issued to construct a complete and systematic legal system for the protection and promotion of overseas investment. Given the lag-behind of China's overseas investment insurance mechanism and the urgency of investment protection along the route, it is feasible for the SC first to issue special laws and regulations and then upgrade them to the legislation of the National People's Congress after forming a relatively complete operational mechanism.

An overseas investment insurance operation mode can be used for references, such as the experience of Germany and Japan, and it can promote our country for the examination and approval of overseas investment insurance institutions and business institutions in the transition from a 'unity mode' to a 'separation' model. The SC should establish a directly affiliated institution (an overseas investment administration bureau), or the overseas investment management committee should be jointly established by the three ministries of commerce, diplomacy and finance to be responsible for the examination and administration of insurance. Furthermore, the SINOSURE should be responsible for the implementation of a specific business. On the one hand, the guidance and supervision role of the MOFCOM, the financial support of the MOFFIN and the coordination ability of the MOFFA can be fully exerted at the level of insurance approval. On the other hand, the intervention of government agencies also conforms to the official nature of overseas investment insurance, which can reflect the guidance and regulation of the state on overseas investment to a certain extent.

Conclusion

This chapter has summarised the overseas investment legal policy system in China, a system that has undergone major transitions in the past 30 years. At the beginning of the 'reform and opening up' period, initial attempts to undertake overseas investment helped to lay the foundations for China's OFDI management system. Then, the Chinese government's approach to OFDI is encapsulated in the 'Going Out' strategy. With the advance of the wider reform process and the trend of economic globalisation, a strategy of support for overseas investment was ultimately established. However, the Chinese government should pay more attention to the clarity and operability of the terms when signing or revising the BIT in the future. In addition, China has an OFDI Regulatory Framework, whereas it has certain defects from the perspective of the development and practice of China's overseas investment. It is urgent to improve the legal protection mechanism of overseas investment from domestic law to international law. In detail, we should improve our legislative system for overseas investment, integrate scattered rules and regulations, and develop a transparent legal mechanism.

References

Bungenberg, Marc et al. (eds.) (2015), *International Investment Law: A Handbook*, Hart Publishing, Oxford.

Chaisse, Julien and Górski, Jędrzej (eds.) (2018), *The Belt and Road Initiative: Law, Economics, and Politics*, Brill Nijhoff, London and Boston.

Cohen, Tyler and Schneiderman, David (2017), "The Political Economy of Chinese Bilateral Investment Treaty Policy", in *The Chinese Journal of Comparative Law*, 5(1), 110–128.

Feng, Da Hsuan and Liang, Haiming (2019), *Belt and Road Initiative: Chinese Version of "Marshall Plan"*? World Scientific Publishing, Singapore.

Frenkel, Michael and Walter, Benedikt (2019), "Do Bilateral Investment Treaties Attract Foreign Direct Investment? The Role of International Dispute Settlement Provisions", in *The World Economy*, 42(5), 1316–1342.

Gu, Jing et al. (2016), "Chinese State Capitalism? Rethinking the Role of the State and Business in Chinese Development Cooperation in Africa", in *World Development*, 81, 24–34.

Himaz, Rozana (2019), "Challenges Associated with the BRI: A Review of Recent Economics Literature", in *The Service Industries Journal*, available at: https://doi.org/10.1080/02642069.2019.1584193.

Maurin, Cristelle and Yeophantong, Pichamon (2013), "Going Global Responsibly? China's Strategies Towards 'Sustainable' Overseas Investments", in *Pacific Affairs*, 86(2), 281–303.

Mumtaz, Muhammad Zubair and Smith, Zachary (2019), "The Determinants of Chinese Outward Foreign Direct Investment: A Closer Look", in *Frontiers of Economics in China*, 13(4), 577–601.

Naughton, Barry (2020), "China's Global Economic Interactions", in Shambaugh, David (ed.), *China & the World*, Oxford University Press, New York, 113–136.

Ohashi, Hideo (2018), "The Belt and Road Initiative (BRI) in the Context of China's Opening-Up Policy", in *Journal of Contemporary East Asia Studies*, 7(2), 85–103.

Pei, Changhong and Zheng, Wen (2015), *China's Outbound Foreign Direct Investment Promotion System: Overall Design*, Springer, Heidelberg, New York, Dordrecht and London.

Sauvant, Karl P. and Chen, Victor Zitian (2013), "China's Regulatory Framework for Outward Foreign Direct Investment", in *EABER Working Paper Series*, 88, available at: http://www.eaber.org/sites/default/files/documents/EABERWorkingPaper88_SauvantandChen.pdf.

Shan, Wenhua and Chen, Hongrui (2016), "China-US BIT Negotiation and the Emerging Chinese BIT 4.0", in Lim, C. L. (ed.), *Alternative Visions of the International Law on Foreign Investment: Essays in Honour of Muthucumaraswamy Sornarajah*, Cambridge University Press, Cambridge, 223–252.

Tong, Jiadong (2012), "WTO Commitment: Further Marketisation and Trade Liberalisation", in Garnaut, Ross and Song, Ligang (eds.), *China: New Engine of World Growth*, Australian National University Press, Canberra, 141–150.

Wang, Heng (2019), "China's Approach to the Belt and Road Initiative: Scope, Character and Sustainability", in *Journal of International Economic Law*, 22(1), 29–55.

Marching to an International Law Powerhouse Through Cities: An Ideational Reflection on China's 'Belt and Road' Initiative

Shisong Jiang

Introduction

To some extent, the emerging concerns about the possibility of a new Cold War between the United States and China seem to be slightly alleviated due to their signing of an agreement on 'phase one' of the trade deal on 15 January 2020.[1] Nevertheless, as with the immediate doubts cast on this trade truce (e.g. Bermingham 2020; Dean 2019), pessimism has continued to shroud the fading of the burgeoning US-China rivalry (Shambaugh 2018). Especially for the Trump administration, the strategic competitor and challenger are the labels that the United States has placed on China in Sino-US relations.[2] The competition between two great powers is evidently comprehensive—albeit the geoeconomic field is positioned as a battlefront—and will hardly be changed in the short term

[1] Document available at: https://ustr.gov/sites/default/files/files/agreements/phase%20one%20agreement/Economic_And_Trade_Agreement_Between_The_United_States_And_China_Text.pdf (accessed on 21 January 2020).

[2] In Trump's first National Security Strategy report, both China and Russia were explicitly categorised as the 'revisionist powers' who intend to 'shape a world antithetical to U.S. values and interests'. Document available at: https://www.whitehouse.gov/wp-content/uploads/2017/12/NSS-Final-12-18-2017-0905.pdf (accessed on 21 January 2020).

S. Jiang (✉)
School of Law, Chongqing University, Chongqing, China
e-mail: shisong.jiang@cqu.edu.cn

G. Martinico and X. WU (eds.), *A Legal Analysis of the Belt and Road Initiative*, https://doi.org/10.1007/978-3-030-46000-6_12

(Zheng 2019). Despite reluctance, it is indeed a political reality that our world has entered a genuinely new era of US-China competition (Breslin 2019).

Among others, the competition in question, inherently, has and will continue to revolve around the role played in the international order. Since the end of the Cold War in 1989, the international order has been constructed, dominated and maintained by the United States and, mainly, its Western partners (Stokes 2018). Regardless of international rules or international institutions, the United States, as the then unipolar superpower (Hansen 2000), has had the absolute discursive power to serve its own national interests. Moreover, as the 'first citizen' of this US-led (or Western) liberal international order, the United States has been quite used to providing hegemonic leadership in the form of 'anchoring the alliances, stabilising the world economy, fostering cooperation and championing "free world" values' (Ikenberry 2018: 7).[3] This get-used-to-it mindset is to a large extent the psychological source that the United States and its Western allies have difficulty accepting the rise of new great powers represented by China on the international stage (Wang 2013: 62–65). From acceptance of China to the US-led liberal international order, which was symbolised by China's accession to the WTO (Kaczmarski 2015), to the demonisation of China as a destroyer of this rule-based order (Lee 2019), the United States and other Western countries have begun to fully guard against the emergence of a new world order in the name of China,[4] including its accumulating ascendancy in global governance and international lawmaking. Just as President Obama declared to the world early, 'America should write the rules. America should call the shots. Other countries should play by the rules that America and our partners set, and not the other way around' (Obama 2016). More importantly, China cannot be allowed to become the maker of the rules of global trade for the twenty-first century (also see Koh 2018).

[3] In addition, as Roberts and her co-authors (2019: 671) describe, '[h]aving underwritten the creation of almost all major international institutions since the end of the Second World War, the USA is used to (disproportionately) setting the rules of international games'.

[4] Since this so-called new world order is primarily characterised and premised by China's strong economic development momentum, it may be more appropriate to call it a new (geo)economic order (see Parmar 2018; Roberts et al. 2019; Shaffer and Gao 2019).

For some, however, the crisis of the US-led liberal international order, if not the end, 'is more deeply threatened by developments within the West itself' (Ikenberry 2018: 7). These threats arise mainly from the prevalent proliferation of, for instance, populism, nationalism, protectionism, exceptionalism and xenophobia in the context of trade, climate change, migration, sustainability and human rights. As a result, these countries have gradually lost their leadership, credibility and influence on these critical global issues. On the one hand, under such circumstances, it seemingly makes sense that China, which has recently held high the banner of, for instance, deepening free trade, strengthening international economic cooperation through partnership, defending multilateralism, prioritising the rights of survival and development, has become more popular and influential in the international community.

On the other hand, the retreat of the United States (and some of its Western allies) from its role as the superpower to address these major global issues and provide international public goods has, conversely, fuelled the enthusiasm and commitment of cities to make their subnational contributions in these regards. By virtue of at least the elasticity in political decision-making, closeness to the local symptoms of global problems, and direct effectiveness of local policy implementation, a growing number of 'frontier cities' (Oomen and Baumgärtel 2018), as well as the city networks, have either substituted or complemented nation-states to tackle the pressing issues of global governance.[5] Furthermore, with the augmentation of the pertinent practices—rather than merely a 'utopian blueprint' (Curtis 2016b: 174)—among cities across the world, an increasing attention has been paid to the role and influence of cities on the formulation and implementation of international legal rules and/or norms, and vice versa, in recent years (see, representatively, Aust 2015; Blank 2006; Frug 1980; Frug and Barron 2006; Oomen and Baumgärtel 2018; Porras 2008). As a collective identity of these intellectual endeavours, 'International Law and Cities' has made strides towards becoming a newly emerging field of international law.

[5] Although the renaissance of cities in the international fora as an architect of the world order in recent decades is remarkable, it does not necessarily represent the failure of the state. Cities' involvement in this regard is also argued as a part of an emerging form of global order (see Curtis 2016a). This chapter, rather than amplifying the abovementioned distinction, loosely attributes the rising of cities in global governance to the deficiency of nation-states (or the failure of the state).

This chapter is developed out of a comprehensive yet provocative consideration of the abovementioned backdrop against which China's Belt and Road Initiative (BRI) is perceived through the prism of the interaction of cities and international law. It attempts to argue that the explorative path of constructing a great power *of* international law[6] would benefit from the firm commitment of promoting the development of the urban dimension of international law and, in this sense, the BRI, which is geographically composed by cities along the Silk Roads (or the Silk Road cities), actually provides China with an innate platform opportunity to enhance its competitiveness in the politics of international law. Nevertheless, this chapter is more an ideational reminder than a concrete elucidation, inviting (especially the Chinese) policy-makers and international lawyers to pay more attention to the role of cities in the field of international law research and practice. To that end, the remainder of this chapter proceeds as follows. Section "From Exotic to Necessity: China's Evolving Engagement with International Law and BRI" will elaborate on China's evolving engagement with international law and the status of BRI in this process. Section "Old Wine in a New Bottle?: Cities as the New Opportunity for International Law" will focus on the rise of cities and transnational city networks in international law and global governance. Section "'Tasting This Bottle of Wine' with BRI: Implications for China's International Legal Strategy" will mainly explain the relevance and importance of cities for China's projection to an international law powerhouse in the context of BRI. Finally, this chapter will end with a concise conclusion.

From Exotic to Necessity: China's Evolving Engagement with International Law and BRI

As an orthodox Chinese international legal and political discourse, international law is treated as an imported good (or exotic) for China (Jiang 2020: 4). Although the de facto operation of international law, in the

[6] The notion of 'great power of international law' is borrowed from Zhipeng He's journal article 走向国际法的强国 [Toward a Great Power of International Law] (2015), which is interchangeably used with 'international law powerhouse' in this chapter. Four components are identified essential for claiming a great power status in international law, namely international legal theory, practice, talents and education, although a clear-cut definition is not provided. Besides, as to great powers ***and*** international law, generally see Bower (2017), Cai (2013), Simpson (2004).

sense of law among nations, can be traced back to the Spring and Autumn Period and the Warring Period of Ancient China (Carrai 2016), the authentic encounter of China with the international law, the Westphalian system of international law exactly, did not occur until the outbreak of the Opium War in the 1840s (Chan 2014). For China, this encounter was, however, 'not the beginning of a beautiful story, but a tragedy that is counting down' (He and Sun 2015: 42). In the presence of guns, cannons and opiums, to the people of the Qing Dynasty, international law was nothing more than a self-verified passport for Western aggression and colonial rule (Zuo 2018). Thus, the forced interactions with the Western-dominated international law in the nineteenth century laid the foundation for China's negative attitude towards international law—i.e. 'a victim-minded underdog, sceptical of the values and utilities of international law' (Li 2019: 305)—for a long time, albeit accelerating the modernisation of China's legal system was one of the by-products of these interactions as well (Burnay 2017).

The demise of China's last imperial dynasty, unfortunately, does not mean the end of the 'most turbulent, humiliating and miserable period for the nation' (Xue 2012: 14). During the Republic of China, China suffered from civil wars and the War of Resistance Against Japan, which led it to a marginal position in the international legal order, even if it participated in the establishment of the United Nations (UN) as a victor of World War II (Muller 2013a: 46–55). After the founding of New China in 1949, the Communist Party's government was affected by the issue of representation in the UN and thus was excluded from the international legal order (Chai 1970). What's worse, China itself chose to stay away from the Western-dominated international law during this period thanks to the fierce ideological struggles and various political movements, for which even the teaching and research of international law (and law in general) were suspended in all Chinese universities between the 1950s and 1970s (Jiang 2020: 8).

The formulation and implementation of the 1978 Reform and Opening-up policy is a historical turning point in China's engagement with international law (Wang and Hu 2010). Since then, China has not only continuously learned and practised how to engage with the existing international rules and institutions as a 'user' but also tried to provide Chinese wisdom and solutions to their reforms and updates as a 'contributor' (Cai 2015). In addition, more importantly, the voices of Chinese representatives have frequently appeared at the negotiating tables for international lawmaking in emerging areas such as cybersecurity, north and south poles and regional trade. It actually indicates a paradigmatic transformation of China's international legal strategy from merely 'improving its compliance record' to 'seek[ing] more influence in international law-making, which not only enhances China's rise but also may bring about important implications for the international legal order' (Cai 2019: 102). Conceiving this transformation in conjunction with China's tragedy in the 'century of humiliation'—i.e. the nineteen century—could (re)confirm that the core of international law, being used as an instrument to maintain and acquire power and serve the national interest, has never changed.

Against the backdrop of the consistent perception of great powers on the nature of international law, the changes that can be identified readily are the distinctive reactions of other states (or the rest) to the divergence and friction of the Chinese and American (or, generally, the Western liberal) approaches to international law. In fact, due to the USA's obsession with 'the adoption of *its* rules as the *neutral* international rules' (Roberts et al. 2019: 671), the burden and complaints of the rest, generated from the strict requirements of joining and playing the game that has been demarcated by these American neutral rules since its inception, such as implementing structural political reform and respecting 'universal' human rights, has been adeptly ignored. For instance, it is essentially the failure of China's compliance with these neutral rules that cause the United States to reflect on the gamble of permitting China's WTO accession, in which it bet that 'China would head towards democracy and the market economy' (*The Economist* 2018).

China's approach to international law is radically different in the sense that it prioritises the supreme significance of the principles of equal sovereignty and non-interference in the internal affairs of states (Muller 2013b; Zheng 2016), the hardening of which has facilitated the popularity of China's norm entrepreneurship especially in the Global South. The South-South Cooperation in human rights is one of the cogent examples in this regard (Zhao and Mao 2018). With the gene of striving for territorial and sovereign integrity and national rejuvenation, which has been injected into China since, again, the 'century of humiliation', China vows to avoid exporting the Chinese model and requiring other countries to replicate its practices in the international legal interactions. On the contrary, China has begun to capitalise on the establishment of coalitions of the willing with like-minded countries, upgrading it into a methodology of achieving its norm entrepreneurship (Cai 2019: 110). It is about cooperation, not coercion. China possesses a deeper understanding in this regard primarily based on the Confucian idea: 'never impose on others what you would not choose for yourself'. This idea, together with other Confucian ideas and principles, contributes to the differentiation between China and the United States in terms of the approaches to international law, the former of which has increasingly linked to the future of international law in recent years. Because there are, as Zhaojie Li summarises,

> [……] reasons to believe that, as a nation on the rise, China will actively take its rightful place at the head table of world politics and enjoy its attendant prerogatives in becoming centrally involved in further international lawmaking. Thus, future decades will see greater increases in China's influence in reshaping the norms and rules of international law and international institution. (Li 2019: 305)

Such a future may have already started from President Xi's initial proposal of BRI in 2013.[7] Ever since then, BRI[8] has become one of the most animated buzzwords in the international arena, although 'it is remarkable how ambiguous the initiative remains' (Stec 2018). However, this kind of ambiguity, which is also argued to be the flexibility that 'constitutes a further benefit' (Bunting 2019: 18), has not extinguished the enthusiastic welcome of the international community to BRI.[9] BRI, no matter how

[7] It is worth noting that the overall strategy of international law has been fundamentally adapted since President Xi came to power in later 2012, the representative of which refers to the adoption of the 'Decision of the CPC Central Committee on Major Issues Pertaining to Comprehensively Promoting the Rule of Law' (《中共中央关于全面推进依法治国若干重大问题的决定》) in 2014, explicitly articulating that China will 'actively take part in international rule-making, promote the rule of law in dealing with foreign economic and social affairs, enhance China's discursive power and influence in international legal affairs, protect sovereignty, security, and development by legal measures'. It is commented by Congyan Cai (2016: 87) that 'this is a major international legal policy announced by China, which indicates that China's international law practice will enter a brand new historical stage'. As to the relationship between this Decision and China's international law, see also Gu (2017).

[8] This initiative is officially launched by the publication of the 'Vision and Actions on Jointly Building Silk Road Economic Belt and 21st Century Maritime Silk Road' in March 2015. The document is available at: http://english.www.gov.cn/archive/publications/2017/06/20/content_281475691873460.htm (accessed on 27 January 2020).

[9] For instance, as Yitzhak Shichor reflects, '[i]n my study of China over fifty years, I have never seen such enthusiastic welcome to any Chinese policy or idea as the Belt and Road Initiative (BRI). Within a short period of time, the 'New Silk Road' vision (as it has also been called) was picked up by the Chinese and international media and discussed

its nature is conceived and interpreted, has had genuine impacts, primary in the form of policy coordination, infrastructure connectivity, trade and investment cooperation, financial integration and people-to-people collaboration, on the world politically, economically, culturally and *legally* (Garlick 2020; Shichor 2018). Given these impacts, BRI has been largely portrayed as the Chinese plan to forge a new world order within which the deprivation of the dominance of the United States would be plausibly inevitable (Maçães 2018), albeit for some such portrayals are unrealistic in practice (Mai 2018).

Although BRI is also often associated with legal challenges,[10] it is more widely agreed—especially among Chinese scholars—that BRI provides China with a great opportunity to 'become an active player in international rule-making' (Shi 2018: 10) and to 'contribute effectively to the international institutions' (He 2017: 14). In effect, there were three interactions between China and international law after the founding of New China, which could also be loosely viewed as *the* opportunity, namely the Reform and Opening-up, WTO accession and maritime territorial disputes with Japan and the Philippines (Li 2016). However, it is noteworthy that while these three interactions represented China's hands-on efforts to be an 'active status-quo keeper of the present international legal order' (Li 2019: 305),[11] BRI has tellingly expressed its dedication to something new which can be encapsulated, from a legal perspective, into a Chinese approach to BRI. By functionally defining (the scope) of BRI,[12] Heng

in scores of conferences all over the world. Even more significant and of longer value, BRI research institutes and centres have been set up in many universities. Although this initiative was launched only in late 2013, hundreds of articles and dozens of books have already been published on this topic' (Shichor 2018: 40).

[10]The legal challenges to BRI, according to for instance Anh and Ha's (2020) summary, revolve around the divergence between China's BRI practices and the four branches of the international law, namely the current international legal framework on human rights, the development of international environmental law, the applicability of current dispute settlement mechanisms (for BRI projects), the issue of transparency of the BRI, see also Wang (2017).

[11]Although China has participated increasingly in the practices of international law since the Reform and Opening-up, the scope, enthusiasm and effectiveness of its participation have been limited due to the long-term prevalence of the basic principle of China's foreign strategy, namely 'keep a low profile, and do something (韬光养晦,有所作为)' (see Cai 2016: 84).

[12]Given that BRI is 'holistic exercise', i.e. 'China promotes the BRI through all possible means and coordinated efforts', Heng Wang (2019) suggests a functional approach

Wang refines the characteristics of China's present approach to BRI as follows:

> (i) China's shaping of the BRI as a hub-and-spoke network; (ii) the lack of rigid institutions and adoption of a three-track approach towards developing and creating BRI-related institutions and mechanisms; and (iii) the adoption of a dual-track normative approach, making greater use of soft law while also utilising hard law treaties. (H. Wang 2019: 35)

Indeed, since BRI is essentially a China-initiated and -led 'grand connectivity project' (Chung 2018), it can be viewed as a hub-and-spoke network in which China plays the role as a hub physically and ideationally connecting the pertinent countries, institutions, mechanisms, rules, peoples, projects and facilities (H. Wang 2019: 35–36). This perceptible trait implies that BRI itself is neither an international organisation nor an international treaty (J. Wang 2019). Besides, more importantly, this network configuration of BRI connotes China's relational approach to international order, and to international law as well. In the context of BRI, Jianyu Wang (2019: 3) specifically argues that 'China adopts a partnership-based, relational approach in ordering bilateral, regional and global economic cooperation'. Rather than relying on a treaty-based institutional arrangement, China has paid extraordinarily attention to the creation of partnerships with BRI countries. He further commends this relational approach as an alternative model for international order because:

> it features a dominate power which controls the direction of cooperation but is willing to share the power (and responsibility) with other stakeholders to achieve mutual benefits, a system in which the participants do not

to delineate the scope of BRI through which 'various measures that serve the purposes of BRI' are taken into consideration in this regard. In detail, in addition to the Joint Communique of Leaders Roundtable of the Belt and Road Forum for International Cooperation (BRF Joint Communique) and the Belt and Road Forum (BRF) itself, which are argued as the 'rudimentary BRI charter' and the only comprehensive BRI institution, respectively, he divides the measures of BRI in question into the external and internal measures. While the former involves seeking 'recognition, legitimacy, or development of the BRI through engagement with international organisations', the latter mainly encompasses the establishment and operation of the China International Commercial Court (CICC) and various Free Trade Zones (FTZs).

> have to surrender sovereignty as much as they have to do in the America-led liberal international order, and regional economic integration achieved through infrastructure-driven connectivity and an investment-led development model. (J. Wang 2019: 3–4)

BRI deserves this compliment largely due to its insistence on the principle of 'wide consultation, joint contribution, and shared benefits', which 'involves trying to find a generally accepted practice to promote win-win cooperation in international affairs and "building a community of shared destiny for mankind"' (A. He 2016: 14). In effect, each of the three elements of this principle has its own (yet interrelated) implications on international law (Gong 2018). 'Wide consultation' denotes that international lawmaking should be approached through consultation and negotiation on the basis of respecting the fundamental principle of equal sovereignty. In so doing, voices from developing countries can be precisely and equally heard and responded in international legal order and mechanism, the realisation of which is crucial for promoting the democratisation of international law. 'Joint contribution' rather emphasises the motivation of participating in the international lawmaking processes whereby the relevance and effectiveness of the rules in question can be secured. Taken together, 'shared benefits' should be understood as a prospect that all countries can share the fruits of its participation in international lawmaking and achieve mutual benefit and win-win results in the process of international governance.

Old Wine in a New Bottle?: Cities as the New Opportunity for International Law

It is undeniable that 'international law has constantly evolved from its inception' (Trachtman 2013: 1). Among others (e.g. Arend 2015), one evolution that has affected the structural landscape of the Westphalian international law is extremely pronounced. It refers to, in a nutshell, the rise of non-state actors in international law and politics, upon which the establishment and prevalence of a dichotomy of state and non-state actors in international legal circles were based.[13] Indeed, there is a vast body of

[13] Although this dichotomy has prevailed for years, it does not necessarily mean there is uncontested consensus on the categorisation in question. For instance, Sandesh Sivakumaran (2017) argues that in addition to state and non-state actors, there is a third

literature on the intricacies between international law and all actors that are not states, such as individuals, multinational corporations, minority groups, nongovernmental organisations (NGOs) and other civil society actors, the growth of which has even resulted in suspension, querying whether the notion of non-state actors *itself*, as well as their roles in international lawmaking, is 'the result of an actual practice' or 'the outcome of an inclination of scholars to expand their material of study' (d'Aspremont 2010: 182). The existence of such suspicion in 'an epoch of nation-states' (Sihvo 2018: 12) introduced by the Westphalia Treaty in 1648 seems to a large extent plausible. After all, as with what Malcolm Shaw (2008: 47) reminds us, the state-centrism of international law, to which the prioritisation of state consent displayed either expressly or tacitly in the creation of treaties and customs is associated, still remain dominant, albeit it has been interrupted by other non-state entities, 'whose importance is likely to grow even further in the future'.

It is hard to deny Shaw's accuracy in terms of describing the constant dominance of states and the increasing prospect of non-state actors in the making and shaping of international law, whereas he, like most of the international law scholars, has neglected to 'talk' to cities (Burke-White 2019). International lawyers' neglect in this regard runs counter to the actuality that '[t]he past two decades have seen the rapid rise of the city as international actor' (Aust 2018: 228). For the sake of brevity, this section intends to omit the review of the long history of the existence of cities which can be traced back to prehistorical times (Lin 2018: 42). Yet, it should by no means omit to reiterate the rise of cities as '[t]he most important characteristic of the 21st century' (Daalder 2015), with which a variety of global problems that have long perplexed the world of sovereign states are more likely to be solved and/or ameliorated.

The entanglement between cities and the field of climate change is regarded as a 'paradigmatic example' (Oomen and Baumgärtel 2018: 610). By identifying drawbacks[14] in the global climate change regime as the 'common starting point' for envisioning 'novel actors' who are capable to overcome this authentic global challenge (Aust 2015: 261), cities have started to exhibit their ambition and potential in the advancement of

category of actors, i.e. state empowered entities, such as the International Law Commission, the UN Human Rights Committee, lying between state and non-state actors.

[14]The shortcomings of the global climate change governance are arguably associated with its universal, state-centric model (see Hoffmann 2008: 141–142).

climate mitigation and adaptation since as early as the 1990s (Smeds and Acuto 2018: 549). Local authorities, especially mayors of these cities, are the vanguard of the urban actions taken to reduce greenhouse gas emission (GHG) mainly due to mayors' recognition that cities, which are the home for more than half of the world's population and are thus responsible for the largest percentage of human-made carbon dioxide emissions, are on the front line of climate change. More importantly, these mayors have already lost patience with states and cannot wait for them 'to come to terms with climate change' (Barber 2013: 131). The exhausted patience of mayors also oftentimes reflects in the form of their prompt response to central (federal) governments' hesitation in or betrayal of implementing the commitment to climate change action.

For instance, when the Bush administration instead stood up for the 'scientific uncertainty and unfairness' of climate change and decided to withdraw its signature from the Kyoto Protocol, a pro-Kyoto cities initiative, i.e. the US Mayors Climate Change Protection Agreement, was launched by the then Seattle mayor Greg Nickels in 2005 whereby signatory cities pledged to 'meet or beat' the Kyoto Protocol targets in their own communities (Lin 2018: 48).[15] Besides, when another climate-change sceptical president, Donald Trump, announced to pull the United States out of the Paris Climate Agreement in 2017, more than 400 mayors from 48 states of the United States have joined the coalition one after another for seeking to bypass Trump with direct role at UN climate talks and committing to upholding the Agreement.[16] With these responses, mayors and their cities have solidified their special status as 'frontrunners' of climate solutions (Schmidt 2019), upon which for instance the appointment of the UN Special Envoy on Cities and Climate Change is plausible and praiseworthy. However, rather than fighting alone, cities have become adept at participating in the global governance of climate change through 'a sprawling genus of city networks' (Smeds and Acuto 2018: 549). Actually, while the number of city networks in general has surged

[15] In addition, the signatory cities have also pledged to urge their state government, as well as the federal government, to meet or beat the greenhouse gas emission reduction target on the one hand and to urge the US Congress to pass legislation in this regard. As of November 2019, 1066 majors have signed this non-binding agreement. See https://www.usmayors.org/mayors-climate-protection-center/ (accessed on 28 January 2020).

[16] See http://climatemayors.org/actions/paris-climate-agreement/ (accessed on 28 January 2020).

since the 1990s, these networks become more environmentally oriented only in the 2000s (Acuto 2016). Some of the transnational climate networks, such as the C40 Cities Climate Leadership Group, Covenant of Mayors, Climate Alliance of European Cities with Indigenous Rainforest Peoples, Energy Cities, have been well known and significant in curbing climate change thanks to their unique advantages in terms of 'information exchange/networking, lobbying, funding operations, research, target and plan provision, and monitoring and certification' (Lee and Jung 2018: 99).

In addition to climate change, the human rights field has also witnessed the rise of cities and city networks over the past decades as a new type of 'human rights user' (Desmet 2014). By engaging with international human rights in multiform and dynamic ways, an increasing number of cities have claimed themselves as human rights cities, the definition of which is summarised as 'local authorities that explicitly base their policies, or some of them, on human rights as laid down in international treaties, and thus distinguish themselves from other local authorities' (Oomen and van den Berg 2014: 163). In fact, the rise of human rights cities should be understood as a resonation of the disillusion of the utopian vision of universal human rights which has already resulted in a series of reconsiderations of the implementation and effectiveness of human rights from below (De Feyter 2007; Merry 2006). Reconsidering international human rights from below allows cities to circumvent constraints of all kinds on human rights imposed by their national governments and reinvigorate the authentic functions of human rights norms mainly in the form of 'a benchmark in urban policies', 'a unifying force to bring together a variety of actors and interests' and 'a way to demarcate local autonomy legally' (Oomen and van den Berg 2014: 160). Cities like San Francisco, New York, Barcelona, Amsterdam, Rotterdam, Rosario and Graz are typical examples of invoking international human rights law locally, who either focus on the general notion of human rights or certain types of human rights like the hot potato—human rights of migrants and refugees (Baumgärtel and Oomen 2019). Exactly like those cities that act together to address climate problems, local authorities have also undertaken cooperation and coordination through creating networks of human rights cities (Roodenburg 2019).

It is noteworthy that both climate change and human rights are part of the increasing trend of accommodating international law in cities in practice. The growing relevance of cities can be readily identified in more areas of global governance like sustainability and terrorism issues. They have engaged with international law not only as 'takers' or 'enforcers'—although implementing the existing international legal rules has so far been the primary form of the urban participation in the international legal process—but also as 'transnational lawmakers' (Lin 2018). This is the partial reason why a range of soft law instruments have emerged and proliferated in various fields through which local authorities are allowed to both 'borrow (formal) legal language' and project 'an image of flexibility and progressiveness' (Oomen and Baumgärtel 2018: 612). Nevertheless, the softness of cities' norm entrepreneurship should not be merely perceived as a product of intention. On the contrary, it is a pragmatic compromise with the state-centric international system that endows nation-states with the exclusive right to make legally binding international treaties. Furthermore, although the discretion of cities in local policy-making and implementation does facilitate the invocation of international law, the hierarchical relationship between local authorities and national governments is the insurmountable obstacle when the establishment of the so-called 'hard' international law is referred to as the goal of the international action of cities and their networks (Lee and Jung 2018: 98).

Thus, the spotlight moves back to the state-centrism of international system/law in which the formal mechanisms still object to guarantee a place of cities and their networks at the global decision-making table. The cliché of international legal subjecthood and personality is actually never absent to exerting its influence to underappreciate the status of the city. Frug and Barron have a clear understanding of this kind of underappreciation and states:

> Until recently, however, the fact that the global and the local were plainly entwined did not make the legal status of cities a distinct subject of international law. The relationship between a sovereign state and its cities has traditionally been considered an internal domestic matter – the type of issue is outside the orbit of international law. International law was concerned with sovereign nation-states, not the sub-state organs subordinate to them. References to cities are few and far between in the classic texts of international law. Indeed, the field's case books, restatements, treatises, and scholarly articles generally ignore cities together. (Frug and Barron 2006: 12–13)

Indeed, it is of importance to distinguish cities with non-state actors in international law. After all, the former is regarded as the subnational entities whose implementation and violation of the international legal obligation are formally attributed to their respective states.[17] The fundamental international legal reality as such underpins the irreplaceable shade of states covering the urban engagement with international law. Under this shade, cities have either purposefully or unintentionally inherited the quintessence of the Western-dominated (or the US-led) international law, namely treating international law as a tool of power politics, the operation of which, this section emphasises, is another pathway to produce inequality in the dichotomy of dominance and subordination of international law.

First and foremost, it should not be ignored that the majority of attention has focused on global cities[18]—rather than the rest—and their roles in the international legal process and vice versa. It is a truism that 'not all cities are equal' and these global cities are more competent and ambitious to 'shape not just the world's economy but also its ideas, its culture, its policies and future' (Daalder 2015). This is also true for the engagement of cities with international law. To name but a few, Jolene Lin (2018) highlights the overarching role of global cities in transnational lawmaking in the field of climate change; Janne Nijman (2011) distinguishes 'global public city' from 'global private city' and emphasises that the future of international law would be shaped by the rise of the global public cities; Helmut Philipp Aust (2015) believes that global cities' lawmaking processes are starting to influence processes of global governance significantly. However, no matter which global city index and alike are used, it is conspicuous that the world's major 'urban superpowers' are located in developed countries (in either Europe or North America). These urban superpowers, such as New York, Los Angeles, London and Pairs, are unexceptionally the pioneers and activists for the urban engagement with international legal order and global governance, during

[17] UN General Assembly, *Responsibility of States for internationally wrongful acts: Resolution adopted by the General Assembly*, 28 January 2002, A/RES/56/83, available at: https://www.refworld.org/docid/3da44ad10.html (accessed on 23 January 2020).

[18] The concept of global city was coined by the Dutch-American sociologist Saskia Sassen in her seminal work *The Global City: New York, London, Tokyo* (Princeton: Princeton University Press, 1991), upon which her prominent status in this areas is based.

which they are more impactful than other cities on the agenda-setting, discursive development and norm-making.

Moreover, in terms of the existing city networks, they are no more than a curing agent for the inequality and unrepresentativeness of international legal politics. Jennifer Bansard and her co-authors (2017) also identify these drawbacks revolving around the transnational city networks (in the field of climate change) with reference to the empirical data. In a nutshell, their findings are mainly associated with the high concentration of cities and city networks in the Global North (Europe and the United States in particular) and the periphery of cities situated within the developing countries. Accordingly, they reach a quite discouraging conclusion, asserting that city networks 'are not an alternative form of climate governance, but rather replicate existing policy networks mainly among the USA and Europe' (Bansard et al. 2017: 242). In effect, this conclusion is not confined to the field of climate change, but compatible with the overall situation of the extant entanglement among cities, city networks and international legal order. Yet, being pessimistic and denying the potential possibilities that cities can bring to international law—as shown in the previous literature—are of arbitrariness as well. Under such circumstances, it not only requires cities and international lawyers to 'start talking to one another' (Burke-White 2019) but also remains wary that, essentially speaking, the participation of cities in the international legal regime is not a substitution but a ramification of the state-centric Western model of international law. In this sense, it is a new bottle with old wine.

"Tasting This Bottle of Wine" with BRI: Implications for China's International Legal Strategy

To taste this new bottle of old wine is to formulate a nuanced perception of the relevance of cities for a country's capacity and competitiveness in the international legal regime. This perception is vital because it can keep the sovereign states system connected to the rise of urban engagement with international law that has actually sunk the place of politics of international law to localities. Keeping this in mind, the question should not be 'what are the contributions that cities can make to international law on the occasion of state failure?', but rather, more strategically, 'how can the sovereign states make full use of their cities to contribute to their interests in international law and the further development of international law as a whole?'. The relevance of cities and their transnational networks for the sovereign states system in the context of international law was delineated as a duplicate of the dominance of the Global North over the Global South in the previous section, which could be viewed as the negative side of the coin. The reverse side of the same coin could have, however, somewhat positive implications at least in the sense of the possibility of the mutual improvement between the sovereign state and its cities in terms of the development level on international law. In other words, although not an axiom or a necessity, a high development level of international law in cities can promote the development of international law in their country, and vice versa. Sondre Torp Helmersen's (2015) statistics on the most important cities in international law can prove the correlation in question, in which academia, state power, international organisations and courts, and private practice are designed as the four parameters. According to this quantification, the most important cities in international law are (in order of ranking): Washington, New York, Paris, London, Geneva, Brussels, The Hague, Frankfurt, Vienna, Berlin, Rome, Tokyo, Beijing, Luxembourg, Moscow, Nairobi, Strasbourg, Singapore, Cambridge UK, Cambridge MA, New Haven, Oxford, Copenhagen, Stockholm, Oslo. Correspondingly, it would not be objective to deny the importance of their respective countries in international law.

The presence of Beijing in this ranking is benefited from the high score on the parameter of state power, which also implies the efforts that have been made by China to elevate its influence in international regulatory affairs as a new great power. As shown in section "From Exotic to Necessity: China's Evolving Engagement with International Law and BRI", China's attitude towards international law is evolving with its rapid economic development and the ambition of becoming an international law powerhouse has steadily navigated its international legal strategies and practices in various areas. However, it is hard to pinpoint the role played by its cities on the road for China to be assertive in international law. The subject has been exclusively and naturally assigned to the central government and its agencies in almost all matters pertaining to international law ranging from law, policy, planning and alike to academic research.[19] Of course, in addition to the stubborn conception of international legal subjecthood, the peculiar political system operating in China should also be taken into account in this regard, in which the administrative power is highly centralised from the subnational (local) governments to the central government (Kostka and Nahm 2017). Combining with, most importantly, the supremacy of the Chinese Communist Party, it is impossible and illegal for local authorities to adopt and implement their own laws, policies, and initiatives in defiance with the central ones. Under this type of regime, therefore, Chinese cities do not have the courage to commit to being the direct enforcer of the existing international law as well as the motivation to bypass the central government to initiate and join transnational city networks that aim to make new international law.

In this sense, China has lagged far behind the Western countries, especially the United States, which is not compatible with its ambition of being an international law powerhouse. For instance, the cogent evidence of China's lag-behind in this area comes from the dearth of participation in transnational city networks, through which China has closed an important door of taking part in global governance by itself. The harder-hit area is human rights, unsurprisingly. Since none of the cities in China has claimed themselves as human rights cities or been the de facto human rights cities, their absence in various human rights cities is logically understandable. In comparison with the sensitivity of human rights issues, China has taken a more friendly position with respect to the environmental issues, because of which Nanjing, Chengdu, and Qingdao became 'the first Chinese cities' to publicly confirm their commitment to Paris Agreement in the framework of the C40 city networks in 2019.[20] However, confirmation as such should not be purely perceived as the enthusiasm generated, as well as the discretion possessed, by cities themselves. After all, firstly, their commitment confirmed at the international level was always 'witnessed' by the companions of, such as, the Chinese Ministry of Ecology and Environment and Ministry of Foreign

[19] In addition to the topics concerning Hong Kong, Macao and especially Taiwan, the interdisciplinary field of cities and international law itself has been paid little (or even zero real) attention by Chinese international lawyers. See a *quasi-exception* in Zhang (2009).

[20] See https://www.c40.org/press_releases/chinese-cities-commit-to-the-paris-agreement (accessed on 29 January 2020).

Affairs.[21] Secondly, in the process of transforming their oral commitment into the concrete action plans, China's national policies and plans were heavily cited as the cornerstone and benchmark.[22] Besides, it is worth noting that membership of the transnational city networks does necessarily give rise to leadership. Even if in the areas that the Chinese cities have gotten involved, their scarce participation in the leadership of these vital city networks makes them vulnerable in the urban process of global governance (Li 2015).

The BRI could be a panacea that provides China and the world with new hope in both the national and subnational dimensions of international law. To a large extent, this is determined by the *very* nature of BRI as an umbrella initiative which has 'no clear and widely accepted statement of' its scope (H. Wang 2019: 31). The ambiguity in terms of the scope of BRI is instead praised as the 'adaptive management' approach (He 2017) or the 'trial-and-error' approach (H. Wang 2019), the core of which is to be flexible enough to continually fine-tune the normative and institutional systems 'according to real situations and new ideas' (He 2017: 32). Premised on this nature, BRI can adequately accommodate the new ideas and practices of 'cities and international law'.

As a grand connectivity initiative, as of January 2020, BRI has already gathered 138 countries across Asia, Europe and Africa and 30 international organisations together by signing 200 cooperation agreements.[23] However, it is more important to know that BRI has also connected thousands of cities located in these countries, among which, according to the statistics of the 65 countries along the Belt and Road, there are

[21] Ibid.

[22] For instance, the preamble of the '13th Five-Year Climate Action Plan of Beijing' (《北京市"十三五"期间应对气候变化规划》), which was issued by the municipal government of Beijing in 2016, explicitly declares that this Plan is based on, to name but few, the 'Recommendations for the 13th Five-Year Plan for Economic and Social Development' (《中共中央关于制定国民经济和社会发展第十三个五年规划的建议》), 'Outline of the 13th Five-Year Plan for the National Economic and Social Development of the People's Republic of China' (《中华人民共和国国民经济和社会发展第十三个五年规划纲要》), 'National Plan on Climate Change (2014–2020)' (《国际应对气候变化规划(2014-2020)》), 'National Plan on Adaptation to Climate Change' (《国家适应气候变化战略), 'Urban Action Plan for Adaptation to Climate Change' (《城市适应气候变化行动方案》). Document available at: http://www.beijing.gov.cn/zfxxgk/110001/szfwj/2016-08/07/content_c7607556c0e74fe58c1c85a5d25183b6.shtml (accessed on 29 January 2020).

[23] Data source available at: https://www.yidaiyilu.gov.cn/gbjg/gbgk/77073.htm (accessed on 29 January 2020).

974 cities with a population of more than 300,000 and 274 major cities with a population of more than one million (Su and Yang 2017: 76). These cities can share, in a broader sense, one name the 'Silk Road Cities' which are often honourably paralleled with the 'Cities alongside the Silk Roads'[24] in ancient time. Apart from these Silk Road cities inside China, Bangkok, Almaty, Moscow, Hamburg, Istanbul, Seoul, Budapest, Saint Petersburg, Prague, Berlin, Busan, Ho Chi Minh City, Cologne and Dubai are regarded as the most important pivot cities (Tu 2019). International organisations and other city networks have also recognised the importance of these Silk Road cities as a whole. The Belt and Road Sustainable Cities Alliance, which was jointly initiated and launched by, for example, the UN Human Settlements Programme, World Health Organization and Energy Foundation, is a good example of this recognition.[25] Moreover, the importance of the Silk Road cities has even been upgraded to the level of challenging 'the "Global Cities" that have thrived during the U.S. led liberal global order', as Ian Klaus and Simon Curtis observe (although seems pessimistic):

> [w]hereas the "Global City" emerged alongside the rise of finance, financial services, and the intermediary relationships needed to further such exchange, Belt and Road cities appear to prioritize infrastructure, supply chain management, legal zoning techniques, and connectivity. And whereas the "Global City" was populated by, at least in part, a nomadic professional class, the Belt and Road City seems to prioritize the needs of Chinese nationals and firms. And whereas the "Global City" coupled liberalism and increasing inequality, the Belt and Road City assumes for urban areas none of the freedoms that have long been associated with cities. (Klaus and Curtis 2019)

Reifying BRI with cities opens a door for China to deepen its approaches to international law largely due to the endogenous compatibility between the logic of the field of international law and cities and the logic of China's approach to BRI (in the legal sense), although policy-makers and international lawyers (especially in China) have not paid sufficient attention to this. As indicated in section "From Exotic

[24] See https://en.unesco.org/silkroad/silk-road-themes/cities-alongside-silk-roads (accessed on 29 January 2020).

[25] See http://fgw.sxxz.gov.cn/bmdt/201905/t20190509_2935428.html (accessed on 29 January 2020).

to Necessity: China's Evolving Engagement with International Law and BRI", after a long period of engagement with international law, BRI is qualified as a flagship product of China's international legal wisdom which simultaneously prioritises partnership in a hub-and-spoke network and soft law. Likewise, the rise of cities in international law (and global governance) is also characterised by, as displayed in section "Old Wine in a New Bottle?: Cities as the New Opportunity for International Law", networking activities and transnational soft lawmaking. Therefore, both network and soft law are the intersection at which the discussion of these Silk Road cities can make sense. Because of the connectivity nature of BRI, the Silk Road cities are a network by nature as well; and this network is distinguished from those of the theme-based model (Fontana 2017: 18–21). In the light of the ambiguous scope of BRI, the Silk Road cities network is not independently about human rights, climate change, sustainability, energy and so forth, but could be all of them. The operation of this composite network of cities is both benefited from and further conducive to the relational normativity of international law, i.e. creating and maintaining partnership (relationship) 'in such a way as to create a fertile soil in which existing norms can find an application, and new ones can gain root' (Vanhullebusch 2018: 6). More importantly, unlike the participation of China's cities in the existing transnational city networks, it seems reasonable for these Chinese cities to take advantage of the leadership opportunities in the network constituted by the Silk Road cities.

Therefore, China's ambition of becoming an international law powerhouse should seriously take account of these Silk Road cities, for which many actions can be taken at both the strategic and operational levels of international law. Explaining all of them is beyond the aim and scope of this chapter, however. Relying on the components of great power *of* international law (He 2015), there are at least four aspects that China needs to (re)consider. Firstly, in terms of international legal theory, it is necessary for China to excavate and mine further the theoretical connotation and extension of the relational approach to international law which has emerged from BRI. As a potential candidate for replacing, or more effectively complementing at least, the liberal international legal theory upon which the predominance of the United States and other Western countries in international legal politics have been based, a relational approach to international law should instead emphasise the primacy of relationships 'between the decision-makers within global governance bodies, between those bodies (of different organizations [international and regional alike]), between (individual) decision-makers and those subject to their decisions, between the different (non-) state actors on the ground' (Vanhullebusch 2018: 6). The primacy of relationships requires Chinese international lawyers—most of them are legal positivists—to be open-minded and willing to compromise with the empirical turn in international legal scholarship (Shaffer and Ginsbury 2012). This compromise would eliminate the metatheoretical barrier of embracing the insights generated from the emerging field of international law and cities. Furthermore, the compromise in question would also facilitate the cross-fertilisation between BRI's relational approach and other pertinent approaches in international law, especially the social network analysis and international law (Puig 2018).

The first (re)consideration concerning international legal theory has radical implications for the remaining three components of an international law powerhouse, namely international legal practice, talents and education, which will be briefly discussed. As to international legal practice, due to the acceptance of the participation of various actors that are not state in international law, China should delegate more power from the central government to local authorities, guaranteeing more policy space for them and most importantly incentivising them initiate and contribute urban agenda on global and regional governance among the Silk Road cities. Besides, there is a possible pathway for China to achieve its norm entrepreneurship through Chinese cities' leadership in the Silk Road cities network. Concerning international legal talents, among others, it is essential for China to alter the assumption that the role of international legal talents, especially international legal scholars, in international legal practice can be assessed only from international and national perspectives. In other words, international legal talents are neither only those who can represent China to sit on the negotiating tables, stand in international courts, work for international institutions, nor those who can serve the central government and its agencies as diplomats, legislators, judges, and brain-trusters. On the contrary, international legal talents should also refer to those who are adept in both international law and urban governance. In this sense, China should firstly revise the mechanism of 'conscription' and 'distribution' in terms of international legal talents, in which the balance should lean more towards urban level. The second response to the problem concerning international legal talents is associated with China's international legal education. In a nutshell, the main point is that realising China's ambition of becoming an international law powerhouse through cities gives rise to a question mark as to the cosmopolitan and internationalist vision of international law towards which international legal education in China has attempted to move. Chinese international law students have gotten so used to *the* international law, which has been proved not as international as they thought (Roberts 2017). In fact, the international community has witnessed a variety of national approaches to international law, the difference of which—including the urban dimension of international law—should be taught in international law classes.

Conclusion

To sum up, this chapter has led us through an evolving process of China's engagement with international law which marks the psychological transition of China from an international law-taker to an international lawmaker in a US-led international regime. It indicated that the adoption and implementation of BRI have reached the pinnacle of China's assertive stance in international law, in which a partnership-based relational approach to especially international economic order has been adopted as one of the fundamental characteristics of China's approach to BRI. This chapter generally appreciated the efforts that have been made by China in this regard but further argued that its ambition of becoming an international law powerhouse could be facilitated by paying nuanced attention to the increasing role of cities in international law and global governance. The rise of cities and their networks, as this chapter underscored, has not only provided new opportunities for international law and global governance but also played a role as the curing agent for the inequality and unrepresentativeness generated by the ongoing international legal politics. Besides, a correlation was discerned between the cities and their respective nation-states in terms of the development of international law. From this point of view, this chapter asserted a gap between China's growing ambition in international law and its sluggishness on the urban development of international law. Taken all together, BRI was upgraded as the antidote with which China can take advantage of the Silk Road cities and its integrated network to deepen the relational approach to international law, which was claimed by this chapter as a potential candidate for replacing and/or competing with the US-led liberal approach to international law.

References

Acuto, Michele (2016), "Give Cities a Seat at the Top Table", in *Nature*, 537(7622), 611–613.

Anh, Nguyen Thi Lan and Ha, Mai Ngan (2020), "Legal Challenges to the Belt and Road Initiative", in Chong, Alan and Pham, Quang Minh (eds.), *Critical Reflections on China's Belt & Road Initiative*, Palgrave Macmillan, Singapore, 159–174.

Arend, Anthony Clark (2015), "The Evolution of International Law", in Mcneill, J.R. and Pomeranz, Kenneth (eds.), *The Cambridge World History: Volume 7, Production, Destruction and Connection, 1750–Present, Part 1, Structures, Spaces, and Boundary Making: Vol. VII*, Cambridge University Press, Cambridge, 285–305.

Aust, Helmut Philipp (2015), "Shining Cities on the Hill? The Global City, Climate Change, and International Law", in *European Journal of International Law*, 26(1), 255–278.

Aust, Helmut Philipp (2018), "Good Urban Citizen", in Hohmann, Jessie and Joyce, Daniel (eds.), *International Law's Objects*, Oxford University Press, Oxford, 225–233.

Bansard, Jennifer S. et al. (2017), "Cities to the Rescue? Assessing the Performance of Transnational Municipal Networks in Global Climate Governance", in *International Environmental Agreements: Politics, Law and Economics*, 17(2), 229–246.

Barber, Benjamin R. (2013), *If Mayors Ruled the World: Dysfunctional Nations, Rising Cities*, Yale University Press, New Haven and London.

Baumgärtel, Moritz and Oomen, Barbara (2019), "Pulling Human Rights Back In? Local Authorities, International Law and the Reception of Undocumented Migrants", in *Journal of Legal Pluralism and Unofficial Law*, 51(2), 172–191.

Bermingham, Finbarr (2020), "China's Trade War Deal 'May Be Doomed from Start' as Scepticism Mounts Overcapacity to Buy US Products", in *South China Morning Post*, 21 January 2020, available at: https://www.scmp.com/economy/china-economy/article/3047018/chinas-trade-war-deal-may-be-doomed-start-scepticism-mounts%0A.

Blank, Yishai (2006), "Localism in the New Global Legal Order", in *Harvard International Law Journal*, 47(1), 263–281.

Bower, Adam (2017), *Norms Without the Great Powers: International Law and Changing Social Standards in World Politics*, Oxford University Press, Oxford.

Breslin, Shaun (2019), "China in 2018: Presidents, Politics, and Power", in *Asian Survey*, 59(1), 21–34.

Bunting, Laura (2019), "The New Great Game in Central Asia? The Belt and Road Initiative and Its Implications for Sino-Russian Relations", in Yang, Yi Edward and Wei, Liang (eds.), *Challenges to China's Economic Statecraft: A Global Perspective*, Lexington Books, Lanham, Boulder, New York and London, 13–32.

Burke-White, William (2019), "Cities and International Lawyers Need to Start Talking to One Another", in *Diplomatic Courier*, 22 November 2019, available at: https://www.diplomaticourier.com/posts/cities-and-international-lawyers-need-to-start-talking-to-one-another.

Burnay, Matthieu (2017), "'Soft Legal Transplants': EU-China Relations at a Glance", in Men, Jing and Linck, Annika (eds.), *China and EU: Reform and Governance*, Routledge, Abingdon and New York, 17–32.

Cai, Congyan (2013), "New Great Powers and International Law in the 21st Century", in *European Journal of International Law*, 24(3), 755–795.

Cai, Congyan (2015), "China as an Acceptor of, User of and Contributor to the Investment Treaty Regime", in *ICSID Review—Foreign Investment Law Journal*, 30(3), 752–755.

Cai, Congyan (2016), "中国国际法学者在国际法实践中的作用 [The Roles of International Legal Scholars in the Practice of International Law]", in 中国法律评论 [*China Law Review*], 3(2), 74–87.

Cai, Congyan (2019), *The Rise of China and International Law: Taking Chinese Exceptionalism Seriously*, Oxford University Press, New York.

Carrai, Maria Adele (2016), "Current Chinese Approaches to a Global History of International Law", in *Storica*, 64(XXII), 23–44.

Chai, Winberg (1970), "China and the United States: Problems of Representation and Alternatives", in *Asian Survey*, 10(5), 397–409.

Chan, Phil C. W. (2014), "China's Approaches to International Law Since the Opium War", in *Leiden Journal of International Law*, 27(4), 859–892.

Chung, Chien-peng (2018), "What are the Strategic and Economic Implications for South Asia of China's Maritime Silk Road Initiative?", in *The Pacific Review*, 31(3), 315–332.

Curtis, Simon (2016a), "Cities and Global Governance: State Failure or a New Global Order?", in *Millennium: Journal of International Studies*, 44(3), 455–477.

Curtis, Simon (2016b), *Global Cities and Global Order*, Oxford University Press, Oxford.

Daalder, Ivo (2015), "A New Global Order of Cities", in *Financial Times*, 26 May 2015, available at: https://www.ft.com/content/a5230756-0395-11e5-a70f-00144feabdc0.

d'Aspremont, Jean (2010), "International Law-Making by Non-State Actors: Changing the Model or Putting the Phenomenon into Perspective?", in Noortmann, Math and Ryngaert, Cedric (eds.), *Non-State Actor Dynamics in International Law: From Law-Takers to Law-Makers*, Ashgate, London and New York, 171–194.

Dean, James (2019), "Doubts Arise Over US-China Trade Deal: Markets Unsettled as Analysts Criticise Viability of Agreement", in *The Times*, 15 October 2019, available at: https://www.thetimes.co.uk/article/wall-street-grows-wary-of-china-trade-deal-jjznlrw8c%0A.

De Feyter, Koen (2007), "Localising Human Rights", in Benedek, Wolfgang et al. (eds.), *Economic Globalisation and Human Rights*, Cambridge University Press, Cambridge, 67–92.

Desmet, Ellen (2014), "Analysing Users' Trajectories in Human Rights: A Conceptual Exploration and Research Agenda", in *Human Rights & International Legal Discourse*, 8(2), 121–141.

The Economist (2018), "How the West Got China Wrong", in *The Economist*, 1 March 2018, available at: https://www.economist.com/leaders/2018/03/01/how-the-west-got-china-wrong%0A.

Fontana, Federico (2017), "City Networking in Urban Strategic Planning", in Karakitsiou, Athanasia et al. (eds.), *City Networks: Collaboration and Planning for Health and Sustainability*, Springer, Cham, 17–38.

Frug, Gerald E. (1980), "The City as a Legal Concept", in *Harvard Law Review*, 93(6), 1057–1154.

Frug, Gerald E. and Barron, David J. (2006), "International Local Government Law", in *Urban Lawyer*, 38(1), 1–62.

Garlick, Jeremy (2020), *The Impact of China's Belt and Road Initiative: From Asia and Europe*, Routledge, Abingdon and New York.

Gong, Bohua (2018), ""三共"原则是构建人类命运共同体的国际法基石 [The Principle of 'Wide Consultation, Joint Contribution, and Shared Benefits' is the International Law Foundation of Building a Community of Shared Destiny for Mankind]", in *东方法学* [*Oriental Law*], 61(1), 30–37.

Gu, Zuxue (2017), "International Law as the Law of Domestic Governance: China's Propositions and Institutional Practice", in *Social Sciences in China*, 38(3), 157–174.

Hansen, Birthe (2000), "The Unipolar World Order and Its Dynamics", in Hansen, Birthe and Heurlin, Bertel (eds.), *The New World Order: Contrasting Theories*, Palgrave Macmillan, London, 112–133.

He, Alex (2016), *The Dragon's Footprints: China in the Global Economic Governance System Under the G20 Framework*, McGill-Queen's University Press, Montreal.

He, Zhipeng (2015), "走向国际法的强国 [Toward a Great Power of International Law]", in *当代法学* [*Contemporary Law Review*], 29(1), 148–160.

He, Zhipeng (2017), "The 'Belt and Road' Initiative and China's Exploration in the Construction of International Institutions", in *Journal of WTO and China*, 7(2), 14–34.

He, Zhipeng and Sun, Lu (2015), "中国的国际法观念:基于国际关系史的分析 [China's Conception of International Law: An Analysis Based on the History of International Relations]", in *国际关系与国际法学刊* [*Journal of International Relations and International Law*], 5, 42–94.

Helmersen, Sondre Torp (2015), "The Most Important Cities in International Law", in *EJIL: Talk!*, 8 June 2015, available at: https://www.ejiltalk.org/the-most-important-cities-in-international-law/.

Hoffmann, Matthew J. (2008), "The Global Regime: Current Status of and Quo Vadis for Kyoto", in Bernstein, Steven et al. (eds.), *A Globally Integrated Climate Policy for Canada*. University of Toronto Press, Toronto, Buffalo and London, 137–157.

Ikenberry, G. John (2018), "The End of Liberal International Order?", in *International Affairs*, 94(1), 7–23.

Jiang, Shisong (2020), "Charting Socio-Legal Approaches to International Law in China: Taking the Interdisciplinary Study of International Law and History as an Example", in *Academic Journal of Interdisciplinary Studies*, 9(1), 1–15.

Kaczmarski, Marcin (2015), *Russia-China Relations in the Post-Crisis International Order*, Routledge, Abingdon and New York.

Klaus, Ian and Curtis, Simon (2019), "Cities of the New Silk Roads", in *Diplomatic Courier*, 27 November 2019, available at: https://www.diplomaticourier.com/posts/cities-of-the-new-silk-roads.

Koh, Harold Hongju (2018), "The Trump Administration and International Law: A Reply", in *Opinio Juris*, 16 October 2018, available at: http://opiniojuris.org/2018/10/16/the-trump-administration-and-international-law-a-reply/.

Kostka, Genia and Nahm, Jonas (2017), "Central-Local Relations: Recentralization and Environment Governance in China", in *The China Quarterly*, 231, 567–582.

Lee, Ann (2019), "The Road to War with China", in *Project Syndicate*, 26 April 2019, available at: https://www.project-syndicate.org/commentary/america-hostile-foreign-policy-toward-china-by-ann-lee-1-2019-04%0A.

Lee, Taedong and Jung, Ha Yoon (2018), "Mapping City-to-City Networks for Climate Change Action: Geographic Bases, Link Modalities, Functions, and Activity", in *Journal of Cleaner Production*, 182, 96–104.

Li, Ming (2016), "国际法与"一带一路"研究 [International Law and the Study on the Belt and Road Initiative]", in *法学杂志* [*Law Science Magazine*], 38(1), 148–160.

Li, Xinlei (2015), "跨国城市网络在全球气候治理中的体系反思:"南北分割"视域下的网络等级性 [The Systematic Reflection of the Transnational Municipal Networks in Global Climate Governance: The Networking Hierarchy from the Perspective of 'North-South Division']", in *太平洋学报* [*Pacific Journal*], 23(7), 38–49.

Li, Zhaojie (2019), "China", in Chesterman, Simon et al. (eds.), *The Oxford Handbook of International Law in Asia and the Pacific*, Oxford University Press, Oxford, 299–319.

Lin, Jolene (2018), *Governing Climate Change: Global Cities and Transnational Lawmaking*, Cambridge University Press, Cambridge.

Maçães, Bruno (2018), *Belt and Road: A Chinese World Order*, Hurst, London.

Mai, Jun (2018), "China's New World Order 'Unrealistic' if Built on Belt and Road Alone, Senior US Diplomatic Observer Says", in *South China Morning Post*, 28 September 2018, available at: https://www.scmp.com/news/china/diplomacy/article/2166159/chinas-new-world-order-unrealistic-if-built-belt-and-road-alone%0A.

Merry, Sally Engle (2006), *Human Rights and Gender Violence: Translating International Law into Local Justice*, The University of Chicago Press, Chicago and London.

Muller, Wim (2013a), *Beyond History and Sovereignty: China and the Future of International Law*, PhD Thesis, European University Institute, available at: http://cadmus.eui.eu/bitstream/handle/1814/29599/2013_Muller_Wim_LAW.pdf?sequence=1&isAllowed=y.

Muller, Wim (2013b), "China's Sovereignty in International Law: From Historical Grievance to Pragmatic Tool", in *China-EU Law Journal*, 1(3–4), 35–59.

Nijman, Janne (2011), "The Future of the City and the International Law of the Future", in Sam, Muller et al. (eds.), *The Law of the Future and the Future of Law*, Torkel Opsahl Academic EPublisher, The Hague, 213–230.

Obama, Barack (2016), "The TPP Would Let America, not China, Lead the Way on Global Trade", in *The Washington Post*, 2 May 2016, available at: https://www.washingtonpost.com/opinions/president-obama-the-tpp-would-let-america-not-china-lead-the-way-on-global-trade/2016/05/02/680540e4-0fd0-11e6-93ae-50921721165d_story.html%0A.

Oomen, Barbara and Baumgärtel, Moritz (2018), "Frontier Cities: The Rise of Local Authorities as an Opportunity for International Human Rights Law", in *European Journal of International Law*, 29(2), 607–630.

Oomen, Barbara and van den Berg, Esther (2014), "Human Rights Cities: Urban Actors as Pragmatic Idealistic Human Rights Users", in *Human Rights & International Legal Discourse*, 8(2), 160–185.

Parmar, Inderjeet (2018), "The US-led Liberal Order: Imperialism by Another Name?", in *International Affairs*, 94(1), 151–172.

Porras, Ileana M. (2008), "The City and International Law: In Pursuit of Sustainable Development", in *Fordham Urban Law Journal*, 36(3), 537–601.

Puig, Sergio (2018), "Network Analysis and the Sociology of International Law", in Moshe, Hirsch and Andrew, Lang (eds.), *Research Handbook on the Sociology of International Law*, Edward Elgar Publishing, Cheltenham and Northampton, 319–332.

Roberts, Anthea (2017), *Is International Law International?* Oxford University Press, New York.

Roberts, Anthea et al. (2019), "Toward a Geoeconomic World Order in International Trade and Investment", in *Journal of International Economic Law*, 22(4), 655–676.

Roodenburg, Lisa (2019), "Urban Approaches to Human Rights: Tracking Networks of Engagement in Amsterdam's Debate on Irregular Migration", in *Journal of Legal Pluralism and Unofficial Law*, 51(2), 192–212.

Schmidt, Jake (2019), "Trump Recklessly Formalizes U.S. Withdrawal from the Pairs Agreement", in *Expert Blog of NRDC*, 4 November 2019, available at: https://www.nrdc.org/experts/jake-schmidt/trump-recklessly-formalizes-us-withdrawal-paris-agreement.

Shaffer, Gregory and Gao, Henry S. (2019), "A New Chinese Economic Law Order?", in *UC Irvine School of Law Research Paper*, No. 2019-21, available at: https://www.law.uci.edu/faculty/full-time/shaffer/pdfs/2019-new-chinese-economic-law-order.pdf.

Shaffer, Gregory and Ginsbury, Tom (2012), "The Empirical Turn in International Legal Scholarship", in *The American Journal of International Law*, 106(1), 1–46.

Shambaugh, David (2018), "U.S.-China Rivalry in Southeast Asia: Power Shift or Competitive Coexistence?", in *International Security*, 42(4), 85–127.

Shaw, Malcolm N. (2008), *International Law*, Sixth Edition, Cambridge University Press, Cambridge.

Shi, Jingxia (2018), "The Belt and Road Initiative and International Law: An International Public Goods Perspective", in Zhao, Yun (ed.), *International Governance and the Rule of Law in China Under the Belt and Road Initiative*, Cambridge University Press, Cambridge, 9–31.

Shichor, Yitzhak (2018), "China's Belt and Road Initiative Revisited: Challenges and Ways Forward", in *China Quarterly of International Strategic Studies*, 4(1), 39–53.

Sihvo, Olena (2018), "Global Constitutionalism and the Idea of Progress", in *Helsinki Law Review*, 12(1), 10–34.

Simpson, Gerry (2004), *Great Powers and Outlaw States: Unequal Sovereigns in the International Legal Order*, Cambridge University Press, New York.

Sivakumaran, Sandesh (2017), "Beyond States and Non-State Actors: The Role of State-Empowered Entities in the Making and Shaping of International Law", in *Columbia Journal of Transnational Law*, 55(2), 343–394.

Smeds, Emilia and Acuto, Michele (2018), "Networking Cities After Paris: Weighing the Ambition of Urban Climate Change Experimentation", in *Global Policy*, 9(4), 549–559.

Stec, Grzegorz (2018), "China's Belt and Road Initiative Is Neither a Strategy, Nor a Vision: It Is a Process", in *EU-Asia at a Glance*, available at: https://www.eias.org/wp-content/uploads/2016/03/EU_Asia_at_a_Glance_Stec_BRI_2018-1.pdf.

Stokes, Doug (2018), "Trump, American Hegemony and the Future of the Liberal International Order", in *International Affairs*, 94(1), 133–150.

Su, Ning and Yang, Chuankai (2017), ""丝路城市":"一带一路"沿线城市节点的特征与发展意义 [Silk Road City: The Characteristics and Development Trends of City Pivots in Belt and Road Region]", in *世界经济研究* [*World Economy Studies*], 36(8), 74–83.

Trachtman, Joel P. (2013), *The Future of International Law: Global Governance*, Cambridge University Press, New York.

Tu, Qiyu (ed.) (2019), *国际城市蓝皮书:国际城市发展报告(2019)*[*Blue Book of World Cities: Report of the Development of World Cities*], 社会科学文献出版社. Social Sciences Academic Press, Beijing.

Vanhullebusch, Matthias (2018), *Global Governance, Conflict and China*, Brill Nijhoff, Leiden and Boston.

Wang, Guiguo (2017), "Legal Challenges to the Belt and Road Initiative", in *Journal of International and Comparative Law*, 4(2), 309–330.

Wang, Heng (2019), "China's Approach to the Belt and Road Initiative: Scope, Character and Sustainability", in *Journal of International Economic Law*, 22(1), 29–55.

Wang, Hung-jen (2013), *The Rise of China and Chinese International Relations Scholarship*, Lexington Books, Lanham and Plymouth.

Wang, Jiangyu (2019), "China's Governance Approach to the Belt and Road Initiative (BRI): Relations, Partnership, and Law", in *NUS Law Working Paper*, 2019/005, available at: https://law.nus.edu.sg/wps/pdfs/005_2019_WangJiangyu.pdf.

Wang, Zonglai and Hu, Bin (2010), "China's Reform and Opening-up and International Law", in *Chinese Journal of International Law*, 9(1), 193–203.

Xue, Hanqin (2012), *Chinese Contemporary Perspectives on International Law: History, Culture and International Law*, Brill Nijhoff, Leiden and Boston.

Zhang, Weibin (2009), "次国家政府的国际法律人格探讨——兼论我国台湾地区参与国际事务问题 [The International Legal Personality of Subnational Government and Taiwan's Participation in International Affairs]", in *广东行政学院学报* [*Journal of Guangdong Institute of Public Administration*], 21(5), 55–59.

Zhao, Shuku and Mao, Kui (2018), "南南人权治理中的中国贡献:理念与实践——以全球人权治理为视域 [China's Contribution of Ideas and Practices in the South-South Human Rights Governance: From the Horizon of Global Human Rights Governance]", in 人权 [*Human Rights*], 18(1), 29–39.

Zheng, Chen (2016), "China Debates the Non-Interference Principle", in *The Chinese Journal of International Politics*, 9(3), 349–374.

Zheng, Yu (2019), "Observations on China-US Strategic Competition and Its Development Trend", in *China-US Focus*, 14 March 2019, available at: https://www.chinausfocus.com/foreign-policy/observations-on-china-us-strategic-competition-and-its-development-trend.

Zuo, Anlei (2018), "China's Approaches to the Western-dominated International Law: A Historical Perspective from the Opium War to the South China Sea Arbitration", in *University of Baltimore Journal of International Law*, 6(1), 21–55.

Construction of the International Commercial Mediation Mechanism Under BRI: A Comparative Study Perspective

Huichun Liu

Introduction

After 'the initiative of jointly building the Silk Road Economic Belt and the 21st Century Maritime Silk Road' (hereinafter referred to as the Belt and Road Initiative, or BRI, or Belt and Road, or One Belt and One Road) was proposed in 2013, it has won positive responses in Asia, Africa and Europe. More than 70 countries have participated in the Belt and Road Initiative which aims to build connectivity and cooperation between China, the land-based Silk Road Economic Belt, and the twenty-first century Maritime Silk Road. Focusing on the objectives to construct a unified large market and make full use of both international and domestic markets, the Belt and Road Initiative has become one of the largest infrastructure and investment projects in history across the Asia Pacific area, Africa and Central and Eastern Europe. However, the increased amount of the investment and trade under the road and belt initiative implies the potential disputes between different entities. To solve the disputes related to BRI, disputants may choose consultation, mediation,

H. Liu (✉)
Human Rights Research Institute of Guangzhou University, Guangzhou, China
e-mail: rally336@163.com

G. Martinico and X. WU (eds.), *A Legal Analysis of the Belt and Road Initiative*, https://doi.org/10.1007/978-3-030-46000-6_13

conciliation, expert determination, neutral evaluation, arbitration or litigation. However, because of the different legal culture and legal system, dispute resolution by litigation will be a big obstacle to overcome, which justifies the alternative dispute resolutions (ADRs) the priority for the settlement of the disputes under BRI. As a universally adopted means for the international commercial disputes, mediation can act separately from or integrally with arbitration for the disputes settlement for the BRI countries. In this article, an attempt to study the possibility of the application of mediation as dispute resolution method will be conducted, and visionary suggestions will be explored for the construction of the mediation mechanism under the BRI.

Mediation and Conciliation and Their Efficacy

In international commercial dispute resolution, arbitration is universally acknowledged due to its advantageous principles like party autonomy, flexibility, fastness and binding force. Standing by arbitration, there are other alternative forms of dispute resolution, among which, mediation and conciliation should be of the second largest importance compared with arbitration.

Unlike arbitration, mediation and conciliation do not provide a binding decision upon the parties. Mediators and conciliators are not empowered to decide the dispute of the parties, but act as catalysts to reach a resolution acceptable to all parties of the dispute (Dress 1988). Noting that the dispute settlement methods referred to as mediation and conciliation are increasingly used in international and domestic commercial practice as an alternative to litigation, the United Nations Commission on International Trade Law (UNCITRAL) issued a model law on the international commercial conciliation to cater to the rapid development of the international trade and e-commerce. According to UNCITRAL Model Law on International Commercial Conciliation,

> 'conciliation' means a process, whether referred to by the expression conciliation, mediation or an expression of similar import, whereby parties request a third person or persons ('the conciliator') to assist them in their attempt to reach an amicable settlement of their dispute arising out of or relating to a contractual or other legal relationship. The conciliator

does not have the authority to impose upon the parties a solution to the dispute.[1]

Starting from the definition of 'conciliation' under the UNCITRAL Model Law, mediation and conciliation refers to the same process for dispute resolution. It utilises a third-party neutral, who works with the parties to settle their dispute arising out of or relating to their contractual or other legal relationship in a friendly way. Unlike arbitrators who need to make the arbitral award after hearing a case, conciliators or mediators have no authority to impose a dispute solution upon the parties. They can guide the parties to discuss the dispute and provide their suggestions or recommendations, but the persuasion of the conciliators or mediators shall never be binding on the disputing parties unless they agree to turn it into an arbitral award.

For purposes of this discussion, the term of 'mediation' will be mostly used, but the term 'conciliation' will be used, as well. They may interchange each other, or both of them will be used together as a combined phrase. One reason for this replacement or overlap is that as an ADR, they share sameness or tremendous similarity as far as their binding force is concerned. The other reason lies in that, in spite of their specific difference in their processes of fact findings and dispute resolution, both the conciliators and the mediators act as the third party, who guides the disputants to solve their legal disputes and provide suggestions and recommendations for the disputants. Be referring mediation and conciliation as the same, this discussion does not ignore the difference between these two terms, especially when they are used in international commercial dispute resolution. To mention some aspects of their difference for example, in mediation, the primary role of the mediator is to facilitate dialogue and communication among the parties in a structured, constructive way. But for the international commercial conciliation, conciliation is a more formal process than mediation, in which the conciliator hears evidence, discusses options with the parties, prepares written recommendations and engages in preliminary fact finding and investigation to facilitate the dispute resolution (Dress 1988). For the purpose of communication in mediation, mediators should be realistic and flexible. Therefore, the position of a mediator is more appropriately to be defined as 'fair proximity'

[1] UNCITRAL Model Law on International Commercial Conciliation (2002), Article 1.

rather than 'equidistance' because he works for the parities without prejudice (Giarrusso 2010). On the other hand, conciliators should be objective and just throughout the proceedings of fact finding and evidence hearing. However, the effectiveness of the suggestions or recommendations of the mediators or conciliators upon the dispute resolution is to be endorsed by the parties rather than by the mediators' or the conciliators'.

As very traditional methods of dispute resolution, mediation and conciliation have been inserted into the international treaties and conventions after World War II. Mediation and conciliation have been used in modern times to successfully solve big and complicated disputes between states, such as 'The Argentine-Chilean Border Conflict', and 'The U.S.-Iran Hostages and Assets Disputes'. The practice of mediation and conciliation used in diplomatic and judicial affairs and issues has a history of several hundred years (Sucharitkul 2001). In Asia, which emphasises the value of oriental harmony, mediation especially exerts an important role in the settlement of regional and domestic disputes. In commercial disputes, mediation and conciliation act as an indispensable and distinct way for dispute resolution. Take the Chinese mediation and conciliation as an example. In the past decades, mediation as a working method has been widely used in civil and commercial litigation and arbitration cases. According to the work reports of the Supreme People's Court of China over the years, from 2013 to 2017, the mediation settlement rate of the people's court of China was between 23 and 33%. According to the data released by the Legal Affairs Office of the State Council, from 2014 to 2016, the proportion of arbitration cases settled by national arbitration institutions through mediation/reconciliation was as high as between 41 and 65%. As reported by the China International Economic and Trade Arbitration Commission (CIETAC), 'In 2016, 121,527 cases were settled through mediation, accounting for 58 percent of the total' (CIETAC 2016). Statistics and data of disputes resolved through mediation and conciliation can absolutely explain the role and function of mediation and conciliation as ADRs.

Mediation as an Option for Dispute Resolution Under BRI

As a cooperative project including more than 70 countries, the BRI will inevitably generate disputes across the border. It is essential to consider the cross-border nature of the disputes arising out of the economic and commercial activities under the BRI framework. Considering the cross-border and cross-cultural situations of the disputes of the BRI, 'it is desirable to resolve disputes by using a method that is not only appropriate to the nature of the dispute, but also acceptable to all the disputing parties' (ICC 2019). While Western parties often resort to arbitration or litigation, Chinese parties and parties form other oriental countries would prefer less adversarial approaches to the resolution of disputes with their business partners. And since there is no 'one size fits all' approach to Belt and Road disputes, mediation and conciliation may be used solely, or be integrated with arbitration or litigation, to efficiently resolve the disputes of the disputants and try to keep the friendly and harmonious relationships between the disputants.

Firstly, mediation as an informal dispute resolution or a formal one has a long history. In Asia, under the influence of Confucianism, informal mediation has been practised in countries such as China, Japan and South Korea. In particular, China has a long history of using mediation as a way to solve civil disputes. In other countries like India, Singapore, Malaysia and Thailand, mediation has also become a good tradition for the dispute settlement. For example, formal mediation was said to have started in Singapore with the launch of the Court Mediation Centre in 1995 (Lim 1997). In India, mediation is used in civil proceedings, commercial proceedings and many other cases. In Italy, one of the European countries under BRI, mediation and conciliation could be tracked back to 1931 in its judicial system. In Africa, as well as in Asia and Europe, regional agreements on mediation have been concluded, such as the '1964 Protocol of the Commission of Mediation and Arbitration of the Organization of African Unity'. In fact, in the countries under BRI, their modern judicial system has, in the early stage of the proceedings or adjudication, used the mediation and conciliation as means to promote the chance of amiable settlement between the disputants, notably in China, Japan, Thailand, Singapore and Italy. Considering the deep root of mediation, it is essential to insert in the alternative dispute resolutions under BRI the mediation and conciliation for the dispute settlement.

Secondly, the legal cultural values of the oriental society favour the mediation under BRI. As is repeatedly quoted, the oriental culture emphasises the value of harmony, which if immersed into the economic cooperation, will benefit the participants, especially the developing countries and small countries along the road and belt. This cultural value of the eastern wisdom and philosophy will also be meaningful when used in the dispute resolution arising out of the cooperative or commercial activities. As the initiator of the project, China will provide its strategies and wisdom for the construction of the mediation and conciliation system under the Belt and Road Initiative. Mediation and conciliation characterised with the oriental wisdom not only coincide with the Chinese culture, but also consist with the current international trends for commercial dispute resolution.

Thirdly, mediation has universally accepted in the international commercial dispute resolution. As has mentioned in the former part of this article, in Asia, countries such as Korea, Malaysia, Singapore and India have cultivated good and healthy environment for mediation and conciliation in the civil and commercial dispute settlement. In Europe, mediation and conciliation have also been broadly integrated into the arbitration system to constitute an effective ADR model. Even in America, where the adversarial common law governs the judiciary system, mediation has currently become an effective resolution of disputes. In the management of the international conflicts, the international mediation still represents one of the most used methods to manage, because mediators are not just bystanders or onlookers in the proceedings, but rather a flexible and active third party to help to shape the final solution of the dispute (Vuković 2014).

Fourthly, the commercial mediation is hybridised with arbitration. It has been a tendency in international commercial arbitration to integrate mediation with arbitration. The common practice is to use mediation at the outset of arbitration, or during the process of arbitration. Although the international community generally supports the integration of international commercial mediation arbitration in the arbitration process, there are some differences about the specific provisions concerning the integration. For example, if mediation fails to facilitate an arbitral award, will the mediators continue to act as arbitrators? There are different opinions on this problem when scholars discuss the building of the BRI dispute resolution mechanism (Wang 2017). And shall the evidence disclosed in the mediation process be kept confidential? The answer is that even in Asia mediation laws and regulations are different between countries and regions like Japan, Singapore, China and Hong Kong on these substantial issues. Solution of this problem ensures the implementation of the mediation agreement under the 'Belt and Road' framework. In fact, international mediation and arbitration research institute findings indicated that international or cross-border mediation and arbitration is on the rise in

Asia. The Hong Kong International Arbitration Centre (HKIAC), for example, reports a 40% increase from 2012 in the number of cases it handles (HKIAC 2014). Following the Asian trend, the BRI countries should make efforts to build the mediation-arbitration dispute resolution mechanism.

Mediation Law of Representative Countries Under BRI for a Comparative Look

In this part, some representatives of the BRI countries will be presented with their mediation law.

Mediation Under Italian Law

Italy has a long history of mediation and conciliation. And in its recent law system, mediation is adopted in civil, commercial and criminal matters. To understand the mediation rule in Italian law system, it is necessary to refer to Code of Civil Procedure (Code 2005), Article 131-8 of which provides for[2]:

> The mediator does not have the power of direction. However, he may, with the consent of the parties and for the purpose of the mediation, hear voluntary third parties. The mediator may not be appointed, in the course of the same proceeding, to execute investigation measures.

Based on this law provision, it is easy to see that the purpose of the mediation is to guide the dissent parties to an agreement concerning their disputes to the degree that the involved parties to be willing to accept. But the mediator is not allowed to conduct investigation measures in the mediation proceeding. Since 1990s, with the support of the mediation laws and bills, chambers of commerce of Italy have begun to establish mediation services for amicable resolution of disputes. For example, after the Italian Parliament passed Law No. 580 in 1993, 'the more than one hundred Chambers of Commerce have established a number of conciliation offices throughout Italy' (De Palo and Cominelli 2003). The purpose of the creation of the mediation system is to make it an alternative dispute

[2] Italian Code of Civil Procedure, Article 131-8.

resolution (ADR) which aims to provide quicker and cheaper solutions of disputes than filing it to the courts.

In accordance with the provisions of the Legislative Decree articles, principles and features of the Italian mediation may be summarised as follows:

Firstly, it is the non-mandatory suggestions of the mediator or conciliators. As a third party, who guides the parties involved in disputes to reach an agreement on the solution of their disputes, will use his professionals and skills to achieve this goal with suggestions or opinions. The mediating party's suggestions and opinions under the agreement are not mandatory to accept. If the mediation is not accepted, the parties involved in the dispute can move on their case to the arbitration or court. Their procedural and substantial rights and interests will not be harmed.

Secondly, it is the impartiality of the mediator. One of the big requirements for determination of the mediators is their objectiveness, justice and impartiality. Mediators should abide by the professional code and conduct the mediation and conciliation between the parties with objectiveness and impartiality. They should not have relationship with either party. Otherwise they need to make it clear to them or abstain from the mediation or conciliation.

Thirdly, it is the rights to autonomy of the involved parties. Autonomy is a significant right of the parties in ADRs, including mediation, conciliation, arbitration and the expert determination. In mediation, autonomy of the parties includes the intention to invite and choose the mediators, to define the extent of the mediation, and the option to accept the mediator's suggestions or not.

Fourthly, it is the confidentiality in and out of the mediation. Alike the other ADRs, confidentiality is clearly stated in the Italian Legislative Decree. The procedure of the mediation is confidential. This confidentiality forms an obligation not only to the mediator, but also to the parties involved in the dispute. Any declarations and statements revealed by the parties during the process of the mediation will not be revealed or used in the later arbitral proceedings or litigant procedures. The same is true with the mediator's or conciliator's suggestions, which will not be disclosed to any other people or parties or entities.

Besides, according to the provisions of law, the Italian mediation may be classified into two categories: mediation under general law provisions (common law mediation) and mediation governed by specific statutes (specific law mediation). The common law mediation is regarded as the out-of-court mediation. This kind of mediation is started with the will of the parties who appoint a professional mediator to guide them to a resolution of their disputes. This process takes place before the arbitration proceeding or court proceeding. If the mediation helps to reach an agreement between the parties, their dispute will be settled without going to the court. The specific law mediation refers to the mediation which is ruled in accordance with the specific law or specific provisions of a law (Giarrusso 2010). In the context of the existing law regulations, Italy has experienced mediation in civil, commercial and criminal matters for many years. Mediation has produced records of appreciation in the consumer disputes, private providers of commercial mediation, mediation in criminal matters (victim offender mediation), family and divorce mediation; public sector ombudsmen; cultural and social mediation (De Palo and Cominelli 2003). In these areas, mediation is conducted in accordance with the specific provisions of the relevant laws.

Mediation and Conciliation of India

In reality, 'mediation' and 'conciliation' are used synonymously in India (Liu 2019). The Supreme Court of India has interpreted it by stating that 'mediation' and 'mediator' should be taken also to mean 'conciliation' and 'conciliator'. According to Rule 4 of the Civil Procedure—Alternate Dispute Resolution and Mediation Rules,[3]

> Settlement by 'Mediation' means the process by which a mediator appointed by parties or by the Court, as the case may be, mediates the dispute between the parties to the suit by the application of the provisions of the Mediation Rules, 2003 in Part II, and in particular, by facilitating discussion between parties directly or by communicating with each other through the mediator, by assisting parties in identifying issues, reducing misunderstandings, clarifying priorities, exploring areas of compromise, generating options in an attempt to solve the dispute and emphasizing that it is the parties own responsibility for making decisions which affect them.

This Rule indicates that mediation in India complies with the principal policies of the international mediation rules, including the voluntariness

[3] Alternate Dispute Resolution and Mediation Rules, Rule 4.

and autonomy of the disputants, impartiality and objectivity of the mediator, communication and negotiation with the disputing parties, and soft power of the mediator's suggestions and opinions.

For the purpose of this discussion, legislation and application of commercial mediation in Indian law will be focused here. Commercial mediation was introduced in Indian law in 1996 when the Civil Procedure Code (CPC) was amended. Rules of governing mediation are provided in Section 89 of this amendment, which empower the courts to direct settlement of disputes by mediation among other means. Combined with the rules and regulations framed by the high courts, Section 89 provides rules to govern the court-annexed mediation. Also in 1996, a specific law concerning conciliation was promulgated. That is the Arbitration and Conciliation Act (ACA), which provides regulations concerning private mediation (conciliation) in addition to the provisions on arbitration in India. Unlike Section 89 of CPC, the ACA deals with private conciliation of disputes arising out of legal relationship, whether contractual or not and to all proceedings relating to the legal relationship. But the revision of CPC in 1999 consolidates the rules set forth by ACA with the provision of settlement of disputes outside the Court inserted in Section 89 of the revision, which states[4]:

> Where a dispute has been referred-(a) for arbitration or conciliation, the provisions of the Arbitration and Conciliation Act, 1996 (26 of 1996) shall apply as if the proceedings for arbitration or conciliation were referred for settlement under the provisions of that Act.

In addition, mediation and conciliation are also means of dispute resolution. In accordance with the propulsion on the 'mediation and conciliation panel' provided for in Section 442 of the 2013 Companies Act, the central government shall maintain a panel of experts to be called as the Mediation and Conciliation Panel consisting of experts having qualifications for mediation between the parties during the pendency of any proceedings before the central government or the Tribunal or the Appellate Tribunal under this Act.

[4]The Code of Civil Procedure 1908 of India, Section 89.

Judging from the legislation of India, mediation and conciliation as a means of dispute resolution are broadly stated in the laws of different sectors, which keeps its law consistent with the world trend of using mediation and conciliation as a way to quickly deal with legal disputes. The mediation and conciliation proceedings of Indian law involve the following main issues (Liu 2019):

Firstly, to initiate the conciliation proceedings, one party shall send a conciliation invitation in writing to the other party. The conciliation proceedings can start when the other party accepts the written invitation to conciliate. If the other party refuses to accept the invitation, there will be no conciliation proceedings.

Secondly, to proceed the conciliation, according to ACA, there shall be one conciliator unless the parties agree that there shall be two or three conciliators. But if there are more than one conciliator, the conciliators shall act jointly. For the appointment of the conciliator(s), if it is one conciliator, the parties may agree on the appointment; if it is two conciliators, each party may appoint one conciliator; if it is three conciliators, each party may appoint one conciliator and the parties may agree on the appointment of the third conciliator who shall act as the presiding conciliator.

Thirdly, as for the role of conciliators, according to ACA, 'the conciliator shall assist the parties in an independent and impartial manner in an attempt to reach an amicable settlement of their dispute'. To fairly guide the parties to an amicable resolution, conciliators shall comply with the principles of objectivity, fairness and justice, and shall give consideration to the rights and obligations of the parties, and the business usages and practice of between the parties. In the course of the conciliation, the conciliators may conduct the proceedings in such a manner as they consider appropriate, and make proposals for a settlement of the dispute, may arrange for administrative assistance by a suitable institution or person with the consent of the parties, may meet with the parties together or separately, or communicate with the parties orally or in written, and disclose factual information from one party to another except for the confidential information. But the conciliator shall not participate in other proceedings as an arbitrator, counsel or witness after the termination of the proceedings and shall keep confidential all matters relating to the proceedings.

Fourthly, conciliation shall be terminated if the conciliator cannot assist the parties to a settlement. In accordance with ACA, under any of the following environments, the conciliation proceedings shall be terminated:

'(*a*) by the signing of the settlement agreement by the parties, or (*b*) by a written declaration of the conciliator; or (*c*) by a written declaration of the parties addressed to the conciliator to the effect that the conciliation proceedings are terminated, on the date of the declaration; or (*d*) by a written declaration of a party to the other party and the conciliator'.[5]

Fifthly, there are special provisions for international commercial conciliation. In fact, ACA does not offer a specific explanation of 'conciliation'. So is the case of 'international commercial conciliation'. However, with its extended application to international commercial disputes, ACA covers not only the domestic conciliation, but also the international commercial conciliation. Understanding and interpretation of the international commercial conciliation is based on the Resolution 35/52 (Conciliation Rules of the UN Commission on International Trade Law) adopted by the General Assembly on 4 December 1980 (hereinafter referred to as UNCITRAL Conciliation Rules), which formed the base of ACA. As convinced by the UNCITRAL Conciliation Rules, the establishment of the international conciliation rules is acceptable in countries with different legal, social and economic systems would significantly contribute to the development of harmonious international economic relations. The international commercial conciliation of Indian ACA law is a specific example of the execution and enforcement of the international rules. In accordance with ACA, international commercial conciliation is the same as international commercial arbitration. Section 2 of the law stipulates clearly the foreign-related elements that make a case an international commercial conciliation. according to Clause (f) of sub-section (1) of Section 2, 'international commercial conciliation' means a conciliation relating to disputes arising out of legal relationships, whether contractual or not, considered as commercial under the law in force in India and where at least one of the parties is (1) a foreign individual; (2) a company established outside India; (3) an association or a body of foreign individuals or (4) a foreign government.[6]

[5] The Arbitration and Conciliation Act of India, 1996, Article 76.

[6] The Arbitration and Conciliation Act of India, 1996, Section 2.

Mediation Mechanism of Singapore

In Singapore, as in other oriental culture, mediation is not a new concept. It is practiced in one way or another for dispute resolution. But the modern adjudicatory system of Singapore has dwindled its mediation as an approach for dispute settlement. Reverse of this situation came in the 1990s, which has started the modern mediation movement in Singapore. In Singapore, mediation is widely used in courts, in arbitral tribunals and in private dispute resolution.

Meaning of 'mediation' in Singapore law can be determined according to the Mediation Act of 2017, which states[7]:

> 'mediation' means a process comprising one or more sessions in which one or more mediators assist the parties to a dispute to do all or any of the following with a view to facilitating the resolution of the whole or part of the dispute: A. identify the issues in dispute; B. explore and generate options; C. communicate with one another; and D. voluntarily reach an agreement.

The concept under the Singapore Mediation Act implies the principles of mediation universally adopted and accepted, including voluntariness of the disputant parties, confidentiality of the process and disclosed information and evidence, neutrality of the mediator(s), and flexibility and practicality of the mediator's action.

Mediation in Singapore is provided for certain qualities similar to arbitration. The mediation agreement is one of these qualities, which makes it get closer to the arbitration, and avoid the nature of its soft power. The Mediation Act states that mediation starts with a mediation agreement, and that 'Mediation Agreement' means an agreement by 2 or more persons to refer the whole or part of a dispute which has arisen, or which may arise, between them for mediation.[8]

Such an agreement may be in the form of a clause in a contract or in the form of a separate agreement. But a mediation agreement must be in writing.

Judiciary support is another reason for the remarkable development of mediation in Singapore. The pre-trial conferences (PTCs) initiated by the

[7] Mediation Act 2017 of Singapore, Article 3.

[8] Mediation Act 2017 of Singapore, Article 4.

judiciary for civil cases in the Supreme and State Courts in 1992 launched the mediation process in adjudication. PTCs present a parallel mechanism for the court to handle the cases, but the summons for directions is initiated by the parties, though the pre-trial conferences are initiated by the courts. According to the relevant provisions, the court may 'at any time before any action or proceedings are tried…direct parties to attend a pre-trial conference relating to the matters arising in the action or proceedings'. Where appropriate, the pre-trial conference may be adjourned, either generally or to a particular date, or the court may dismiss the action or proceedings or strike out the conference. The pre-trial conference provides an opportunity for the parties to settle during the conference (Chen and Eunice Chua 2018).[9] The use of PTCs was formalised in 1996 in the High Court and State Courts through O34A of the Rules of Court of Singapore. As the provision of the Rules of Court of 2014 states,[10]

> no communication made in the course of a pre-trial conference in any action or proceedings shall be disclosed to the Court conducting the trial of the action or proceedings if such communication —
> (a) has been stated by any of the parties to the action or proceedings to be "confidential" or "without prejudice"; or
> (b) has been marked by the Registrar as being "confidential" or "without prejudice".

This order gives the High Court and the State Courts the power to make orders and give directions for the just, expeditious and economical disposal of proceedings. It also empowers mediation as a parallel approach of dispute resolution or as an integral part of the adjudication.

Mediation law and practice in Singapore is absolutely a good example for other BRI countries. It has provided for measures such as the mediation agreement to strengthen the mediation power. And the international mediation development in Singapore has greatly improved. This development is attributable to the construction of the mechanism construction of international mediation institutes and system. As for the international constitutes, in Singapore, there are globally famous mediation centres like

[9] See Chen, Siyuan and Eunice Chua, Hui Han. *Civil Procedure in Singapore*, Third Edition, Kluwer Law International.

[10] Court of Judicature Act (Chapter 322, Section 80) (2016) of Singapore.

the Singapore Mediation Centre (SMC), Singapore International Mediation Centre (SIMC) and International Chamber of Commerce (ICC), which has launched the new ICC Rules of Mediation. The mediation rules enacted by these mediation centres or committees have built a comprehensive system for mediation concerning the international disputes.

One big event for the international mediation is that the UNCITRAL agreed to create the United Nations Convention on International Settlement Agreements Resulting from Mediation (The Singapore Convention). The Convention was signed in Singapore in August 2019. A contracting state to this Convention will be obliged to enforce a mediated settlement agreement according to its domestic procedural rules. The Convention applies to cross-border commercial disputes resolved through mediation. It eases the enforcement of settlement agreements resulting from mediation and expedites the procedure of enforcement of the agreements. That is why the Singapore Convention is regarded as a framework for the cross-border recognition and enforcement of mediated settlement.

Mediation in China and Its Development for BRI

As the initiator of BRI, China has been making efforts to promote the amicable methods to settle the possible legal disputes arising from the economic and business activities under the BRI. The mediation mechanism is one of the two core approaches, with the other being arbitration.

In China, mediation is used alone and in combination with adjudicatory procedures such as litigation and arbitration. In general, the mediation system of China can be divided into five categories: (1) people's mediation, which is conducted by the people's mediation committees; (2) administrative mediation, which is undertaken by the local people's governments or administrative departments; (3) mediation within litigation proceedings, which is conducted by the people's court; (4) mediation within arbitral proceedings, which is combined with arbitration; and (5) industry mediation, which is conducted by respected associations within a particular industry. The establishment of mediation system could be traced back to 1991, when the Civil Procedure Law (CPL) was adopted, which was lately revised in 2017.

The CPL emphasised the following rules: (1) Mediation shall be conducted on the consent of the disputant parties, without coercion on either party. (2) Mediation can be carried out in simple and easy ways, including the presiding over by a single judge or by a collegiate panel, or inviting units and individuals concerned to assist the mediation. (3) A settlement agreement reached between the parties must be made on their own free will and without compulsion. (4) The content of the mediation agreement shall not violate the provisions of law. (5) The mediation document shall be legally binding on the disputant parties upon their signature and receipt of it. (6) If no agreement has been reached through mediation or if one party reneges before the mediation statement is served, the people's court shall render a judgement without delay.[11] In other words, according to the CPL, the people's court shall carry out mediation in the trial of cases based on the principle of voluntariness and in accordance with the law. If mediation has reached and signed, it shall have legal effect on the disputant parties. Otherwise, judgements shall be rendered without delay.

Starting from the 1991 CPL, rules of mediation have been inserted into different laws. Laws involve mediation regulations mainly include the following laws and regulations beside the procedure law. They are the Arbitration Law of 1994, People's Mediation Law of 2010 and 'Several Provisions of the Supreme People's Court on the Judicial Confirmation Procedure for the People's Mediation Agreements' issued by the Supreme People's Court in 2011. The People's Mediation Law, for example, reiterates the main principles for mediation, including '(1) Mediating on the basis of free will and equality of the parties concerned; (2) Abiding by laws, regulations and policies of the state; and (3) Respecting the rights of the parties concerned, and refraining from stopping the parties concerned from protecting their rights through arbitration, administrative means or judicial means in the name of mediation'.[12]

Although mediation has been exerting an important role in the dispute settlement proceedings, the legislation on mediation is mainly concerning the resolution of private disputes. That is the mediation conducted by the court. To apt to the dispute resolution under the BRI, international commercial mediation mechanism should be facilitated and improved.

Based on the five categories of mediation mentioned above,the development of the mediation in China will be unfolded from the following aspects:

[11] Civil Procedure Law of PRC, Chapter 8.

[12] The People's Mediation Law of PRC, Article 3.

Firstly, it is the legislative and judiciary development. According to a data-based research, since the founding of New China 70 years ago, China's litigation on mediation has formed a framework from the introduction of judicial policies to the enactment of law, to the change of judicial policies and to the amendment of laws and regulations. This development pattern reflects the rationales of mediation, including the voluntariness of mediation, combination of mediation and adjudication, priority of mediation to litigation and standardisation of mediation. The 70-year development of the mediation in legislation, mainly represented by the enactment of the 'People's Mediation Law' and the amendment of the 'Civil Procedure Law', has outlined forms of mediation, qualifications for mediation, protection of rights of the disputant parties, selection of mediators and procedures for judicial confirmation of mediated settlements, and has established regulatory institutions for the judiciary practice of mediation. Research results indicated that whether it is due to the emphasis of mediation or due to the respect of the subject status of the parties, judicial policy accomplished its goal through its influence on the trial of the courts. This kind of influence actually does not considerably influence the exercise of the litigant's litigation rights. The enactment and amendment of laws and regulations have proportionally and synchronously influenced the mediation rate.

Secondly, it is the development of mediation in practice. After the practice for 70 years, mediation in China has been directed in a dramatically professional way. Lawyers, arbitrators and experts have been appointed as mediators. More sources are used to train the mediators. Mediation centres have been established to deal with domestic and international disputes. Currently, in cities like Beijing, Shanghai, Guangzhou and Shenzhen, international commercial mediation institutes and international commercial arbitration institutes have been built to a 'one-stop' diversified international commercial dispute resolution mechanism (Liu 2018). Besides, professional mediation organisations have emerged in insurance, securities, intellectual property and other sectors.

A big movement of the Chinese mediation development occurred in 2012, when 'The White Paper on China's Judicial Reform' was issued.[13] The White Paper initiated the Grand Mediation (translation from the

[13] *White Paper on China's Judicial Reform* was issued by the State Council Information Office of PRC in October 2012, available at: http://www.scio.gov.cn/zxbd/tt/Document/1226132/1226132.htm (last consulted: 4 April 2017).

Chinese *Da Tiaojie*), which focuses as follows: according to the Law on People's Mediation, the Opinions on Establishing and Improving Conflict and Dispute Resolution Mechanisms by Linking Litigation and Non-litigation Cases, and the Guidelines on Encouraging the Use of Mediation to Solve Conflicts and Disputes, development and improvement of non-litigation dispute resolution mechanisms is encouraged, dispute resolution mechanisms by linking litigation and non-litigation cases is strengthened, and the role of people's mediation organisations, social groups, lawyers, experts and arbitration agencies is highlighted. A 'grand mediation' work system is established to integrate people's administrative and judicial mediation, and to improve coordination among the three in terms of procedure linkage, validity confirmation and legal guidance. The Grand Mediation reshuffles the mediation practice by being utilised as a caseload management tool and by saving judicial economy as well. The deployment of court resources to keep disputes out of the judicial system (chiefly by settling disputes using court-annexed and other out-of-court mediation programmes) has evolved into a type of judicial convention in China (Chan 2017). Mediation holds the legacy of amicable relationship by avoiding the adversarial allegation in the court.

Thirdly, it is the development of international commercial mediation for the BRI project. For this purpose, China has taken actions, especially the measures for the 'one-stop' diversified international commercial dispute resolution mechanism. Here are some facts: (1) In order to implement the Opinions on the Establishment of 'One Belt And One Road' International Commercial Dispute Settlement Mechanism and Institution issued by the central government, the China International Commercial Court (CICC) was established by the Supreme People's Court of China (SPC) to adjudicate international commercial cases. The First International Commercial Court (in Shenzhen) and The Second International Commercial Court (in Shaanxi) started to operate in June 2018. According to Articles 11, 12 and 13 of the Rules on the Establishment of the International Commercial Courts (hereinafter referred to as Rules), the Supreme Court of China will select competent international mediation agencies and international arbitration agencies to cooperate with the International Commercial Courts to build a dispute resolution platform for mediation, arbitration and litigation and to construct a 'one-stop' international commercial dispute resolution mechanism. If the mediation succeeds, the court may prepare and issue a mediation statement or a written judgement giving force to the mediation. Mediation, arbitration and litigation will form an integral part of the dispute resolution under the BRI framework.[14] (2) China has participated and played a main role in the negotiation of the Regional Comprehensive Economic Partnership ('RCEP') agreement, which all of the 15 negotiating countries will predicatively sign in February 2020. Though it is difficult to figure out the specific provisions of the dispute resolution mechanism of the RCEP prior to the release of the RCEP text, the Guiding Principles and Objectives of RCEP at least offers some conception of the dispute resolution procedures. The efficient and transparent dispute resolution mechanism proposed by the Guiding Principles and Objectives of RCEP will not only solve the disputes under RCEP, but also will consider other issues under the FTAs signed between RCEP participating countries as well as newly emerging issues related to commercial activities. As academically interpreted, such an efficient and transparent mechanism may hopefully be established on the bases of consultation, mediation, arbitration and other legal approaches (Wang and Gao 2018). (3) China has signed the Singapore Mediation Convention. Including China, 46 states signed the Convention. The Singapore Mediation Convention, an international agreement regarding the recognition of mediated settlements, states apparently the rational in the Preamble to the Convention 'that the establishment of a framework for international settlement agreements resulting from mediation that is acceptable to States with different legal, social and economic systems would contribute to the development of harmonious international economic relations'. Based on this general framework, the Convention empowers the cross-border commercial disputes resolved through mediation and facilitates the enforcement procedure of properties located in another contracting State. According to Article 1.1(a), 'the Convention applies to cross-border commercial disputes resolved through mediation, where at least two parties to the [written] settlement agreement have their places of business in different States'.[15] For countries which are on the Road and Belt, the Convention will utilise the mediation system to promote the settlement of disputes of commercial entities. And for other BRI countries not signing this Convention, China may follow this model to build a dispute resolution mechanism to solve commercial disputes and

[14] The Rules on the Establishment of the International Commercial Courts, Articles 11, 12 and13.

[15] The Singapore Convention on Mediation, Article 1.1(a).

maintain good relations of international trade. At least, dispute resolution agencies between China and Singapore have started this motivation. For example, The Singapore International Mediation Centre ('SIMC') signed a Memorandum of Understanding ('MOU') with the China Council for the Promotion of International Trade ('CCPIT'). Under the MOU, the SIMC and CCPIT will jointly develop the rules, case management protocol and enforcement procedures for disputes submitted to mediation and establish a panel of mediators to resolve disputes arising out of The Central People's Government of China's Belt and Road Initiative ('BRI') projects (Alert 2019).

In fact, apart from the participation in the RCEP, Singapore Convention, China has paid attention to other international, regional and bilateral instruments to development of the mediation approach for dispute resolution. Examples include signing treaties such as choice of court agreements (the Hague Choice of Court Convention), and court judgements (the Hague Judgements Convention).

Vision for the Construction of BRI Mediation Mechanism

As is repeatedly quoted, the mediation system is regarded as the oriental value, oriental treasure and oriental wisdom (Wang 2017; Zhang and Chen 2017). Under the BRI, the mediation system may not only facilitate dispute settlement in an amicable and friendly environment, but also expedite the BRI goals of common development and common prosperity by respecting the traditional culture and legal system, especially the culture of harmony rooted on the Confucian philosophy. A vision for the BRI mediation system construction may include the following ideas.

Firstly, it is to start the top-level design of the dispute settlement mechanism. Considering that the BRI countries are from Asia, Africa and Europe, with many of them being developing countries or small countries, and with the political, economic and legal difference among them, a top-level design can guarantee the construction of the mediation mechanism. The top-level design includes the institutional arrangement and strategy and policy plan. All of the efforts made on the participant countries' level will provide guidance and credibility for the development of an efficient and convincing mediation mechanism for the dispute resolution under BRI. At the same time, such the top-level cooperation will produce possibility for the integrity of the mediation system with arbitration and litigation mechanism, forming a reliable system for the resolution of disputes. As the initiator of the BRI, China has exerted a significant role as one of the top-level designers in the dispute settlement mechanism. For example, the BRI (China) Arbitration Committee has been established as the first BRI-based arbitration committee, whose integration of mediation and arbitration has settled five cases concerning Libya, Kuwait and Vietnam with the value of ¥600 million (Zhao 2019).

Secondly, it is to initiate a mediation-and-arbitration dispute settlement mechanism. As is well known, the international commercial dispute settlement has tended to hybridise mediation and arbitration for the commercial dispute settlement. In fact, upon the entry into the twenty-first century, 'arbitration and mediation, together with other proceedings, have become the available methods of dispute resolution system because they satisfy the five-factor resolution of a (1) prompt, (2) affordable, (3) fair proceeding conducted by a (4) neutral expert who decides the case, (5) based on the merits' (Liu 2018). Under the BRI, the cross-border dispute settlement mechanism should adopt the diversified approaches to integrate consultation, mediation and arbitration on a multilevel. This multimodel of dispute resolution represents not only the domestic mediation legislation and practice but also the international trend of the international commercial mediation and arbitration. The convergence of mediation and arbitration reduces the cost of the dispute resolution proceedings, promote the proceedings from a free will resolution model to an arbitral model or to a litigation model. In this area, China, as the BRI initiator, has made attempts to kick off the ball. The Opinions on the Establishment of 'One Belt And One Road' International Commercial Dispute Settlement Mechanism and Institutions issued in January 2018 announced that the international commercial dispute settlement mechanisms and institutions should apply diversified means to resolve disputes, to foster the linkage of mediation, arbitration and litigation to improve the dispute settlement services and to guarantee dispute resolution mechanism work in a healthy mode. In this process, the mediation step can provide a flexible negotiation for a package of strategies for the dispute resolutions, which gears with the rationales of *peaceful harmony* and *win-win cooperation*. The Chinese experience of years' of development of the diversified dispute resolution mechanism serves as a good example for the BRI mediation-arbitration dispute resolution system.

Thirdly, it is to improve the bilateral and multilateral agreements on mediation. Construction of the mediation mechanism, to stand alone or to be integrally applied with arbitration and litigation, is an issue which deserves consideration for BRI. The answer lies in the cultural, legal and political elements of the countries alongside the belt and road, with reference to the development of the international commercial dispute rules. So it is core to negotiate or renegotiate the bilateral and multilateral agreements on mediation under the BRI framework to improve the mediation mechanism under BRI. The negotiation or renegotiation has their justifications. First, in the first stage of the BRI, with a growth of just seven years since the issuance of this cooperative vision, it is impossible to establish a comprehensive mediation system to effectively deal with the legal issues concerning the business activities under the BRI framework. Secondly, it is not an ideal policy to create a completely new mediation system for the BRI because it takes time for the countries to converge the dispute resolution rules through consensual understanding and acceptance. Therefore, based on the existing bilateral or multilateral mechanisms and systems treaties or agreements, parties of the BRI will facilitate the interconnection and cooperation.[16] Also, during the beginning years, the investor-state disputes resolution (ISDS) will also be based on the bilateral or multilateral agreements for its development and improvement. The Chinese projects and elements contribute here too (Shi and Dong 2018).

In terms of the international dispute resolution mechanism between China and African countries for the BRI, the existing China–Africa cooperative relationships have already provided groping experience. In fact, before the Chinese central government formally proposed the establishment of the 'One Belt And One Road' dispute settlement mechanism, China and Africa started to explore the construction of a joint dispute settlement mechanism between them in 2015. The Forum on China–Africa Cooperation Johannesburg Action Plan (2016–2018) stated the establishment of the China–Africa Joint Arbitration Centre (CAJAC) to settle the disputes resulting from the economic, trade and investment exchanges between China and Africa through mediation, arbitration and other ADRs. The brotherly relationship principle, one of the three basic principles the Center adheres to in mediation and arbitration, implies the oriental and amicable values for the dispute resolution.

[16]Vision and Proposed Actions Outlined on Jointly Building Silk Road Economic Belt and Twenty-First-Century Maritime Silk Road issued by the National Development and Reform Commission, Ministry of Foreign Affairs and Ministry of Commerce of PRC.

Fourthly, it is to propose fundamental principles to govern the BRI mediation. Construction of the BRI mediation system, main principles suggested below deserve the necessary consideration:

1. Autonomy of mediation. As apparently stated in various mediation rules and laws, mediation procedures should be motivated by the disputant parties. Mediators should completely respect the consensual intention of the parties for the motion of mediation, and for the discussion of the disputes. The disputant parties shall have the autonomy to choose the mediators, and choose the procedures or methods to manage the mediation.
2. Freedom of terminating the mediation. As a derivative right of the autonomy principle, parties shall have the right to decide whether and when to terminate the mediation. After entering into the mediation proceedings, either party has the freedom to step out of the mediation proceedings. Upon the termination of the mediation, resumption of arbitration or initiation of litigation shall start (Shi and Dong 2018).
3. Hybridisation of mediation, conciliation and arbitration. Merge of mediation and arbitration has become a popular tendency of the international ADR forms. As an oriental wisdom, the legal value of combining the three has even a longer history than in other places of the world. But in Asian mediation system, there exist difference about the continuity of whether a mediator will continue to work as an arbitrator for the same case after the mediation is terminated due to one party's or both parties' reluctance to go on with the mediation. In commercial mediation in China, mediators usually shall not work as arbitrators to continue their role in the same case. But in countries such as South Korea and Malaysia, the rules are unlike that of China. The mediators may move on to the arbitration section after the termination of the mediation proceedings. As for the mediation system of BRI, a system of separating the mediators from the arbitrators shall be executed. Separation of the mediators and arbitrators will guarantee the efficiency, objectivity and amicability of the case stopped by the mediation, and for the purpose of the avoidance of the interruption of the information and facts obtained by arbitrator who worked as the mediator in the previous mediation proceedings.

4. Partial mediation agreement. Mediation and arbitration fall into the same frame as ADR forms, which makes them share some values and functions in common. One identity is that either may solve part of the whole dispute. In arbitration, when disputants can reach agreement on some of their disputes, they can sign a temporary arbitration agreement, which facilitates the solution of part of their disputes. Enlightened with this model, mediation can insert this temporary resolution way into its system to partially solve the problems prior to the arbitration agreement has been concluded.
5. Confidentiality of the mediation. Confidentiality forms an essential principle of mediation. For the mediation of the BRI disputes, the principle of confidentiality is of equal importance for the dispute resolution. Without confidentiality, disputants would be unwilling to disclose any information unknown to the other party, which will be a big obstacle for the solution of the disagreements. Application of confidentiality shall be controlled within some limitation. It will be limited to the procedures not open to the public, information unveiled by the disputants, including statements, opinions and views, which can be used as evidence in the consequential arbitration proceedings. Prevention of the leakage of the confidential information forms one of the core values of mediation and conciliation.

Fifthly, it is to adopt the successful experience of international mediation. Mediation has become a common trend for the cross-board dispute resolutions. Countries from oriental culture or adversarial culture tend to sign international mediation treaties and conventions. This international tendency sheds light on the mediation system construction for the BRI. For example, ICC mediation can help parties reach an amicable settlement quickly and inexpensively, often with minimal damage to their overall relationship. As ICC states, in cross-border, cross-cultural situations like these, it is essential to resolve disputes by using a method that is not only appropriate to the nature of the dispute, but also acceptable to all the disputing parties. Therefore, its mediation is particularly suitable for high-stakes, cross-border disputes of the type that Belt and Road may generate, without endangering the underlying project or parties' relationships. Another very important convention that can support the BRI mediation mechanism is the Singapore Convention on Mediation. Combining the oriental wisdom and the Western adversarial essence, the Singapore Convention integrally put the mediation tradition and the enforcement of the dispute resolution into consideration for the healthy development of the Singapore Convention. Besides, many countries under BRI have signed the Singapore Convention, which make it easy for the BRI countries to set up rules of the BRI mediation. Of course, good experience of the existing bilateral and multilateral agreements can all be examples for the BRI mediation mechanism to learn from.

Conclusion

'Mediation', as a flexible and consensual technique with which a neutral third party helps the disputant parties to settle their disputes through negotiation and discussion, should be used as an important dispute resolution for BRI. It caters to the peaceful harmony value of the oriental culture; it aims to solve the disputes between parties while attempting to keep the friendly business relationships between them; it also tries to avoid the conflicts possibly caused by the different law systems of the BRI countries and undeniably it has become a common effective technique for the cross-border commercial disputes around the world. Considering the facts that more than 70 countries participated in the BRI, that the tremendous business activities can possibly cause disputes, and that efficient and successful resolution of the disputes in a harmonious relationship will benefit all the participants, a constructive mediation mechanism under the BRI should be given priority and privilege. In the course of the BRI mediation system construction, the initiator of the cross-border and cross-century project, China, should provide its strategies and policies. It should work with the other countries to reach the best and optimal dispute resolutions by depending on their domestic mediation law and practice, and by improving the bilateral and multilateral agreements involving mediation system. When the BRI mediation mechanism is established, it will facilitate settlement of disputes, help to fulfil the mission of common development and common prosperity, and contribute to the development of the international mediation system.

References

Alert (2019), "Memorandum Signed to Develop Mediation Rules for Disputes Over China BRI Projects", available at: https://www.jonesday.com/en/insights/2019/02/memorandum-signed-to-develop-mediation/.

Chan, Peter (2017), "China's Grand Mediation Strategy for Social Stability: A Study on Out-of-Court Mediation Procedures", in *Revista de Processo Comparado*, 6(3), 81–111.

Chen, Siyuan and Eunice Chua, Hui Han (2018), *Civil Procedure in Singapore*, Third Edition, Kluwer Law International B. V.

CIETAC (2016), "Annual Report of China International Commercial Arbitration", available at: http://www.cietac.org/Uploads/201710/59df3824b2849.pdf/.

De Palo, Giuseppe and Cominelli, Luigi (2003), "Crises of Courts and the Mediation Debate: The Case of Italy", in Alexander, Nadja (ed.), *Global Trends in Mediation*, Centrale für Mediation GmbH & Co. KG, 213–232.

Dress, Tobi (1988), "International Commercial Mediation and Conciliation", in *Loyola of Los Angeles International and Comparative Law Review*, 10(3), 569–582.

Giarrusso, Valentina (2010), "Mediation Under Italian Law", in Campbell, Denise (ed.), *International Dispute Resolution: The Comparative Law Yearbook of International Business*, Volume 31A, Kluwer Law International, 249–266.

HKIAC (2014), "Arbitration and Mediation in Asia-Pacific: Interviews with Mediation and Arbitral Centers and Law Department Best Practices", available at: https://www.researchgate.net/publication/323227946/.

ICC (2019), "Guidance Notes on Resolving Belt and Road Disputes Using Mediation and Arbitration", available at: https://iccwbo.org/content/uploads/sites/3/2019/02/icc-guidance-notes-belt-and-road-disputes-pdf.pdf/.

Lim, Lan Yuan (1997), *The Theory and Practice of Mediation*, Singapore F T Law & Tax Asia Pacific, Singapore.

Liu, Huichun (2018), "Evolution of Arbitration System Under the China FTZ Template", in *World Scientific*, 1(3), 1–26.

Liu, Huichun (2019), "Analysis of Indian Conciliation System", in *Legal System and Society*, 1(1), 20–21.

Liu, Tingmei (2018), "The China International Commercial Court (CICC) in 2018", available at: http://cicc.court.gov.cn/html/1/219/208/209/1316.html/.

Shi, Jingxia and Dong, Nuan (2018), "The Construction of Investor-State Dispute Settlement Mechanism Under 'The Belt and Road' Initiative", in *Wuhan University International Law Review*, 3, 1–24.

Sucharitkul, Sompong (2001), "Mediation and Conciliation as Alternative Means of Settling International Disputes", in *Golden Gate University School of Law GGU Law Digital Commons*, November, 1–22.

Vuković, S. (2014), "International Mediation as a Distinct Form of Conflict Management", in *International Journal of Conflict Management*, 25(1), 61–80.

Wang, Guiguo (2017), "On the Dispute Resolution Mechanism of the Belt and Road", in *Chinese Law Science (Digest)*, 6, 56–71.

Wang, Qian and Gao, Jinhan (2018), "An Exploratory Study of the Establishment of Dispute Settlement Mechanisms for RCEP", in *Guoji Zhanwang*, 2, 134–152.

Zhang, Xiaojun and Chen, Zhe (2017), "Construction of the Belt and Road Regional Investment Dispute Settlement Mechanism", in *Academic Forum*, 3, 50–56.

Zhao, Qingshu (2019), "Constructing and Perfecting the International Commercial Dispute Settlement Mechanism Under the Belt and Road Initiative", in *Knowledge Economy*, 6, 65–66.

Index

A

B

C

G. Martinico and X. WU (eds.), *A Legal Analysis of the Belt and Road Initiative*, https://doi.org/10.1007/978-3-030-46000-6

The manufacturer's authorised representative in the EU is Springer Nature Customer Service Centre GmbH, Europaplatz 3, 69115 Heidelberg, Germany. If you have any concerns regarding our products, please contact ProductSafety@springernature.com

Printed and bound by CPI Group (UK) Ltd, Croydon, CR0 4YY
25/09/2026
02222902-0006